vegetables
for vitality

vegetables for vitality

more than **200 delicious recipes** that use
less meat, more vegetables

Reader's
Digest

Montreal • New York

Copyright © 2011 by The Reader's Digest Association Inc.
Copyright © 2011 by Reader's Digest Association (Canada) ULC
Copyright © by The Reader's Digest Association Far East Ltd.
Philippine Copyright © The Reader's Digest Far East Ltd.
All rights reserved. Unauthorized reproduction, in any manner,
is prohibited. Reader's Digest and the Pegasus logo are registered
trademarks of The Reader's Digest Association, Inc.

Library and Archives Canada Cataloguing in Publication

Vegetables for vitality : more than 200 delicious recipes that
use less meat, more vegetables / editors of Reader's Digest.

Includes index.
ISBN 978-1-55475-084-9

1. Cooking (Vegetables). 2. Cookbooks. I. Reader's Digest
Association (Canada)

TX801.V426 2012   641.6'5   C2011-904541-9

Printed in China

We are committed both to the quality of our products and the service
we provide to our customers. If you have any comments about the
content of this book, write to
Book Editor, Reader's Digest Association (Canada) ULC,
1100 René-Lévesque Blvd. W., Montreal QC H3B 5H5

To order copies of **Vegetables for Vitality**, visit us at our online store:
www.rd.com in the US
www.readersdigest.ca in Canada

Note to Readers
The information in this book should not be substituted for, or used to
alter, medical therapy without your doctor's advice. For a specific
health problem, consult your physician for guidance. The mention of
any products, retail businesses or Web sites in this book does not
imply or constitute an endorsement by the authors or by
The Reader's Digest Association Inc. or by Reader's Digest Association
(Canada) ULC.

Front cover *(main image)* Asian noodle salad, p. 154; *(bottom left)*
gazpacho, p. 72; *(bottom centre)* beef salad niçoise, p. 111; *(bottom
right)* grilled chicken breast with corn & pepper relish, p. 94; **Back
cover** *(bottom left)* chicken breasts stuffed with spinach & cheese,
p.104; *(bottom centre)* stir-fried shrimp & snow peas,
p. 129; *(bottom right)* baked sweet potato fries, p. 193;
Title page *(left)* grilled tuna steaks with corn & tomato, p. 138;
(centre) vegetable tart provençale, p. 169; *(right)* mustard-glazed
brussels sprouts & new potatoes, p. 183; **Page 6** *(left)* grilled steak
with portobello mushrooms, p. 116; *(center)* baked sweet potato
fries, p. 193; *(right)* spring vegetable sauté with tarragon, p. 199;
Page 7 *(left)* chili with beans, tomatoes & corn, p. 173; *(centre)*
raspberry-beet-berry smoothie, p. 48; *(right)* grilled eggplant &
tomato sandwiches, p. 56

Project Staff

Project Editor Jesse Corbeil

Senior Designers Donna Heldon, Andrée Payette

Production/Art Chris A. Cant

Recipe Developers/Retesters Elaine Khosrova, Michael
Krondl, Anton Li, Wendye Pardue, Michele Peters

Photographers Sang An, Martin Brigdale, Christine
Bronico, Beatric daCosta, Gus Filgate, Mark Ferri, Ian
Hofstetter (*Stylist* Katy Holder), William Lingwood, Steven
Mays, Andrew McCul, David Murray, Sean Myers, Mark
Needham, Alan Richardson, Jules Selmes, Lisa Koenig,
Elizabeth Watt

Indexer Diane Harriman

Proofreaders Madeline Coleman, Judy Yelon

Reader's Digest Association (Canada) ULC

Manager, Book Editorial Pamela Johnson

Vice-President, Editorial Robert Goyette

The Reader's Digest Association

President and Chief Executive Officer Tom Williams

**Executive Vice-President, RDA and President, North
America** Dan Lagani

**Executive Vice-President, RDA and President,
Allrecipes.com** Lisa Sharples

**Executive Vice-President, RDA and President,
Europe** Dawn Zier

introduction

Vegetables are the perfect food for energy, disease prevention and weight loss. And as a bonus, they taste great, too. Yet, many of us don't make the most of the abundance of varieties available or the benefits that they offer.

Vegetables have crunch, color and distinctive flavors and aromas. They pair well with one another and with meats, seafood, fish and poultry. They team with pasta, legumes and rice and their flavors are complemented and enhanced by herbs, spices and sauces. Better still, they're inexpensive and easy to prepare. And, best of all, you can eat generous amounts of them thanks to their low-calorie, high fiber and high-nutrient content.

The wide range of recipes in this book will show you how to make vegetables a greater part of your daily diet. Some are classics that use traditional ingredients and cooking methods. Others are modern variations of old favorites that have been reworked to incorporate ingredients from the different world cuisines that are becoming part of daily life. Yet others introduce healthier cooking techniques that still retain veggies' optimum flavors and textures.

This book has been developed for all types of health levels and all levels of cooking expertise. There are vegetable-only recipes, as well as ones that are designed to accompany or incorporate meat, fish, poultry and seafood. There are breakfast dishes, appetizers, lunch or supper main courses, side dishes, and even desserts. Each and every one of them is made with at least one vegetable.

All the recipes include easy instructions, complete preparation and cooking times and nutritional data. There is also a comprehensive A–Z guide to buying, cooking and storing more than 30 widely available vegetables.

With this book as your guide, you'll soon be including the recommended daily servings of vegetables in your diet and chances are, you'll find you're eating even more.

The Editors

key to recipes

Recipes in this book are marked as follows.

QUICK RECIPE	MAKE AHEAD	HEART HEALTHY
The recipe can be prepared in 30 minutes or less, from start to finish.	The dish can be made in advance and reheated. Or just one small step is needed to complete it.	Less than 30% of the calories in the recipe come from fat.

How to use Nutrition Information Compare the nutrition analysis at the end of each recipe with the following average guidelines to design daily menus that are within healthy limits.

			daily nutrition information			
	calories	protein	total fat (limit to 30% of total calories)	cholesterol	sodium (1,200–2,300 if aged 70 or over)	fiber
women	2,000	50 grams	66 grams	300 mg	1,500–2,300 mg	25 grams
men	2,700	63 grams	90 grams	300 mg	1,500–2,300 mg	38 grams

contents

the rewards of vegetables

vegetable variations

The world of vegetables is flourishing. All year round, new flavors, colors, sizes and shapes are widely available.

anyone who cooks or shops for food will have noticed the quiet revolution that's taken place in the world of vegetables over the last 20 years. Today, there are an astonishing number of choices. Most supermarkets carry three or four kinds of cabbages, five different potatoes and six types of lettuce. Tomatoes, too, come in many shapes and sizes. There are red and yellow cherry tomatoes and grape and roma varieties as well as vine-ripened, greenhouse and heirloom to choose from.

Other newcomers include bok choy and a wide variety of Chinese cabbages; cooking greens and okra; broccoli rabe (rapini) and broccolini; beans, squash and carrots of many colors. There are many new vegetables to experiment with.

One of the main forces behind this change is our expanding knowledge of the health benefits that come from eating vegetables. We know that nothing can beat a vegetable for providing rich amounts of fiber, nutrients, vitamins and fuel in a convenient, low-calorie form. Then there are the health benefits beyond simply daily nutrition. Phytochemicals – the natural chemicals in vegetables that display significant healing powers – are thought to bolster immunity, battle cancer, reduce stress, improve skin and hair… and much more.

Thanks to this new evidence, the medical world began campaigning to encourage people to eat at least seven to 10 servings of fruits and vegetables a day. Add to that the fact that food distribution ensures there are plenty of choices available year-round, not to mention the ever-growing variety of vegetables on the market.

If you, like so many people, don't want to buy produce that's traveled long distances to get to you, there are excellent alternatives closer to home. Over the past few years, there's been a steady, welcome growth in farmers' markets right around the country. Small growers bring their freshly picked, and often organically grown or vine-ripened, produce to these weekend markets, attracting discerning customers who are happy to have the opportunity to buy from them direct.

our sources for vegetables

Some farmers rely on cutting-edge science, while others have gone natural. Never before has there been so much debate about how vegetables are grown.

Most vegetables in North America are grown on farms specializing in one or two varieties of a particular plant. The varieties destined for market rather than a food processing plant have been bred to withstand long trips to market and to have a long shelf life.

The farms that grow these vegetables are remarkably efficient operations that skillfully use irrigation systems, chemical pesticides, herbicides and fertilizers to ensure bumper crops. The result can be good-looking, nutritious vegetables with very little flavor.

the organic alternative

Organic does not simply mean chemical-free, it also refers to the way that food is grown and handled. An increasing number of people are choosing to buy organic vegetables, knowing that they are grown under environmentally friendly conditions, rather than on commercial farms that use chemical pesticides, herbicides and fertilizers.

Both the US and Canada have clear laws on what consitiutes an organic product, but the best way to know is to buy *certified* organic foods. Certified organic growers do not use synthetic chemicals, fertilizers or genetically modified organisms (GMOs) in their farming practices, in keeping with the set standards and principles that certification requires. Look for the USDA or Canada Organic certification logo on the product. Certification ensures you're buying an item that fulfills all of the requirements for being considered "organic."

Slowly but surely, as farmers' markets have proliferated, organic foods have worked their way into the mainstream. In fact, some of the larger supermarket chains also stock organic foods (both dried and fresh), which will ultimately help to lower the higher cost of buying organic produce.

to clean

Vegetables should be cleaned before they're eaten, especially when the skin will be consumed. Some, such as potatoes, mushrooms and spinach, hold on to the dirt they were grown in and require more careful cleaning than others.

leafy greens Soak them in a sink filled with cold water, swirling the leaves around a few times to be sure all grit and sand is removed. Remove the greens from the water and inspect them for signs of dirt and grit. If still dirty, wash them again in clean water. Greens that come straight from the farm may need washing several times.

mushrooms Wipe them with a dry paper towel or use a soft-bristled brush designed for the purpose to remove surface dirt. Avoid cleaning mushrooms with water as they will become soggy.

root vegetables such as potatoes, carrots and sweet potatoes require a good scrubbing with a vegetable brush to remove all pockets of dirt. Cut out any soft, moldy or soggy parts with a knife.

You should not have to peel carrots unless the skin has dried out or is unusually dirty.

smooth-skinned vegetables such as zucchini, tomatoes, eggplant and peppers should be held under cool water and gently rubbed to remove residual dirt and chemicals.

biotechnology and the food supply

When biology, biochemistry, chemical engineering, genetics and computer science merged to form the science of food biotechnology, new forms of plant and animal life were created, as well as a means of enhancing the quality and quantity of commercially produced agricultural products.

Genetically modified (GM) foods are a controversial result of this science. Genetic engineering is the transfer of genes among plants and animals, allowing scientists to copy a gene for a desirable trait in one organism and implant it into another. And while it sounds positive, many consumers have concerns about the safety of GM foods.

The two major concerns are the possibility of allergic reactions in some people, and what is referred to as "gene pollution," or the escape of genetically engineered genes into the wild through natural cross-pollination, which is a very real concern, coinsidering that many of these organisms are grown in fields adjacent to non-GMO farms. Some 60 percent of processed foods – both imported and local – now contain GM ingredients, additives or processing.

food irradiation

Irradiation helps preserve food using ionizing radiation to destroy disease-causing bacteria and other pathogens on food. Also known as *cold pasteurization*, it can be used to make fresh and dried fruits, vegetables, herbs and spices safer for consumers. Irradiation extends the shelf life of fresh vegetables by delaying the ripening process in some vegetables and by inhibiting sprouting in others.

According to both the US FDA and the Canadian Food Inspection Agency, irradiated products must be labeled (either on the packaging, or in the case of unpackaged food, on an adjacent card) with both the international Radura logo and an accompanying statement that reads "treated by radiation," "treated with radiation" or "irradiated."

csa and u-pick

Short of growing your own, there's no better way to get fresh fruit and vegetables than by visiting a pick-your-own farm or supporting a Community-Supported Agriculture farm (in the US) or Community Shared Agriculture farm (in Canada).

For a U-pick, each farm will have its own set of rules, but you may have to pay an admission fee. In general, though, you pay on a price-per-pound/kilo basis at a U-pick.

A CSA will usually charge a yearly membership fee, and some will require you to spend some time digging out at the farm. Your fee will get you a regular basket of fresh produce that you can pick up at a central location.

Here are some tips to help you get the most out of your pick-you-own farm experience:

Some pick-your-own farms don't provide buckets, so go armed with your own.

It's a farm out there. Take a hat, sturdy shoes, protective clothing, insect repellent and sunscreen.

Don't expect picture-perfect, pristine produce. This is not a factory farm that uses chemicals and genetic engineering to create perfectly round tomatoes. What the goods lack in appearance, they will make up for in flavor.

hydroponic farming

Hydroponics is a method of growing plants in nutrient-enriched (fertilized) water, rather than in soil. Among the most popular and widely cultivated hydroponic crops are tomatoes, cucumbers, lettuces and herbs, because these are the most cost-effective. Hydroponic farming is not a cheaper way of farming, especially when crops are grown in greenhouses, and the plant nutrients used can be twice as expensive as field fertilizer. It's also a time-consuming technique requiring constant attention and special skills.

On the positive side, hydroponically grown plants are larger and grow faster than those that are grown in soil because they routinely receive high-grade nutrients and their growing conditions are so well controlled. The growing season is extended because the plants are frequently grown indoors, where temperature, light and humidity are controlled. Also, hydroponic crops can be farmed in places where the soil may be deemed unsuitable for growing similar crops. Since they grow in water, hydroponic crops also use much less extra water than crops grown in fields. Perhaps the greatest commercial advantage is that, with a hydroponic system in place, significantly more crops can be grown in a smaller amount of space. A hydroponic farm can yield more tomatoes per acre than a conventional farm because plants can be grown closer together.

farmers' markets

Not only has the way vegetables are grown undergone major changes; so has the way vegetables are sold. The supermarket is no longer your main option.

today, country and city dwellers alike can enjoy, in an unprecedented way, the benefits of truly fresh and varied produce from the many small farmers who are willing to load up their trucks in the early morning darkness and drive to urban or suburban markets to sell their vegetables, fruits and other agricultural products.

Farmers' markets have provided a real alternative to those export markets that force farmers to both overproduce and overuse chemical sprays and fertilizers, and then pay them less and less for their crops. Partly as a result of that and partly because people are seeking out organic and locally produced fruits and vegetables more and more, farmers' markets are on the rise. At a farmers' market – also sometimes called a growers' market – small producers have the necessary platform to sell their food directly to the public.

In most of the markets, management or a centralized municipal or governmental association rents a space to each individual grower or artisan, and takes care of running the market facilities. The benefit of this arrangement is passed on to you in the form of affordable produce and a pleasant shopping experience.

a friendly way to shop

Wandering through farmers' markets is not only a pleasant way to come across fresh, local foods, it's also a wonderful opportunity to get to know the men and women who grow them. They can tell you about the different varieties of produce that they grow and the best ways to prepare, cook and serve them. They will also alert you to the crops that will be arriving in the coming weeks. It is no wonder that these markets have become so popular that they rank as major tourist attractions in many towns and cities.

Farmers, consumers and community members at large all benefit from farmers' markets. Many small farmers are in business only because of the popularity of urban open-air markets. With no middlemen, they're able to charge low prices and still make a profit because they keep the money that would otherwise be lost to shipping, distribution and marketing through supermarkets. As a result, city dwellers get to enjoy such things as corn picked the same day, vine-ripened tomatoes, tree-ripened peaches and richly flavored honey, straight from the hive, all at decent prices.

a boost to nutrition

There are many ways vendors at farmers' markets help to promote good health besides selling fresh, seasonal food. Small farmers frequently offer unusual varieties of fruits and vegetables that aren't found in regular supermarkets because they are not grown on larger commercial farms.

Farmers' markets do more than provide fresh food and preserve a tradition of small family farms. They help bring a sense of purpose and pride to the areas where they are located. In many cities, the presence of a farmers' market has brought about neighborhood improvements and helped to stimulate further commercial development in the area. Not surprisingly, it looks like they are not only here to stay, but will expand into more areas.

websites

In the US www.localharvest.org (Local Harvest, Inc.) lists farms, farmers' markets and Community Supported Agriculture (CSA) farms across the US and some parts of Canada.

In Canada www.farmersmarketscanada.ca (Farmers' Markets Canada) has a directory of markets listed by province.

how to shop at a farmers' market

Go early in the day. The market is likely to be less crowded, nothing will have run out and you will have the pick of the crop.

Browse before you buy. Wander around the market to see everything that is offered and to compare quality and prices.

Talk to the vendors. Many market stands are set up by the farmers or producers themselves. They can provide ideas, tips and sometimes even recipes for using their products.

Plan your meals around what is available. Farmers' markets sell seasonal, locally grown vegetables and fruits. Whatever is there is at its peak, so it's best to see what's available rather than shop with a set menu in mind.

Taste the samples. Many stalls will offer a taste tester or sample of their products for you to try before you buy.

Bring a large shopping bag or trolley. Stallholders may not provide bags, although environmentally friendly bags are sometimes on sale at the market.

vegetables as health superstars

You may have thought that seven servings of vegetables each day were enough. But research indicates that an even larger number of servings is advisable. Here are seven compelling reasons to eat more vegetables:

white rice) causes blood sugar spikes and can contribute to weight gain, that doesn't hold true for most vegetables. The carbohydrates contained in vegetables are usually complex, which means that they need to be broken down substantially before they can be available to the cells for fuel. In fact, nutrition experts recommend getting up to 60 percent of your daily calories from carbohydrates, in particular the complex carbohydrates found in grains, beans and starchy vegetables like corn and peas.

2 rich in fiber

Fiber, simply defined, is the material in a plant that your body cannot digest. On the surface, it would seem that fiber would provide little benefit, as it passes undigested through your body. But the opposite is true. There are two types of fiber – soluble and insoluble – and each has unique benefits.

"Soluble" refers to something that dissolves in water. Soluble fiber mixes with water and food in the digestive tract to form a gooey gel that slows digestion and makes blood sugar enter the bloodstream more gradually; this is a particularly good benefit for people with Type 2 diabetes. This gel also binds with fats and cholesterol, making it beneficial for the heart.

Insoluble fiber has many benefits as well. It creates a feeling of fullness, making it important for weight loss; it helps bulk up stools, preventing constipation; it cleans the digestive tract as it passes through, which doctors believe may help prevent gastrointestinal diseases such as colon cancer and diverticulosis.

Grains and vegetables, not surprisingly, are excellent sources of fiber. Cauliflower, green beans and potatoes are especially rich in the fiber your body needs.

1 provide great fuel

The human body needs a very wide range of nutrients for general health and daily function. But it has need of only one for energy: glucose, commonly known as blood sugar. The human body is equipped to digest just about any food into glucose, including fats and protein. But without doubt, the best source of fuel for your body is the carbohydrates found in vegetables.

The emergence of high-protein weight-loss programs has contributed to a lot of confusion over whether starches or carbohydrates are as good for you as once thought. While it's true that eating too many simple carbohydrates (foods easily converted to glucose, such as white flour, sugar and

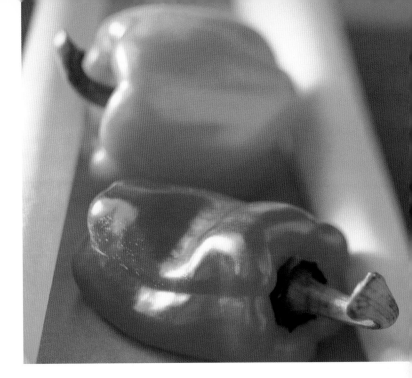

provide quality protein

Although proteins supplied by vegetables and other plant foods are considered "incomplete" when compared to protein from animal sources, they find each other in the body, hook up and form complete proteins that are equal in quality to protein from meat. A diet that includes lots of vegetables, grains and legumes supplies the nine essential amino acids. That is why a balanced vegetarian diet can provide all the protein a person needs.

virtually fat-free

Reducing your total fat intake reduces the risk of developing heart disease, certain cancers and other chronic diseases. Interestingly, some dietary fats that are considered most healthy are oils that come from vegetable sources such as olives and corn. These fats help keep blood cholesterol levels down, while fats from animal sources tend to raise cholesterol and total fat in the blood.

help with weight loss

Vegetables are the perfect food for weight loss. Most vegetables – particularly leafy greens – are low in calories. As a result, they can be eaten in large quantities and are an excellent source of nutrients.

Then there's the fiber in vegetables, which makes you feel full more quickly, and which binds with fats on its way through the digestive tract. Vegetable carbohydrates are mostly complex, meaning that they provide great fuel, but in healthy, steady ways. Even starchy plant foods such as grains, legumes, sweet potatoes, corn and squashes have a place in a weight-loss program. While not especially low in calories, they are high in fiber and nutrients and can be very filling in small amounts.

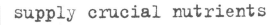
supply crucial nutrients

For everyday function, your body needs proteins, fats and carbohydrates for fuel and cellular growth. Your body also needs vitamins, minerals, and other substances for the chemistry of life – the manufacturing of hormones, the creation of immune cells, the functioning of the brain and nervous system. Your body also needs ingredients like calcium and magnesium for bones and teeth, and iron and potassium for blood.

Vegetables are an outstanding source for all these nutrients. Plants are dense with the minerals, vitamins and important chemicals you need to function.

help prevent disease

For untold centuries, many human cultures have used food as part of the healing process. But only in the past 20 years or so have scientists dived deeply into the science of phytochemicals and the healing power of vegetables, fruit and grains.

Phytochemicals are natural chemicals in plants that are beneficial to human health. Technically, vitamins and minerals in vegetables are phytochemicals, but the term is used for a whole group of ingredients with complicated names and very specific usages. For example, broccoli, cabbage and other types of green vegetables are rich in chemicals called glucosinolates that research reveals can be used in the battle against cancers. Garlic and onions are rich in sulfur compounds such as allicin that also battle cancer and cholesterol. Peppers contain bioflavonoids, which help to neutralize free radicals in the bloodstream.

A single plant food can contain many hundreds of these disease-fighting nutrients. These nutrients give vegetables their brilliant colors, distinctive flavors and appetizing aromas. They protect the plants from insects, bacteria, viruses, UV light and other environmental threats. In the human body, their benefits are similarly broad. They help the body to dispose of potentially hazardous substances such as carcinogens and free radicals. They stimulate the body's immune cells and infection-fighting enzymes.

While an increasing number of these plant chemicals are being sold in supplement form, doctors maintain that the best thing to do is to eat a diversity of fresh produce, spanning a wide range of colors and sources.

the big 10

All vegetables are good for you, but some do more than others to keep you healthy. The 10 discussed here are the superstars and feature in many of the recipes in this book. They all contain macronutrients for fuel, micronutrients for daily chemistry and phytochemicals for long-term health.

broccoli is a prime source of calcium; vitamins A and C; antioxidant beta-carotene; folate, which helps reduce the risk of cancer and heart disease; insoluble fiber; and potassium. While that's a good start, broccoli's super status is based on the properties of its many other phytochemicals. Among these are dithiolethiones, which are anti-cancer agents; indoles, which help combat hormone-related cancers; isothiocyanates, which stimulate cancer-fighting enzymes and also neutralize cancer-causing substances such as smoke; lutein, which fights colon cancer and eye diseases; and sulforaphane, which reduces tumor formation and stimulates cancer-fighting enzymes.

brussels sprouts are part of the family of cruciferous vegetables to which broccoli belongs, and contain many of the same vitamins and phytochemicals, including isothiocyanates, indoles and sulforaphane.

cabbage is a third member of the phytochemical-rich cruciferous vegetable family. Cabbage is thought to reduce hormone-related cancers as well as cancers of the colon and rectum. It is also a great source of vitamin C, carotenoids and folate.

peppers of all types contain good amounts of vitamin C. Red peppers contain lutein and zeaxanthin, carotenoids that may lower the risk of age-related blindness due to macular degeneration and cataracts, as well as forms of cancer. Chili peppers contain concentrated amounts of capsaicin, which is used topically to treat pain and can help to inhibit cholesterol formation. Chlorophyll in peppers may protect against environmental carcinogens.

carrots are super sources of beta-carotene, an antioxidant and a precursor to vitamin A, which maintains healthy eyesight, cell growth, skin and hair. They are rich in calcium pectate, which helps remove cholesterol from the body, and insoluble fiber, preventing constipation.

cauliflower is another crucifer that is rich in vitamin C and folate and provides such phytochemicals as indoles and isothiocyanates. In scientific studies, indoles have been shown to interfere with hormones that fuel the growth of breast cancer tumors.

dark leafy greens such as kale, spinach and Swiss chard contain disease-fighting phytochemicals as well as rich amounts of vitamin C, bone-building and anti-clotting vitamin K, beta-carotene and fiber. Chlorophyll in these greens may help block the changes that turn healthy cells into pre-cancerous ones. Kale is a rich source of lutein and zeaxanthin, both linked to the prevention of macular degeneration and some cancers.

pumpkin & squash are super-rich in beta-carotene, potassium, vitamin B_6, vitamin C and lutein. They contain large amounts of soluble fiber, which helps lower cholesterol. They are also a source of brain-boosting thiamine and magnesium, a valuable mineral that may help control allergies and prevent heart disease.

sweet potatoes are extremely high in beta-carotene, which helps prevent cancers such as those of the stomach, pancreas, mouth and gums; potassium, which is associated with lower blood pressure; vitamin B_6, which may help prevent heart disease; vitamin C, which bolsters immunity; and, when eaten with the skin on, insoluble fiber prevents constipation and diverticulosis. Sweet potatoes also contain caffeic acid, which may help fight cancer and the AIDS virus; cancer-fighting chlorogenic acid; lutein and zeaxanthin to protect against cancer and eye diseases; and cholesterol-lowering plant sterols.

tomatoes and tomato products, such as sauce, paste and juice, are rich sources of cancer-fighting beta-carotene and immunity-boosting vitamin C. Tomatoes contain lycopene, a carotenoid that suppresses damage caused by free radicals and is associated with the reduced risk of heart attack and prostate cancer; caffeic and ferulic acids, which enhance the body's production of cancer-fighting enzymes; and chlorogenic acid, which may help to guard against cancer by blocking the effects of toxins.

top 10 vitamins & minerals

vitamin/mineral	may be helpful for	where to find it
calcium	anxiety and stress, high blood pressure, hyperthyroidism, osteoporosis, overweight, peri-menopause and menopause, PMS, pregnancy	broccoli, dairy products, salmon or sardines with bones, tofu
folate	anemia, cancer, depression, heart disease, infertility and impotence, insomnia, osteoporosis, pregnancy, rheumatoid arthritis	asparagus, avocados, beans, beets, broccoli, cabbage family, citrus fruit, cooking greens, corn, lentils, peas, rice, spinach
iron	anemia, immune deficiency, memory loss, pregnancy	apricots, fatty fish, figs, lentils, meat, peas, poultry, shellfish
magnesium	allergies and asthma, anxiety and stress, chronic fatigue syndrome, constipation, diabetes, high blood pressure, kidney stones, migraine, PMS	avocados, grains, nuts, pumpkin and squash, rice, seeds, shellfish, spinach
selenium	allergies and asthma, cancer, hypothyroidism, infertility and impotence, macular degeneration, prostate problems	meat, mushrooms, nuts, poultry, rice, seeds, shellfish, whole grains
vitamin B_6	acne, anemia, anxiety and stress, depression, heart disease, hypothyroidism, insomnia, memory loss, PMS, pregnancy	asparagus, bananas, fatty fish, figs, mushrooms, peas, potatoes, poultry, pumpkin and squash, rice, sweet potatoes
vitamin B_{12}	anemia, depression, heart disease, infertility and impotence	dairy products, fatty fish, meat, poultry, shellfish
vitamin C	allergies and asthma, anemia, bronchitis, cancer, cataracts, chronic fatigue syndrome, cold sores, colds and flu, diabetes, eczema, hemorrhoids, heart disease, infertility and impotence, high blood pressure, hyperthyroidism, immune deficiency, macular degeneration, osteoarthritis, osteoporosis, rheumatoid arthritis, sinusitis, sprains	berries, cabbage family, peppers, citrus fruit, kiwis, melons, peas, pineapple, potatoes, pumpkins and squash, salad greens, spinach, sweet potatoes, tomatoes, turnips
vitamin E	bronchitis, cancer, cataracts, eczema, hyperthyroidism, immune deficiency, infertility and impotence, macular degeneration, memory loss, osteoarthritis, prostate problems, rheumatoid arthritis	avocados, grains, nuts, olive oil, salad greens, seeds
zinc	acne, bronchitis, chronic fatigue syndrome, colds, eczema, hemorrhoids, hypothyroidism, immunity, infertility and impotence, macular degeneration, rosacea, sinusitis	beans, grains, meat, poultry, seeds, shellfish

the vegetable arsenal

Researchers are discovering that phytonutrients can help to heal many medical conditions. Here's a sampling of vegetables that contain healing agents for 16 common health conditions or concerns.

condition	vegetable	healing nutrient
allergies & asthma	red onions	quercetin
	broccoli	vitamin C
	peppers and chili peppers	vitamin C
cancer prevention	garlic	allium compounds
	onions	allium compounds
	carrots	beta-carotene
	sweet potatoes	beta-carotene
	broccoli	flavonoids, glucosinolates
	asparagus	folate
	beets	folate
	spinach	folate
	brussels sprouts	glucosinolates
	cabbage	glucosinolates
	tomatoes	lycopene
	mushrooms	selenium
	peppers	vitamin C
diabetes	asparagus	fiber
	canola oil	monounsaturated fat
	olive oil	monounsaturated fat
	peppers	vitamin C
	broccoli	vitamin C
heart disease	asparagus	folate
	spinach	folate
	carrots	soluble fiber
	soy foods	soy protein
high blood pressure	broccoli	calcium
	cooking greens	calcium
	asparagus	dietary fiber
	potatoes	potassium
	peppers	vitamin C
high cholesterol	onions	flavonoids
	tomatoes	lycopene
	carrots	soluble fiber
	garlic	sulfur compounds
immune deficiency	carrots	carotenoids
	sweet potatoes	carotenoids
	tomatoes	carotenoids
	onions	flavonoids
	peppers and chili peppers	vitamin C

condition	vegetable	healing nutrient
macular degeneration	carrots	beta-carotene
	spinach	beta-carotene
	pumpkins and squash	beta-carotene
	collard greens	lutein and zeaxanthin
	peppers and chili peppers	lutein and zeaxanthin
	spinach	lutein and zeaxanthin
	sweet potatoes	lutein and zeaxanthin
	tomatoes	lycopene
	broccoli	vitamin C
osteoarthritis	sweet potatoes	folate
	peppers and chili peppers	vitamin C
osteoporosis	cooking greens	calcium
	peppers and chili peppers	vitamin C
	kale	vitamin K
	spinach	vitamin K
overweight	broccoli	calcium
	cooking greens	calcium
	asparagus	dietary fiber
	beets	dietary fiber
skin problems	broccoli	antioxidants
	carrots	antioxidants
	tomatoes	antioxidants
	asparagus	beta-carotene
	sweet potatoes	beta-carotene
	pumpkins and squash	beta-carotene
	potatoes	vitamin B6
stress	broccoli	calcium
	cooking greens	calcium
	asparagus	folate
	peas	folate
	salad greens	folate
	peas	tryptophan
	turnips	tryptophan
	potatoes	vitamin B6
stroke	broccoli	calcium
	asparagus	dietary fiber
	beets	dietary fiber
	onions	flavonoids
	potatoes	potassium
	peppers and chili peppers	vitamin C
tooth and mouth conditions	broccoli	calcium
	cooking greens	calcium
	celery	insoluble fiber
	salad greens	insoluble fiber
	peppers and chili peppers	vitamin C
yeast infections	garlic	allicin
	artichokes	fructo-oligosaccharides
	onions	fructo-oligosaccharides

10 ways to eat more vegetables

Your goal is to include more vegetables in your diet. Trying new recipes will help, of course, but there are many other simple ways to add vegetables to your meals. Here are 10 to get you started that will be easy to adopt.

 serve them straight up
Put a platter of sliced raw vegetables on the table each suppertime. Particularly enjoyable for their crunchiness and fresh taste are tomatoes, carrots, celery, cucumbers and green peppers. Serve them with a dip, salsa or vinaigrette.

have a nightly salad
A handful of prepackaged salad greens, a few cherry tomatoes, sliced cucumber or apple and you have a healthy salad in barely a minute. It's a great way to start supper.

 roast them
Many vegetables develop a full-bodied, intense flavor when roasted in the oven. In winter, go for root vegetables such as parsnips, turnips, beets and potatoes. In summertime, mushrooms, zucchini, tomatoes, peppers and onions work well. Cut the larger vegetables into chunks, toss them in oil, vinegar and seasonings and place in a roasting pan. Cook at a medium heat for about 30 minutes, depending on their thickness. To ensure even cooking, be sure to cook vegetables of similar textures and piece sizes in the one pan.

 purée into soup
Potatoes, carrots, squash, cauliflower and broccoli – just about any cooked (or leftover) vegetable can be made into a creamy, comforting soup.

 do a fast sauté
Select two or three favorite vegetables and cut into bite-sized pieces. Heat a frying pan or small wok to a high temperature. Swirl a little olive oil in the pan until hot and add the vegetables. Toss until cooked through. Add salt, pepper and thyme or soy sauce and a little sesame oil and toss to combine. Serve at once.

 make into sauce
Quick and easy cooked and uncooked sauces and salsas can be made with tomatoes, onions, peppers or mushrooms, on their own or in combination with other vegetables.

fill an omelette
There are few vegetables that aren't suitable to include in an omelette, especially when a little grated or crumbled cheese is added. Good ones to try are onions, peppers, tomatoes, mushrooms and potatoes.

grate into ground meat
To enhance the flavor and nutritional value of ground meat for burgers and meat loaves, add up to a cup of grated or finely chopped raw vegetables to the mixture before shaping and cooking. Carrots, zucchini, peppers, mushrooms, spinach and onions work well.

 cook in the oven
Finely chopped peppers or onions flavor the meat beautifully when placed inside rolled fillets of pork, beef or chicken.

 try a recipe makeover
Add chopped cooked spinach or grated carrot to the sauce you use to make lasagna. Increase the amount of vegetables and decrease the amount of meat you use to make homemade soups, stews and casseroles.

seasoning guide

Sometimes all you need is the right herb, spice, fruit or juice to turn a plain vegetable into a spectacular side dish. And sometimes the best way to season a vegetable is by cooking it with another vegetable.

artichokes	lemon, butter, garlic, oregano
asparagus	lemon, mustard, dill, parmesan cheese, soy sauce, dark sesame oil, capers
avocados	chili powder, cumin, grapefruit, lemon, lime, orange, oregano
beans	olive oil, parsley, lemon, sesame seeds, soy sauce
beets	balsamic vinegar, dill, lemon, rosemary, apple, pecans
broccoli	grapefruit, orange, garlic, soy sauce, dark sesame oil, a mustard/mayonnaise blend
broccoli rabe (rapini)	olive oil, garlic, chili flakes, chili sauce, soy sauce
brussels sprouts	chives, scallions, mustard
cabbage	caraway seeds, garlic, sugar and vinegar (sweet and sour), soy sauce, dark sesame oil, ginger, apple
peppers	balsamic vinegar, garlic, cured olives, capers, thyme, soy sauce and ginger, chili powder, cumin
carrots	citrus, curry powder, honey, ginger, lemon, dill, raspberry vinegar
cauliflower	basil, lemon thyme, curry powder, a mustard/mayonnaise blend
celery	garlic, oregano, soy sauce, dark sesame oil
corn	basil, butter, chili powder

cucumbers	dill, sugar and vinegar (sweet and sour), sesame seeds, soy sauce
eggplants	basil, garlic, tomato, chili sauce, sesame oil
fennel	bay leaf, tomato, parmesan cheese
green beans	garlic, soy sauce, sesame seeds
leafy greens	(such as spinach) citrus, dill, garlic, pine nuts, raisins, sesame seeds
mushrooms	balsamic vinegar, chives, scallions, parsley, thyme
okra	lemon, marjoram, tomato, thyme
parsnips	parmesan cheese, thyme
peas	mint, dark sesame oil, sesame seeds
potatoes	chives, curry powder, garlic, yogurt, roast pepper, rosemary
pumpkin & squash	maple syrup, nuts, citrus, garlic, ginger, cinnamon, apples, pears, cranberries, dried fruit, rosemary
spinach	raisins, garlic, cracked pepper, sea salt, soy sauce
sweet potatoes	maple syrup, butter, citrus, ginger, cinnamon, cranberries, dried fruit
tomatoes	balsamic or white wine vinegar, basil, garlic, oregano, parmesan or romano cheese
turnips	honey, apple, pear, lemon, walnuts

herbs & spices

allspice tastes like a mix of ginger, nutmeg, cinnamon and pepper.

anise has a strong licorice flavor that works well in cakes and biscuits.

basil has a warm, anise flavor. It is a major ingredient in pesto and also boosts the flavor of tomato-based dishes.

bay leaf, with its woodsy flavor, is a staple in meat dishes and stews. Add the dry leaf at the start of cooking; remove just before serving.

black peppercorns are sharp and aromatic. Grind black pepper as needed.

caraway seeds impart an aromatic, anise flavor to breads and cakes and cheese, vegetable and meat dishes. The seeds have a nutty texture.

cardamom is a relative of ginger. One of the main ingredients in curry powder, it is used in cakes, ice-cream and mulled wine. Lightly crush whole pods to flavor slow-cooked dishes, as well as milk to be used in sauces.

cayenne, ground from dried red chili peppers, adds a hot, peppery taste to sauces and stews. It is widely used in Mexican dishes.

celery seeds may be tiny but they pack a punch, adding a strong celery flavor to sauces, dips and soups.

one of the tastiest and healthiest ways to enhance the flavor of foods is to cook with herbs and spices.

choose fragrant, fresh-looking herbs with no wilted, yellowing leaves or brown spots. Store loosely wrapped in a damp paper towel and then in plastic, in the crisper drawer of the refrigerator. Most fresh herbs will last only a few days. Basil and mint do best standing upright in a jar of water in the fridge, loosely covered with a paper towel and then plastic.

chop fresh herbs and crush the seeds just before using. Add herbs to cooked dishes during the last 30 minutes of cooking time or they will lose their pungency. Add herbs to uncooked dishes at least 1 hour before serving so that their flavors have time to marry with other ingredients.

spices are sold dried; you can grind them yourself for the freshest taste or buy them ready-ground, in which case replenish your stocks regularly.

chervil tastes of anise and parsley. It enhances chicken, egg, prawn, potato and salad dishes.

chili powder varies in its degree of heat depending on what type of chili it is made from. Taste a tiny bit before using to gauge how much to use.

chives add a sweet onion flavor to dips, salads and sauces. They're easy to grow yourself in a pot or they can be bought fresh, frozen or freeze-dried.

cilantro is a herb and coriander is a spice made from the seeds. Either form has a pungent taste that is popular in Mexican or southwest cooking and Asian cuisines. The seeds are included in most curry powders and spice mixes.

cinnamon in stick form can be used to flavor milk for sauce and custard recipes. Ground cinnamon is a popular flavoring in desserts and baking. It is also used in Moroccan and Greek cuisines. It is mixed with sugar to make cinnamon toast.

cloves have a very intense, musky taste that mellows during cooking. They can be used to stud hams before baking and to spike apples for cider punch or for pies. Use ground cloves in cookies, cakes and sauces.

cumin seeds and ground cumin both have an earthy flavor that adds richness to bean and shellfish recipes and Mexican cooking.

 **dill** seeds and the feathery leaves (both fresh and dried) are used. Chopped leaves lift the flavor of eggs and seafood, as well as beets, cucumber and potatoes. Dill seeds are used in pickling.

 fennel seeds have an anise taste that complements the rich flavor of pork.

 ginger has a warm, slight lemony flavor. Fresh ginger is peeled and grated or diced and added to Asian dishes such as stir-fries and to spicy curries and stews. Store fresh ginger in the freezer. Ground dried ginger is used for cakes and cookies.

mace is the external covering of the nutmeg seed that is also ground as a spice. It is hotter than nutmeg and a classic spice for pound cake.

 marjoram has a spicy, cleansing taste that goes with most vegetables, especially those that are used in Mediterranean dishes and Mexican recipes.

 mint is a refreshing herb that enlivens salads, fruit salads and fruit drinks such as lemonade. In jelly or sauce form, it enhances the taste of roast lamb. It works well with fish.

mustard seeds are used to make many popular commercial mustards ranging from fairly mild Dijon to fiery English mustard. Pungent ground mustard seed (powder) is used in homemade mayonnaise and many sauces that can be served with fish, poultry and meat.

 nutmeg has a warm, nutty flavor that complements spinach, pumpkin and savoury dishes, as well as baked goods and custards.

 **oregano** tastes like a stronger version of marjoram. A feature of Mediterranean cuisines, it enhances poultry, beef, veal and lamb dishes, tomatoes and cabbage.

paprika, like cayenne, is a product of ground dried red chili peppers. However, it is sweeter and milder than chili powder. Hungarian paprika is among the best and is particularly aromatic. It is used in goulashes and other slow-cooked dishes.

 parsley comes in curly-leaf and flat-leaf varieties. They are interchangeable, both adding a fresh taste to potatoes, grains, mushrooms, salads, sauces and meat dishes. Chewing fresh parsley is said to freshen the breath.

 rosemary has an intense, earthy taste. Use it in marinades and for flavoring barbecued, grilled and roast meat such as lamb. It also complements beans, peas, mushrooms and zucchini.

saffron, the most expensive of all spices, is obtained from the stamens of a single variety of crocus. Its very fine threads are used to flavor and color rice dishes, vegetable soups, seafood dishes and sweet rolls.

 sage has a woodsy, aromatic flavor that is popular in Italian cooking. It teams well with tomatoes and garlic and also complements onions, legumes, pork, poultry and stuffing.

sea salt comes in coarse granules. Depending on its source, it has subtle flavors from trace minerals. As well as its use as a food flavoring, it is a preserving medium in pickling and drying. It is used to make Asian soy and fish sauces and shrimp paste. Food without any salt added will be bland. While too much salt is bad for the heart, too little is a danger in hot climates and during exercise when the body loses salt through sweating.

 **summer savory** is a peppery herb that spices up green beans, dried beans, cabbages, potatoes and brussels sprouts, as well as fish, poultry and pork.

tarragon, popular in French cuisine, has a mild anise flavor. Stir through scrambled eggs or sprinkle on carrots, greens, seafood and chicken.

 thyme has a light, spicy flavor that complements salad greens, carrots and mushrooms. It goes well with oil-rich fish. It is a key ingredient, with parsley and bay, in a bouquet garni.

a world of flavors

There are so many popular herbs and spices, you could spend a lifetime exploring them. But if you really want to add some flair and personality to your cooking, you need to explore the cuisines of the world.

each of the world's cuisines has its trademark fruit or vegetable and signature dishes that set it apart from the food of other countries. But the thing that most defines a cusine is the blend of seasonings and spices that it utilizes.

Following are some of the basic seasonings and condiments that help give each cuisine its distinct flavor.

chinese

chili paste A peppery condiment that varies in intensity depending on the brand. Test before adding to food.

five-spice powder A blend of cinnamon, fennel, cloves, star anise and Szechuan peppercorns. Often used in marinades or as a seasoning for soups, stews and stir-fries.

hoisin sauce A dark, thick, sweet and salty sauce made from fermented soybeans. Use it in stir-fries and as a condiment served at the table.

hot mustard A very vinegary mustard used as a dipping sauce.

sesame oil Light sesame oil has a slightly nutty flavor; add it sparingly at the end of cooking. Dark sesame oil is fragrant and intensely flavored. Nut oils tend to turn rancid in a hot environment so store in a cool place.

soy sauce The most important and commonly used seasoning in China and all of Asia, this salty sauce made from fermented soybeans comes in several varieties. Light soy sauce is

warm spices *include cloves, allspice berries, star anise, cumin (seeds and ground) and caraway seeds.*

thinner and saltier. Dark soy sauce is thicker and less salty. Chinese black soy sauce and Japanese tamari are very dark and sweet.

star anise This pretty star-shaped spice has a strong anise flavor. It comes from a Chinese evergreen tree. Use in soups and stews.

french

chestnut purée Used to add rich, nutty flavor to sauces, baked goods and vegetable side dishes.

mustard The most popular is from the Dijon region; it is sharp and of a medium intensity. Serve at the table or use to add piquancy to sauces and salad dressings.

nut oils These are richly flavored seasoning oils made from hazelnuts, walnuts, almonds and pine nuts. High heat destroys their flavor and also puts them at risk of catching fire. Add a few drops to other milder oils such as peanut oil to impart a little of their flavor. Also use in vinaigrettes or drizzle over cooked vegetables.

peppercorns Green and pink peppercorns feature in dishes where a milder pepper flavor is desired.

greek

kalamata olive spread A purée of olives, olive oil, capers and herbs used as a spread on different breads.

olive oil Extra virgin olive oil with its distinctive strong, fruity flavor is a basic condiment in Greek cuisine. It is always used in vinaigrettes and drizzled over vegetables.

pomegranate syrup This tangy fruit sauce is used in vinaigrettes, sauces and marinades.

indian

chutney A spicy, sometimes sweet, condiment used as a relish with rice dishes and curries. Coriander, mango, lemon, mint and date are among the most common chutneys.

curry powder An aromatic blend of seeds and spices used to flavor curries, lentils, meat, poultry, sauces and vegetable dishes. Some powders are much hotter than others.

olive oil is rich in phytochemicals, vitamin E and monounsaturated fat.

garam masala A blend of cumin, cinnamon, black pepper, coriander, cloves and cardamom that is used to flavor curries, rice, beans, potatoes, eggplant and meat dishes. Like all other dried spices, garam masala will quickly lose its flavor unless stored in tightly sealed jars well away from heat and light.

italian

balsamic vinegar The intense flavor of this vinegar comes from boiling down white grapes to about 50 percent of their original volume and fermenting the resultant "must." During an aging process in wooden casks over as many as 25 years, the vinegar becomes sweet, viscous and very concentrated. Flavor depends on the type of wood used to make the casks. Use as a simple flavoring for fish, meats, green salads, vegetables and even citrus fruits and berries.

extra virgin olive oil This deep green, intensely flavored, fragrant, high-grade olive oil is used for pastas, salads and cooked vegetables.

olive paste A rich purée of black or green olives and olive oils. Add it to pasta sauces and salad dressings.

Olive paste is also used as a spread for breads and toast.

sweet pepper paste A purée of roasted peppers, olive oil, vinegar and soft cheese.

japanese

miso Fermented soybean paste used in soups, salad dressings and marinades.

tamari soy sauce Darker and more intense than regular soy sauce.

wasabi A blast-furnace hot, slightly bitter powder or paste. Use sparingly in dips, dressings and sauces.

korean

chili sauce A garlicky sauce used on salads and also as a marinade.

korean barbecue sauce Sweet soy-based sauce for glazing food for grilling or as a condiment to pass at the table.

latin american

adobo sauce A sauce or marinade made with finely chopped or puréed chili peppers, garlic and vinegar and often onions and tomatoes. The blend of ingredients varies depending on the region the sauce is from.

annatto (achiote) A deep red seed that is most often mixed into a paste with vinegar, garlic and other seasonings and used to flavor and color vegetables, soups and meats.

chili powder A blend that usually includes dried chili peppers, oregano, garlic and cumin. Chili powders vary from brand to brand, depending on which chili is used and its ratio to the other ingredients used.

picante sauce A hot sauce used as a table condiment and to flavor soups, salads and salsas. It is also served as a table condiment.

recaito This mild cilantro-based Mexican sauce includes garlic, green peppers, onion and olive oil. Use to season beans, rice and stews.

sofrito A blend of annatto seeds, onions, red and green peppers, garlic, cilantro, tomatoes and other seasonings. It is a basis for many Puerto Rican dishes. Add to beans, rice and soups.

tomatillos Small, green tomato-like fruits with a fruity, sharp and rather sour flavor. Used in salsas, salads and guacamole.

thai

chili paste Includes chili peppers and sweet basil. Use to flavor stir-fries, curries, sauces and marinades.

lemongrass Its sour lemon flavor works well in soups, stews, stir-fries, teas and curries.

tamarind paste Adds an intense sweet-and-sour flavor to stews and curried dishes.

vietnamese

fish sauce A salty, fermented anchovy sauce that is used in small amounts to flavor soups, stir-fries and dipping sauces.

sweet soy sauce A thick, sweet, molasses-like sauce used extensively in Vietnamese and Thai cooking as a marinade or dipping sauce.

hot spices include chili peppers (fresh, dried and ground), pepper-corns (black, white, green and pink) and mustard (seeds and ground).

kitchen essentials

Life in the kitchen is made easier if you have a few small appliances and utensils on hand. To prepare vegetables, invest in some or all of the following.

blender A good appliance for chopping, puréeing or liquefying. Not as versatile as a food processor, but preferable when only a small amount of food is involved. A hand blender is a narrow, handheld appliance that is convenient for making sauces and purées. This type of blender can be immersed right into the cooking pot to purée a soup or a batch of tomato sauce. It can also be immersed into liquid substances in a tall glass to blend a smoothie or shake.

colander Made of plastic or metal, with large holes to let liquids drain quickly. A metal colander can be inserted into a large saucepan for use as a steamer.

cutting board Made of wood, hard rubber, acrylic or plastic. There is no evidence that one type is better, or safer, than another. The important thing is to use separate cutting boards for animal foods and plant foods to eliminate the risk of cross-contamination from raw meat, poultry or seafood to uncooked fruit or vegetables. Also, be sure to wash all types of boards very thoroughly in very hot water.

food processor Handy when needing to chop, grate or purée large amounts. Mini food processors are perfect for chopping or grinding smaller amounts of food or herbs. To chop or grate very small quantities, it is more efficient (and less messy) to use a knife or grater.

How many knives do you need? Not many, really. Start with these three (buy the best quality you can afford) and build up from there.

small paring knife Has a 3 in. (9 cm) blade suitable for scraping carrots, paring asparagus stalks, peeling avocados and removing the strings from celery.

medium-sized serrated knife Slices tomatoes and other soft, juicy vegetables and fruits. It can also be used for slicing bread.

large chef's knife Has an 8–10 in. (20–25 cm) blade for precise, quick and easy slicing, dicing and chopping.

grater Comes in a variety of sizes and types. A four-sided box grater is good for grating, shredding and slicing vegetables and cheese. Extra-fine grating can be done with a small hand-held grater.

mandoline Ideal for slicing a variety of fruits and vegetables. The classic mandoline has interchangeable blades to slice, julienne, crinkle and waffle cut. Keep a mandoline's guard in place to prevent injury.

potato masher Not just useful for potatoes: works on cooked squash, carrots, sweet potatoes and many other root vegetables.

salad spinner Handy for drying salad greens and herbs quickly and evenly.

shears Use for snipping fresh parsley and other herbs. Shears come in handy for other culinary tasks such as trimming pastry and meats and chopping through poultry bones.

steamer Consists of an upper pot with a mesh or perforated bottom that fits into a larger pot, which holds water, stock or some other mixture of liquids. Stackable bamboo or metal steamers which are designed to hold two or three layers of food can be

what's in a serving?

Health experts and nutritionists recommend eating seven to 10 servings of fruits and vegetables every day and as many as nine, if possible. Each of the following constitutes a serving of fruits or vegetables.

1 cup (250 mL) raw, leafy greens such as lettuce, spinach or cabbage

½ cup (125 mL) juice

½ cup (125 mL) cut-up, raw, non-leafy vegetables such as carrot sticks or cucumber rounds

½ cup (125 mL) cooked vegetables

1 piece of fresh fruit

cooking to preserve nutrients

Cooking fresh vegetables helps release certain nutrients and phyto-chemicals, making them more available to your body. But at the same time, improper handling and cooking can destroy essential nutrients, especially vitamin C and folate. Here's how to make sure you preserve these vital nutrients.

store vegetables with care The crisper section of the refrigerator, where many vegetables are stored, is designed to be several degrees cooler and more humid than the upper part of the refrigerator. (Refer to the storage instructions under the individual vegetable headings in the A–Z Guide to Vegetables, page 254.)

leave skins on vegetables such as carrots and potatoes when cooking. Vitamins and minerals are often concentrated in and near the skin. Clean vegetables very thoroughly when the skins are left on.

chop and slice vegetables into larger pieces to reduce the surface area exposed, thereby minimizing nutrient loss. Cook vegetables whole whenever possible. For example, boil potatoes whole in their skins to retain nutrients, then slice or chop them after cooking.

cook vegetables in the minimum amount of water Water-soluble vitamins leach out into cooking water and vanish down the drain when the water is discarded.

cook vegetables only as long as necessary Long cooking times destroy vitamins that are susceptible to heat.

reheat leftover vegetables as quickly as possible to avoid any further nutrient loss.

placed over a frying pan or saucepan. For small amounts of food, a metal, collapsible steamer that fits inside a large or medium-sized pot is useful and inexpensive. Collapsible steamers made of plastic are suitable for use in a microwave oven. If you don't have a steamer, improvise by standing a metal colander or a wire-mesh strainer in a large saucepan. Tightly cover the pan to retain the steaming heat. Steaming is an easy, quick cooking method that is ideal for retaining essential nutrients.

strainers Use over a bowl to drain liquids from solids. Strainers are also used to sift and separate out fine particles. They are available in a range of sizes and made of different gauges of wire mesh attached to a ring frame.

vegetable peeler Many people find these easier to use than a knife to pare vegetables. It is not worth spending a lot of money on one. Discard and replace once the blade grows dull.

cook smart

Stir-frying, blanching, steaming or microwaving are the cooking methods that best preserve the taste, texture and nutritional value of vegetables, but there are other cooking techniques that will also produce great results.

barbecuing Cooking vegetables over hot coals enhances their flavor. Gas and electric barbecues produce a good result, too. Either set the grill to medium-hot or allow hot coals to die down for about 30 minutes before placing vegetables on the rack. Rub all vegetables with cooking oil or toss them in an oil-based marinade or vinaigrette before cooking. Use long-handled tongs to turn the vegetables once, halfway through cooking time, or when they are lightly charred and almost tender.

blanching Cooking vegetables in a large amount of boiling water for a brief period of time. The vegetables can then be immersed in cold water to arrest the cooking process and to retain their bright color.

boiling Cooking vegetables in a pot of rapidly boiling water to cover. Use this method for hard vegetables such as green beans, broccoli spears and carrots. Cook the vegetable just long enough to freshen its color and soften the texture. Bring water to the boil first, add the vegetable and cook uncovered or partially covered.

braising Sautéing vegetables briefly in fat before adding liquid to finish the cooking process. Braising works well with fibrous vegetables such as celery hearts, celeriac, leeks and fennel. Root vegetables and leafy greens also become very tender when they are braised.

frying Cooking vegetables in very hot fat. Pan-frying uses up to ¾ in. (2 cm) of fat in a pan to cook larger pieces of food such as crumb-coated slices of eggplant. Deep frying, where food is completely immersed in hot fat, is the method for cooking batter-coated vegetables, such as those cooked in the Japanese tempura style.

Broiling Browning the surface of vegetables with intense dry heat while cooking the inside. Marinate vegetables or brush with oil before broiling. Fibrous vegetables such as celery and leeks are best if they are first blanched. The broiler should be preheated first. Place the vegetables 4–6 in. (10–15 cm) from the heat.

microwaving Microwaving is a fast, clean and convenient method for cooking many vegetables and retains their nutrients, crispness and color. Place vegetables in a microwave-safe dish with a vented cover and add a small amount of water. The greater the volume of vegetables, the longer it will take for them to be cooked.

roasting Cooking vegetables slowly in an oven with dry heat. When vegetables are roasted, they are usually tossed first in oil or melted butter. High-temperature roasting 400°F–450°F (200°C–230°C) results in well-browned, crisp food.

sautéing Cooking vegetables quickly in a small amount of fat over a relatively high heat. Shaking the sauté pan frequently during cooking keeps the food from sticking. Tender vegetables such as onions, zucchini and mushrooms can be cut up and sautéed very quickly. Hard ones such as carrots, broccoli and cauliflower may benefit from a blanching so as to soften them slightly before sautéing.

steaming Cooking food on a rack above boiling or simmering liquid, usually water. Cooking vegetables in the oven encased in parchment paper or aluminum foil with a little liquid is also a form of steaming.

stir-frying Cooking small pieces of food fast in a wok or frying pan in a small amount of oil over high heat, stirring constantly. Stir-fry just until crisp-tender. Organized preparation is essential for successful stir-frying. Chop vegetables and measure out seasonings ahead of time.

taking stock

roast vegetable broth

The flavor of vegetables is intensified by roasting, resulting in a full-bodied stock.

Makes about 6 cups

2 tablespoons olive oil
3 large carrots
2 medium parsnips, peeled
2 onions, cut into eighths
2 stalks celery, with leaves, halved
4 cloves garlic, unpeeled
3 roma tomatoes, halved
8 cups water
6 sprigs parsley
3 thin slices ginger, unpeeled
1 teaspoon salt
1 teaspoon dried rosemary

1 Preheat oven to 400°F (200°C). Pour oil into a large roasting pan. Add carrots, parsnips, onion, celery and garlic. Stir to coat vegetables well with oil. Roast until vegetables are lightly colored, 30 minutes. Scrape up any browned bits from the bottom of the pan.

2 Transfer vegetables to a large casserole or other heatproof dish. Add the tomato, water, parsley, ginger, salt and rosemary. Bring to a boil over high heat. Reduce heat to low. Partially cover dish. Simmer until vegetables are very tender and stock is richly flavored, about 1 hour.

3 Line a wire strainer with two layers of dampened cheesecloth. Strain stock into a large bowl. Discard vegetables and herbs. Cool stock completely.

tips for success

Be sure the vegetables are very clean before using, even if they are to be peeled. Simmer for just 1 hour or the stock may become bitter. For a richer taste, cook the strained stock for a further 30 minutes to reduce the liquid and concentrate the flavor.

basic vegetable stock

For this essential staple, minimum effort is required to produce maximum results.

Makes about 4 cups

2 large carrots, coarsely chopped
1 large onion, coarsely chopped
2 stalks celery, coarsely chopped
1 large tomato, cut into 2 cm chunks
1 medium turnip, coarsely chopped
1 small parsnip, coarsely chopped
1 cup shredded crisp lettuce
small handful of parsley
1 clove garlic
1 bay leaf
1 teaspoon dried thyme
7 cups water

1 Place all the vegetables and herbs in a large saucepan. Add water. Bring to a boil over medium heat, skimming foam from the surface, as needed. Reduce the heat to low. Partially cover pan; simmer for 1 hour.

2 Line a wire strainer or metal colander with two layers of dampened cheesecloth. Strain stock into a large bowl. Discard vegetables and herbs. Cool stock completely. Stocks can be frozen for up to 6 months.

eggs &
breakfasts

'mostly whites' spinach omelette with tomato-mushroom sauce

A phytochemical in spinach known as lutein helps keep eyes bright and healthy.

Serves 2   Preparation 10 minutes   Cooking 25 minutes

1½ teaspoons olive oil
1⅔ cups mushrooms, sliced
1 cup tomato pasta sauce
4 large egg whites
1 large egg
¼ teaspoon black pepper
1 small onion, chopped
⅔ cup cooked chopped spinach
pinch of salt
2 teaspoons grated parmesan cheese

1 Heat ½ tsp oil in a small non-stick pot over medium-high heat. Add the mushrooms; cook until softened, 4 minutes, stirring once. Add pasta sauce; simmer until thickened, about 5 minutes. Remove from heat. Cover to keep warm.

2 Beat egg whites, egg and pepper in a small bowl.

3 Heat the remaining oil in a large non-stick frying pan over medium heat. Add onion; sauté until softened, 4 minutes. Stir in spinach and salt; cook until heated through. Stir half of the spinach mixture into the egg mixture.

4 Coat the same frying pan with non-stick cooking spray. Heat over medium heat. Pour in spinach-egg mixture; spread evenly. Cook, without stirring, until the eggs begin to thicken slightly around the edge, about 1 minute. Run a thin spatula around the edge of the pan, lifting mixture so the uncooked portion flows under the cooked one. Cook until center is still moist but not runny, about 3 minutes.

5 Spread remaining spinach mixture over one half of the omelette; sprinkle with parmesan. Fold omelette over to cover filling. Reduce heat to low. Cover; cook until egg component is set but still soft, 3 to 4 minutes. Slide omelette onto serving plate. Top with mushroom sauce.

per serving 205 calories, 17 g protein, 7 g fat (including 2 g saturated fat), 108 mg cholesterol, 22 g carbohydrates, 6 g fiber, 1,144 mg sodium

broccoli, tomato & cheese omelette

1 cup of cooked broccoli contains more vitamin C than a fresh orange.

Serves 2   Preparation 10 minutes   `QUICK RECIPE`
Cooking 8 minutes

3 large eggs
1 large egg white
1 tablespoon milk
pinch of salt
1 cup cooked chopped broccoli
1 large roma tomato, sliced
½ cup coarsely grated reduced-fat
    Swiss-style cheese

1 Coat a 10-in. (25 cm) non-stick frying pan with non-stick cooking spray. Heat over medium heat. Beat eggs, egg white, milk and salt in a medium bowl until combined. Add broccoli. Pour into pan, spreading evenly. Cook, without stirring, until the mixture starts to thicken slightly around the edge, about 1 minute. Run a thin spatula around the edge of the pan, lifting mixture so the uncooked portion flows underneath the cooked one. Cook until center is still moist but not runny, about 3 minutes.

2 Arrange tomato slices over one half of omelette. Top with cheese. Fold omelette over to cover filling. Reduce heat to low. Cover; cook until the egg component is set but still soft, 3 to 4 minutes. Slide omelette onto serving plate.

per serving 225 calories, 22 g protein, 11 g fat (including 4 g saturated fat), 365 mg cholesterol, 8 g carbohydrates, 3 g fiber, 365 mg sodium

pepper & ham quiche

All peppers are rich in vitamin C, but red ones are an especially good source.

Serves 6   Preparation 10 minutes   MAKE AHEAD
Cooking 1 hour 5 minutes

1 unbaked, 9½-in. (24 cm), deep-dish pastry crust (made from 1 sheet frozen shortcrust pastry)
1 tablespoon vegetable oil
1 medium onion, finely chopped
1 medium red pepper, seeded and finely chopped
½ cup finely chopped lean ham
1 cup reduced-fat ricotta cheese
1 cup low-fat plain yogurt
3 large eggs
¼ teaspoon salt
freshly ground black pepper, to taste

1 Preheat oven to 410°F (210°C). Prick bottom of pastry crust with a fork. Bake 8 minutes. Remove from oven. Reduce temperature to 325°F (160°C).

2 Heat oil in a large non-stick frying pan over medium heat. Add onion; sauté until softened, 5 minutes. Add pepper; sauté 2 minutes. Stir in ham. Spoon mixture into pastry crust.

3 Process the ricotta, yogurt, eggs, and salt and pepper in a blender or food processor until very smooth, about 2 minutes. Pour over mixture in pastry crust; stir gently.

4 Bake until mixture is set but still slightly wobbly in the center, 45 to 55 minutes. Remove to a wire rack; cool slightly. Serve warm or at room temperature.

per serving 275 calories, 13 g protein, 16 g fat (including 6 g saturated fat), 126 mg cholesterol, 20 g carbohydrates, 1 g fiber, 472 mg sodium

spanish omelette

The potatoes, tomato and peppers all add a substantial supply of vitamin C to this dish.

Serves 4   Preparation 10 minutes   Cooking 22 minutes

1 tablespoon olive oil
1 medium onion, coarsely chopped
2 cloves garlic, chopped
1 small green pepper, seeded and coarsely chopped
1 small tomato, seeded and coarsely chopped
1 medium roasted red pepper *(see page 291)*, coarsely chopped
2 small cooked potatoes, cut into ½ in. (2 cm) dice
½ teaspoon salt
4 large eggs, lightly beaten

1 Heat 2 tsp oil in a large non-stick frying pan over medium heat. Add the onion and garlic; sauté 5 minutes. Add green pepper and tomato; sauté 3 minutes. Add roasted pepper, potato and salt. Cover and cook, stirring frequently, until the vegetables are tender, about 10 minutes. Add a little water if the vegetables begin to stick.

2 Coat a large non-stick frying pan with non-stick cooking spray. Heat over medium heat. Swirl in remaining oil. Add the eggs; cook, without stirring, until they begin to thicken slightly around the edge of the pan, about 1 minute. Run a thin spatula around the edge of the pan, lifting mixture so uncooked egg flows under the cooked portion. Cook until center is still moist but no longer runny, about 3 minutes. Slide the omelette onto a plate. Top with vegetable mixture.

per serving 163 calories, 8 g protein, 11 g fat (including 2 g saturated fat), 213 mg cholesterol, 9 g carbohydrates, 2 g fiber, 74 mg sodium

HINT helpful HINT HINTHINTHINT

To make a crustless quiche that's much lower in fat and calories, coat the bottom and side of a 9-in. (23 cm) pie plate with non-stick cooking spray. Combine the sautéed vegetables and the ricotta mixture; pour into the pan. Bake as for the main recipe, but start checking how well the quiche is cooked after 30 minutes.

A traditional Spanish omelette, also called tortilla española, is open-faced and topped with a combination of potatoes and onions. **Add tomatoes** and peppers to enliven the mix. A flat omelette is a versatile dish and there are many variables you can try. **Other additions:** zucchini and diced ham; marinated artichokes and pitted olives; cooked chicken and grated cheese. Serve with a green salad.

Look out for omega-3 fat enhanced eggs. Laid by hens fed a diet high in canola seed, the yolks contain omega-3 fats, which are the polyunsaturated fats associated with lower risk of heart disease and stroke. These eggs are also low in saturated fat and are a better source of vitamin E than regular eggs.

summer spinach scramble

Leafy green vegetables such as kale and spinach contain calcium, folic acid and fiber. These are key nutrients for a healthy heart.

Serves 4   Preparation 10 minutes   **QUICK RECIPE**
Cooking 10 minutes

2 cups shredded fresh spinach
   or kale, stems removed
5 large eggs
5 large egg whites
¼ teaspoon ground cumin
¼ teaspoon salt
⅓ cup chopped lean ham
2 scallions, trimmed and thinly sliced

1 Cook spinach in a large pot of boiling salted water until tender, 3 to 5 minutes. Drain. Rinse under cold water. Drain well.

2 Whisk eggs, egg whites, cumin and salt in a large bowl.

3 Coat a large non-stick frying pan with non-stick cooking spray. Heat over medium heat. Add egg mixture; stir until eggs start to thicken slightly, 2 to 3 minutes. Stir in spinach, ham and scallion. Cook, stirring occasionally, until eggs are soft-scrambled, 2 to 3 minutes.

per serving 145 calories, 15 g protein, 7 g fat (including 2 g saturated fat), 270 mg cholesterol, 5 g carbohydrates, 1 g fiber, 385 mg sodium

fresh ideas

Spinach can be served raw or cooked. Stir-frying or steaming helps to retain its flavor and texture.

mushroom & pepper frittata

Mushrooms contain niacin, a B vitamin that helps your body produce energy.

Serves 4   Preparation 10 minutes   **MAKE AHEAD**
Cooking 26 minutes

2 tablespoons olive oil
1 medium red or orange pepper, seeded
   and cut into ¼-in. (5 mm) slices
1 medium yellow pepper, seeded and
   cut into ¼-in. (5 mm) slices
2 cups sliced mushrooms
8 large eggs
¼ teaspoon salt
¼ teaspoon black pepper
⅓ cup grated Parmesan cheese
10 basil leaves, torn into small pieces

1 Heat oil in a large non-stick frying pan over medium-high heat. Add the red and yellow peppers; sauté until softened, about 4 minutes. Add mushrooms; sauté until vegetables are lightly browned, about 5 minutes. Reduce heat to medium.

2 Whisk eggs, salt and pepper in a bowl. Pour into pan; cook, stirring frequently, until soft-scrambled, 3 to 4 minutes. Reduce heat to medium-low. Stir in the Parmesan and basil; smooth top. Cook 5 minutes. Cover and cook until eggs are firm and bottom is browned, about 8 minutes.

3 To serve, loosen frittata around the edge with a spatula. Invert onto a large plate and cut into 4 equal wedges. Serve warm or at room temperature.

per serving 269 calories, 17 g protein, 19 g fat (including 5 g saturated fat), 430 mg cholesterol, 8 g carbohydrates, 2 g fiber, 397 mg sodium

on the menu

A hearty strata is an ideal and easy centerpiece for a brunch menu. Serve it with orange juice and plenty of strong fresh coffee. Fresh fruit such as strawberries or slices of melon makes a good, light accompaniment.

tomato & bacon strata

The soluble fiber found in oat-bran bread helps lower cholesterol.

Serves 8   Preparation 10 minutes
Cooking 45 minutes   MAKE AHEAD

4 large eggs
4 large egg whites
1½ cups 1% milk
1½ teaspoons curry powder
¼ teaspoon salt
freshly ground black pepper, to taste
2 teaspoons vegetable oil
10 slices oat-bran bread
2 medium tomatoes, thinly sliced
1 cup coarsely grated sharp
    cheddar cheese
4 slices bacon

1 Whisk eggs, egg whites, milk, curry powder, salt and pepper in a large bowl.

2 Grease a 12 x 9 x 2 in. (30 x 23 x 5 cm) baking dish with oil. Place 5 slices of bread in a layer in the bottom, cutting 1 slice to fit, if necessary. Layer on tomato slices; scatter ½ cup cheddar on top. Repeat layering. Pour egg mixture over the top, pushing bread down into the liquid – it should come almost to the top of the bread. Cover. Let stand 1 hour.

3 Preheat oven to 350°F (180°C). Bake uncovered strata until puffed and golden, about 45 minutes. For the final 10 minutes, place bacon on top. Let stand 5 to 10 minutes before serving.

per serving 244 calories, 15 g protein, 12 g fat (including 5 g saturated fat), 129 mg cholesterol, 19 g carbohydrates, 2 g fiber, 562 mg sodium

HINT helpful HINT HINTHINTHINT

If you're planning a breakfast party for a crowd, Eggs in Tomato Cups (right) is an easy option for the busy cook. The filling and tomatoes can be prepared several hours in advance. Fill tomatoes and top with the eggs just before guests arrive. While the tomatoes are baking, grill some bacon and sausages and make hash-brown potatoes to complete the menu.

eggs in tomato cups

Tomatoes are rich in cancer-fighting lycopene and vitamin C.

Serves 6   Preparation 35 minutes
Cooking 30 minutes   MAKE AHEAD

6 large beefsteak tomatoes
1½ teaspoons salt
1 bunch spinach,
    stems removed
1 tablespoon olive oil
¼ cup finely chopped onion
10½ oz (300 g) mushrooms, finely chopped
⅓ cup fresh bread crumbs
2 tablespoons grated Parmesan cheese
¼ teaspoon black pepper
6 large eggs

1 Cut a ¼ in. (5 mm) thick slice off the top of each tomato. Core and seed. Sprinkle inside of tomatoes evenly with 1 tsp salt. Place tomatoes upside down on paper towels to drain.

2 Wash spinach, letting water cling to the leaves. Place in a very large pan. Cover and cook over medium heat until leaves are wilted, 1 to 2 minutes.

3 Preheat oven to 350°F (180°C). Lightly coat 12 x 9 x 2 in. (30 x 23 x 5 cm) baking dish with non-stick cooking spray. Heat the oil in a large frying pan over medium heat. Add onion; sauté until softened, about 3 minutes. Add mushrooms; sauté until moisture evaporates, 5 minutes. Stir in spinach, bread crumbs, Parmesan, remaining salt and the pepper.

4 Pat insides of tomatoes dry with paper towels. Stuff each tomato with spinach mixture. Arrange in baking dish. Crack an egg on top of each tomato cup. Cover loosely with foil and bake until eggs are set, 20 to 25 minutes.

per serving 163 calories, 11 g protein, 9 g fat (including 2 g saturated fat), 214 mg cholesterol, 13 g carbohydrates, 4 g fiber, 739 mg sodium

huevos rancheros

Peppers, tomatoes and avocado make this classic dish a hothouse of vitamins.

Serves 6   Preparation 15 minutes
Cooking 15 minutes

QUICK RECIPE

1 tablespoon olive oil
1 medium red or yellow pepper seeded and cut into $\frac{1}{4}$-in. (5 mm) pieces
2 medium tomatoes, seeded and cut into $\frac{1}{2}$-in. (1 cm) pieces
1 cup bottled salsa
$3\frac{1}{2}$ oz (100 g) drained, pickled green chili peppers
$\frac{1}{2}$ teaspoon ground cumin
6 large eggs
$\frac{1}{4}$ cup shredded light cheddar cheese
6 large flour tortillas, warmed (see Hint)
2 tablespoons chopped cilantro
1 avocado, pitted, peeled and chopped

1 Heat oil in a medium frying pan over medium heat. Add pepper; sauté until slightly softened, about 3 minutes. Add tomato, salsa, chili peppers and cumin. Simmer for 7 to 10 minutes, until thickened.

2 Crack eggs onto sauce without breaking yolks; top with cheese. Cook, covered, until whites are set, 3 to 5 minutes.

3 To serve, place an egg with sauce on top of each tortilla. Sprinkle with cilantro and avocado.

per serving 294 calories, 13 g protein, 12 g fat (including 3 g saturated fat), 215 mg cholesterol, 34 g carbohydrates, 4 g fiber, 595 mg sodium

egg burritos with roasted pepper

The vitamin C in peppers and the protein in eggs are essential for healthy skin.

Serves 4   Preparation 5 minutes
Cooking 5 minutes

QUICK RECIPE

4 large flour tortillas, warmed (see Hint)
1 tablespoon vegetable oil
8 large eggs, lightly beaten
$\frac{1}{4}$ teaspoon salt
$\frac{1}{4}$ teaspoon black pepper
1 large roasted red pepper (see page 291), coarsely chopped
2 tablespoons chopped cilantro
$\frac{1}{4}$ cup bottled salsa, at room temperature

1 Heat oil in a medium non-stick frying pan over medium heat. Whisk eggs with salt and pepper. Stir until eggs start to thicken slightly, 1 to 2 minutes. Stir in the pepper and cilantro; cook, stirring occasionally, until the eggs are soft-scrambled, 2 to 3 minutes.

2 Spoon a quarter of the egg mixture in the middle of each tortilla; top each one with 1 tbsp salsa. Fold the edges of each tortilla over, then roll to enclose filling.

per serving 364 calories, 17 g protein, 17 g fat (including 4 g saturated fat), 425 mg cholesterol, 36 g carbohydrates, 2 g fiber, 688 mg sodium

HINT helpful HINT HINTHINTHINT

To warm tortillas, preheat oven to 350°F (180°C). Stack tortillas (up to 6 at a time) and wrap loosely in aluminum foil. Warm for 8 to 10 minutes. Leave wrapped until ready to serve.

asparagus & eggs on toast with tomatoes & ham

The folic acid, vitamin C and beta carotene in asparagus help protect against heart disease.

Serves 4   Preparation 15 minutes
Cooking 6 minutes   QUICK RECIPE

24 thin stalks asparagus or 12 thick stalks,
   trimmed
4 slices grainy whole wheat bread
4 teaspoons Dijon mustard
8 slices lean ham
2 hard-boiled eggs, peeled and sliced
8 thin slices of tomato
2 slices provolone cheese,
   cut into thin strips

1 Preheat the grill. Place the asparagus in a pot of simmering water; cook until crisp-tender, 3 to 4 minutes. Drain well.

2 Place sliced bread on baking sheet. Grill 10 cm from heat until toasted, about 1 minute each side.

3 Spread 1 tsp mustard on each slice. Place 2 slices of ham, 6 thin or 3 thick asparagus spears, half a sliced hard-boiled egg, 2 tomato slices and a quarter of the provolone on top.

4 Grill open sandwiches until heated through and cheese is melted and golden brown, 1 to 2 minutes.

per serving 199 calories, 15 g protein, 9 g fat (including 4 g saturated fat), 128 mg cholesterol, 17 g carbohydrates, 3 g fiber, 738 mg sodium

HINT **helpful HINT** HINTHINTHINThintHINThelpfulHINT

Choose spears of asparagus (green, white or purple) that are a bright, clear color. Whether buying thin or thick asparagus, the stalks should be firm, full and round, with compact tips and tight scales. If the stalks are limp or bend easily, or the color is dull, the asparagus is well past its best. Remove the tough ends of the stalks before cooking, keeping these trimmings to flavor a homemade vegetable stock.

potato pancakes
with apple rings

The carrot in these potato cakes gives them a big beta-carotene boost, while the potatoes and apples supply plenty of vitamins C and B_6 – both useful for fighting arthritis.

Makes 12 (2¾ in. / 7 cm) pancakes   Preparation 20 minutes
Cooking 45 minutes

2 teaspoons unsalted butter
2 medium apples, cored and sliced
    into ¼ in. (5 mm) thick rings
1 pound (500 g) desirée potatoes, grated and
    blotted dry
1 medium carrot, peeled, grated,
    and blotted dry
⅓ cup grated onion
2 large eggs, lightly beaten
2 tablespoons all-purpose flour
¾ teaspoon salt
¼ cup vegetable oil

1 Preheat oven to 250°F (120°C). Melt the butter in a large non-stick frying pan over medium heat. Add apple rings; cook, turning occasionally, until tender, 10 to 12 minutes. Place in oven to keep warm.

2 Combine potato, carrot, onion and eggs in a large bowl. Stir in flour and salt until well combined.

3 Heat 2 tbsp oil in a large non-stick frying pan over medium heat. Measure a generous ¼ cup batter for each pancake and cook, 4 pancakes at a time, until well browned and crisp on the bottom, about 4 minutes. Turn pancakes over; flatten slightly with a spatula. Cook until browned, crisp and cooked through, a further 4 minutes. Drain on paper towels. Place on a baking sheet and keep warm in the oven. Make another 8 pancakes, using remaining oil as needed. Serve topped with apple rings.

per pancake 123 calories, 2 g protein, 6 g fat (including 1 g saturated fat), 37 mg cholesterol, 15 g carbohydrates, 2 g fiber, 162 mg sodium

fresh ideas

Apples are a good source of vitamin C as well as potassium. Eating the peel ensures that you get the full measure of fiber. There are **many apple varieties** to try, including Cortland, Spartan, McIntosh, Honeycrisp and Delicious.

drinks, snacks & starters

raspberry-beet-berry smoothie

The vibrant color and luxurious texture of this vitamin C-packed beet-and-berry mix appeals to the eye and the tastebuds, too.

Serves 4
Preparation 10 minutes

QUICK RECIPE
HEART HEALTHY

2 cooked beets, cooled and
    coarsely chopped
2 oz (60 g) fresh or frozen raspberries
1 cup cranberry juice, chilled
1 cup low-fat plain yogurt
chilled raspberries for garnish *(optional)*

1 In a food processor or blender, purée beets, raspberries and cranberry juice until smooth.

2 Pour purée through a strainer into a large jug. Whisk in most of the yogurt.

3 Pour into 4 glasses and top with remaining yogurt. Garnish with extra raspberries, if desired. Serve immediately.

per serving 90 calories, 4 g protein, 1 g fat (including 1 g saturated fat), 5 mg cholesterol, 18 g carbohydrates, 2 g fiber, 75 mg sodium

fresh ideas

Add fresh herbs to your smoothie, such as chopped parsley or crushed mint, or feathery fronds of dill or fennel.

spicy vegetable cocktail

The cancer-fighting phytochemical lycopene is highly concentrated in commercial tomato products such as tomato juice.

Serves 4
Preparation 8 minutes

QUICK RECIPE
MAKE AHEAD
HEART HEALTHY

3 cups tomato juice
¼ cup coarsely chopped, seeded
    green pepper
1 scallion, trimmed to 4 in. (10 cm),
    thinly sliced
1 tablespoon coarsely chopped parsley
1 tablespoon horseradish
1 teaspoon Worcestershire sauce
½ teaspoon sugar
½ teaspoon Tabasco, or to taste
celery stalks and lemon slices,
    for garnish *(optional)*

1 In a blender, process the tomato juice, pepper, scallion, parsley, horseradish , Worcestershire sauce, sugar and Tabasco until smooth, 2 to 3 minutes.

2 Serve over ice. Garnish with celery and lemon, if desired.

per serving 46 calories, 2 g protein, 0 g fat (including 0 g saturated fat), 0 mg cholesterol, 9 g carbohydrates, 1 g fiber, 687 mg sodium

tomato smoothie

This smoothie is a good bone-builder, thanks to the calcium from the yogurt.

Serves 2
Preparation 5 minutes

QUICK RECIPE
HEART HEALTHY

1 cup plain low-fat yogurt
2 large ripe plum tomatoes, peeled,
    seeded and chopped
½ teaspoon dried basil
½ teaspoon salt

In a blender, whirl yogurt, tomatoes, basil and salt until very smooth, 2 minutes. Serve over ice, if desired.

per serving 91 calories, 7 g protein, 2 g fat (including 1 g saturated fat), 7 mg cholesterol, 12 g carbohydrates, 1 g fiber, 382 mg sodium

carrot-orange juice

This immune-boosting antioxidant cocktail supplies all your vitamin A for the day and more than half the required vitamin C.

Serves 2
Preparation 5 minutes

QUICK RECIPE
MAKE AHEAD
HEART HEALTHY

1½ cups fresh or bottled carrot juice, chilled
⅔ cup freshly squeezed
    orange juice (3 oranges)
¾ in. (2 cm) thick slice peeled fresh ginger

Combine carrot juice and orange juice in a bowl. Crush ginger in garlic press to make ½ tsp. Stir into juice mixture and serve. (If making ahead, stir just before serving.)

per serving 75 calories, 2 g protein, 0 g fat (including 0 g saturated fat), 0 mg cholesterol, 17 g carbohydrates, 0 g fiber, 93 mg sodium

DID YOU KNOW

...that you need a special appliance to make your own vegetable juices? Food processors and blenders purée vegetables to a suitable consistency for soup, but a juicer is needed to separate out a vegetable's liquid. Some extractors can press juice out of citrus fruits, but that's a separate process.

Many different vegetables can be used to scoop up dips. Try sticks of fennel or celery, whole endive leaves, the firm ribs of bok choy, slices of cucumber or small radicchio leaves.

steamed vegetables with peanut dip

This easy-to-make party favorite is rich in fiber and bursting with flavor.

Serves 8   Preparation 20 minutes
Cooking 20 minutes

MAKE AHEAD

⅔ cup water
⅓ cup smooth peanut butter
1 clove garlic, minced
2 teaspoons grated fresh ginger
2 scallions, chopped
2 tablespoons brown sugar
2 tablespoons soy sauce
pinch of chili powder
1 tablespoon freshly squeezed lemon juice
6 large carrots, peeled, halved lengthways,
    cut in 3 x ¼ in. (5 mm) sticks or 16 baby carrots
    with tops
2 large red or yellow peppers, halved
    and seeded, sliced ¼ in. (5 mm) thick
½ pound (250 g) snow peas or green
    beans, trimmed
8 radishes, thinly sliced

1 To make the peanut dip, bring the water to a boil in a small pot. Stir in the peanut butter, garlic, ginger, scallion, sugar, soy sauce and chili powder. Simmer 2 minutes. Remove from heat. Stir in lemon juice. Set aside to cool slightly or refrigerate until ready to serve.

2 In a large pot with a steamer basket, bring water to a boil. Fill a bowl with ice water. Steam carrots for 3 minutes, lift out and plunge into ice water to cool. Steam pepper for 1 minute, lift out and plunge into ice water to cool. Steam snow peas or beans for 2 minutes, lift out and plunge into ice water to cool. Drain vegetables and dry with paper towels.

3 Spoon peanut dip into a small bowl and place on a serving platter. Arrange the carrot sticks, pepper, snow peas or green beans around the bowl. Add the radish as a garnish.

per serving 136 calories, 5 g protein, 6 g fat (including 1 g saturated fat),
0 mg cholesterol, 19 g carbohydrates, 5 g fiber, 305 mg sodium

creamy spinach dip

Leafy green vegetables such as spinach are rich in folate, which helps protect against heart disease and birth defects.

Serves 6
Preparation 10 minutes

QUICK RECIPE
MAKE AHEAD

½ pound (250 g) frozen chopped spinach, thawed
    and squeezed dry
1 cup low-fat plain yogurt
½ cup light mayonnaise
2 teaspoons dried dill
½ teaspoon celery seeds
pinch of salt
1 clove garlic, crushed

Whirl spinach, yogurt, mayonnaise, dill, celery seeds, salt and garlic in a food processor until smooth and creamy. Refrigerate for 1 hour before serving.

per serving 106 calories, 4 g protein, 8 g fat (including 2 g saturated fat),
9 mg cholesterol, 7 g carbohydrates, 2 g fiber, 273 mg sodium

HINT helpful HINT HINTHINTHINT

Make dips well ahead of serving time. Leaving them in the refrigerator for an hour or more lets the mixture become thoroughly chilled. It also allows the flavors to develop fully so that they better complement one another.

chili peppers con queso with vegetables

Antioxidant-rich fresh vegetables are ideal scoops for this spicy starter.

Serves 8   Preparation 20 minutes
Cooking 12 minutes

MAKE AHEAD

2 teaspoons olive oil
1 medium green pepper, seeded
    and chopped
1 medium onion, chopped
3½ oz. (100 g) drained pickled chili peppers, chopped
1 cup chopped tomato
1½ teaspoons ground cumin
½ teaspoon salt
8 oz (225 g) cream cheese
3 tablespoons chopped cilantro
2 teaspoons Tabasco
1 medium red pepper, seeded and sliced
2 small carrots, peeled and cut into sticks
1 medium celery stalk, cut into sticks

1 Heat oil in a large non-stick frying pan over medium heat. Add green pepper and onion; sauté until softened, about 5 minutes. Add chili pepper, tomato, cumin and salt; cook for about 3 minutes.

2 Add cheese, cilantro and Tabasco. Reduce heat to low. Cook, stirring, until cheese melts and mixture is creamy, about 3 minutes. Serve warm with red pepper, carrots and celery.

per serving 147 calories, 4 g protein, 11 g fat (including 6 g saturated fat), 31 mg cholesterol, 9 g carbohydrates, 3 g fiber, 339 mg sodium

vegetable-stuffed mushrooms

This simple, attractive first course is packed with fiber.

Serves 4   Preparation 20 minutes
Cooking 20 minutes

MAKE AHEAD

24 large or 12 extra-large mushrooms,
    stems removed
2 teaspoons canola oil
1 medium onion, finely chopped
3 cloves garlic, minced
1 medium carrot, finely chopped
1 medium red pepper, finely chopped
½ cup salt-reduced chicken stock
½ teaspoon dried oregano
3 tablespoons grated Parmesan cheese
2 tablespoons chopped parsley

1 Preheat oven to 400°F (200°C). Blanch mushroom caps in a pan of boiling water for 2 minutes. Drain on paper towels.

2 Heat oil in a large frying pan over medium heat. Add onion and garlic; sauté for 5 minutes. Add carrot and pepper; cook for 4 minutes. Add the stock and oregano; cook for 4 minutes or until the vegetables are very soft. Remove from heat; stir in Parmesan and parsley.

3 Spoon mixture into the mushroom caps and place on a baking tray. Bake for 10 minutes or until piping hot.

per serving 48 calories, 1 g protein, 2 g fat (including 0 g saturated fat), 0 mg cholesterol, 8 g carbohydrates, 2 g fiber, 202 mg sodium

DID YOU KNOW

...that cooking mushrooms breaks down their fibrous cell walls, which makes some of their nutrients more available to the body?

grilled tomato & pepper salsa

Each red and yellow pepper contains about 2 teaspoons of natural sugar, resulting in the slightly sweet taste of this salsa.

Serves 6   Preparation 20 minutes   MAKE AHEAD
Cooking 12 minutes

2 medium firm, ripe tomatoes
1 small onion, cut into ¾ in. (2 cm) thick slices
2 teaspoons olive oil
1 corn cob, inner layer of husk intact
1 small red pepper, seeded and
    finely chopped
1 small yellow pepper, seeded and
    finely chopped
2 cloves garlic, finely chopped
½ teaspoon ground cumin
½ teaspoon dried oregano
½ teaspoon salt
¼ teaspoon chili powder
2 tablespoons chopped cilantro

1 Heat grill to medium hot. Brush tomatoes and onion with oil and place, with the corn, on the grill.

2 Grill 4 in. (10 cm) from heat, turning frequently, until lightly browned, 10 to 12 minutes.

3 When cool enough to handle, finely chop tomatoes and onion. Remove husk from corn and cut kernels from cob.

4 Combine all the ingredients in a serving bowl. Refrigerate until ready to serve.

per serving 48 calories, 1 g protein, 2 g fat (including 0 g saturated fat), 0 mg cholesterol, 8 g carbohydrates, 2 g fiber, 202 mg sodium

HINT helpful HINT HINTHINTHINT

Cilantro's distinctive flavor does not please every palate. If it is too intrusive for you, try dill, chervil or Italian flat-leaf parsley in your salsa.

on the menu

Thin slices of ham could be used in place of the beef. Sprinkle finished dish with chopped flat-leaf parsley instead of cilantro for a milder flavor.

beef, scallion & asparagus roll-ups

The green tops of scallions are a good source of vitamin C and beta-carotene, antioxidants that protect against all types of chronic disease.

Serves 4 (2 roll-ups per serving)   QUICK RECIPE
Preparation 15 minutes   Cooking 6 minutes

8 asparagus stalks, trimmed to 6-in. (15 cm) lengths
8 thin slices sirloin steak
4 scallions, trimmed to 6-in. (15 cm) lengths
2 teaspoons canola oil
3 tablespoons bottled teriyaki sauce
1 tablespoon sesame seeds, toasted
1 tablespoon chopped cilantro

1 Bring a pot of water to a boil. Cut each asparagus stalk in half. Blanch in boiling water 1 minute; drain. Pound sirloin slices until very thin. Cut each scallion in half.

2 Place 2 pieces of asparagus and 1 piece of scallion near one end of each beef strip. Roll beef around middle of vegetables to form 8 bundles.

3 Heat oil in a large non-stick frying pan over medium-high heat. Add rolls. Brown 2 minutes, turning rolls frequently. Add teriyaki sauce. Lower heat to medium; boil 3 minutes.

4 Transfer rolls to serving platter. Sprinkle with sesame seeds and cilantro.

per serving 91 calories, 7 g protein, 5 g fat (including 1 g saturated fat), 16 mg cholesterol, 4 g carbohydrates, 1 g fiber, 533 mg sodium

DID YOU KNOW

...that when you see the word "negamaki" on a Japanese menu, the term refers to beef roll-ups, such as Beef, Scallion & Asparagus Roll-Ups, as in the recipe above?

pita pizzas

Eating pepper can help reduce the risk of stroke because they're rich in vitamin C.

Serves 4   Preparation 10 minutes   QUICK RECIPE
Cooking 3 minutes   HEART HEALTHY

1 small roasted red pepper (see page 291),
    seeded and coarsely chopped
1/4 teaspoon crushed fennel seeds or
    dried oregano
1/4 teaspoon salt
freshly ground black pepper, to taste
1/4 cup light mozzarella cheese,
    coarsely grated
2 tablespoons Swiss cheese,
    coarsely grated
2 whole-wheat pita breads
8 teaspoons bottled tomato sauce or pizza sauce
1/2 small red onion, thinly sliced

1 Preheat broiler. Combine pepper, fennel seeds or oregano, salt and pepper in a small bowl. Combine the mozzarella and Swiss cheese in another bowl.

2 Separate each pita bread into 2 flat rounds. Place rounds, insides facing up, on baking tray. Broil 4 in. (10 cm)) from heat until golden brown around edges, about 1 minute.

3 Spread 2 tsp sauce up to the edges of each pita round. Spoon 2 tbsp pepper mixture over the top. Sprinkle evenly with cheese; top with onion.

4 Grill until cheese is melted and pizzas are hot, about 2 minutes.

per serving 137 calories, 7 g protein, 4 g fat (including 2 g saturated fat), 7 mg cholesterol, 22 g carbohydrates, 3 g fiber, 475 mg sodium

spinach-stuffed clams

Clams are packed with iron for healthy blood and zinc for a strong immune system.

Serves 4   Preparation 15 minutes
Cooking 20 minutes

HEART HEALTHY

2 pounds (1 kg) fresh clams, washed and cleaned
3 teaspoons olive oil
¼ cup finely chopped onion
2 cloves garlic, minced
4 teaspoons flour
⅔ cup 1% milk
pinch of cayenne pepper
⅓ cup frozen chopped spinach, thawed
   and squeezed dry
⅓ cup fresh bread crumbs
4 teaspoons grated Parmesan cheese

1 Place clams in a large frying pan with ½ in. (1 cm) water. Bring to a boil and cover. Cook 4 minutes or until clams open. Start checking after 2 minutes. Remove clams as they open; discard any that do not. Transfer clams to a bowl; when cool enough to handle, discard top shell halves. Place shell halves with clams attached on a baking tray.

2 Preheat oven to 450°F (220°C). In a small pot, heat 2 tsp oil over low heat. Add the onion and garlic; sauté for 5 minutes or until soft. Whisk in flour and cook for 1 minute. Whisk in milk and cayenne; cook for 3 minutes or until lightly thickened. Stir in spinach. Spoon spinach mixture over clams.

3 Combine bread crumbs and Parmesan in a small bowl. Top clams with bread crumb mixture and drizzle with remaining oil. Bake just until clams are bubbly and hot, about 5 minutes.

per serving 150 calories, 19 g protein, 5 g fat (including 1 g saturated fat),
16 mg cholesterol, 16 g carbohydrates, 1 g fiber, 330 mg sodium

grilled eggplant & tomato sandwiches

You'll get heart-protective nutrients in every bite.

Serves 6   Preparation 15 minutes
Cooking 12 minutes

QUICK RECIPE

2 oz (60 g) goat cheese, crumbled
1 tablespoon snipped fresh chives
¼ cup dry bread crumbs
2 tablespoons grated Parmesan cheese
½ teaspoon dried basil
1 large egg
1 large egg white
¼ teaspoon salt
12 slices peeled eggplant, ¼ in. (5 mm) thick
6 thin slices tomato, blotted dry
2 tablespoons olive oil

1 Combine goat cheese and chives in a small bowl. Combine bread crumbs, Parmesan and basil in a shallow dish. Beat egg, egg white and salt in a second shallow dish.

2 Spread about 2 tsp goat cheese mixture onto a slice of eggplant. Top with a tomato slice and an eggplant slice. Make 5 more sandwiches the same way.

3 Dip each sandwich in egg mixture, then bread crumb mixture to coat both sides. Place on wax paper.

4 In large non-stick frying pan over medium-low heat, heat about 1½ tbsp oil. Add sandwiches in a single layer, working in batches, if necessary. Cook until fork-tender and golden brown, 10 to 12 minutes, turning over halfway through cooking. Add more oil as needed if pan becomes dry. Serve warm.

per serving 133 calories, 6 g protein, 10 g fat (including 4 g saturated fat),
47 mg cholesterol, 6 g carbohydrates, 1 g fiber, 213 mg sodium

fresh ideas

For a sharper taste, substitute feta cheese or a more aged goat's milk or sheep's milk cheese for mild goat's milk cheese in recipes. Goat's milk and sheep's milk are higher in fat than whole cow's milk, but lower in cholesterol. The longer these cheeses are aged, the more tart their flavor becomes. Feta, made from sheep's or goat's milk, is brined and must be rinsed in cold water to reduce the salt content.

on the menu

These Tex-Mex snacks are delicious eaten as they are, but for added taste, top with a spoonful of salsa and a dollop of yogurt or sour cream. To fill out a lunch, add a mixed green salad and serve fresh fruit for dessert.

chili-cheese quesadillas with tomato

Chillies contain phytonutrients that protect against cancer and other chronic diseases.

Serves 4 (3 wedges per serving) QUICK RECIPE
Preparation 15 minutes   Cooking 12 minutes

6 flour tortillas (8 in./20 cm)
1 large tomato, seeded and finely chopped
1 cup coarsely grated cheddar cheese
4½ oz (125 g) drained pickled chili peppers, chopped
1 tablespoon chopped fresh cilantro
¼ teaspoon salt
freshly ground black pepper, to taste

1 Preheat oven to 250°F (120°C). Place 3 tortillas on a work surface. Sprinkle equally with tomato, cheese, chili pepper, cilantro, salt and pepper. Place the remaining tortillas on top. Gently press the quesadillas to flatten.

2 Coat a large non-stick frying pan with non-stick cooking spray. Heat over medium-high heat. Place one quesadilla at a time in the pan; cook until lightly browned on both sides and cheese is melted, 2 minutes per side. Transfer to a baking tray; place in the oven to keep warm. Repeat with the remaining quesadillas. To serve, cut each quesadilla into 4 wedges.

per serving 359 calories, 14 g protein, 14 g fat (including 7 g saturated fat), 25 mg cholesterol, 44 g carbohydrates, 4 g fiber, 769 mg sodium

DID YOU KNOW

...that pan-grilled sandwiches in Italy are called panini? While their close relation, the classic grilled cheese sandwich, uses cheddar and butter, panini use mozzarella and olive oil. Italian sandwiches are very versatile and can be filled with herbs, mushrooms, olives and many other fresh and pickled ingredients.

pan-grilled tomato, mozzarella & basil sandwich

Fresh green herbs such as basil contain small quantities of protective antioxidant nutrients such as vitamin C and beta-carotene.

Makes 4 sandwiches QUICK RECIPE
Preparation 10 minutes   Cooking 4 minutes

4 thin slices mozzarella cheese (4½ oz/125 g total)
8 thin slices tomato, seeded
8 thin slices red onion
8 basil leaves, shredded
8 small slices Italian sandwich bread
¼ teaspoon salt
freshly ground black pepper, to taste
4 teaspoons olive oil

1 Pat dry mozzarella and tomato with paper towels.

2 Place 1 mozzarella slice, 2 tomato slices, 2 onion slices and 2 shredded basil leaves on each of 4 slices of bread. Sprinkle with salt and pepper. Top with remaining bread.

3 Heat oil in a large non-stick frying pan over medium heat. Add sandwiches; cook, firmly pressing down with a spatula, until lightly browned, about 2 minutes. Turn sandwiches over. Cook, pressing down, until sandwiches are browned and the cheese is melted, about 2 minutes.

per sandwich 206 calories, 8 g protein, 12 g fat (including 5 g saturated fat), 23 mg cholesterol, 17 g carbohydrates, 1 g fiber, 343 mg sodium

bean & vegetable tostadas

Fiber from beans and vegetables keeps the digestive system healthy and can help lower cholesterol levels.

Makes 6 tostadas   Preparation 15 minutes
Cooking 10 minutes

QUICK RECIPE
HEART HEALTHY

6 corn tortillas (6 in./15 cm)
14-oz (398 mL) can black beans,
   drained and rinsed
14-oz (398 mL) can corn kernels,
   drained and rinsed
1 small tomato, cored and chopped
2 tablespoons finely chopped red onion
1 small jalapeño or other hot chili pepper, seeded
   and finely chopped
2 tablespoons chopped cilantro
1 tablespoon freshly squeezed lime juice
½ teaspoon salt
dash of Tabasco
1 small ripe avocado, pitted, peeled
   and chopped

1 Preheat oven to 425°F (220°C). Place tortillas in a single layer on a baking tray; coat both sides of each one with cooking spray. Bake until lightly browned and crisp, about 10 minutes; turn them over halfway through. Transfer to wire racks to cool.

2 Combine beans, corn, tomato, onion, chili pepper, cilantro, lime juice, salt and Tabasco in a large bowl. Gently fold in avocado. Top each tortilla evenly with bean mixture.

per tostada 130 calories, 5 g protein, 1 g fat (including 0 g saturated fat),
0 mg cholesterol, 26 g carbohydrates, 5 g fiber, 390 mg sodium

corned beef & cabbage calzones

Cabbage and other cruciferous vegetables help to protect against cancers of the breast and prostate.

Makes 12 calzones   Preparation 20 minutes
Cooking 35 minutes

MAKE AHEAD
HEART HEALTHY

2 teaspoons canola oil
1 large onion, finely chopped
4 cups shredded green cabbage
   (half a small head)
1 medium carrot, peeled and chopped
2 teaspoons Dijon mustard
¼ teaspoon salt
freshly ground black pepper, to taste
1 cup shredded light Swiss cheese
   or Jarlsberg
2 oz (60 g) corned beef, chopped
16 oz (500 g) homemade pizza dough or 12 flour tortillas

1 Preheat oven to 400°F (200°C). Heat oil in a large non-stick frying pan over medium heat. Add onion; sauté until a little softened, about 3 minutes. Stir in the cabbage, carrot, mustard, salt and pepper. Cover; reduce heat to low. Cook until the cabbage is wilted, 10 to 15 minutes, adding water if necessary to prevent mixture sticking to the pan. Uncover; cook 1 minute, stirring. Let cool slightly. Stir in cheese and corned beef.

2 On a lightly floured board, shape dough into a log 12 in. (30 cm) long; add flour as needed to prevent sticking. Divide dough into 12 equal pieces. Roll or pat out each piece to form a circle 6 in. (15 cm) in diameter. Spoon ¼ cup filling over lower half of each round. Fold dough over to enclose filling. Press edges firmly to seal and crimp with a fork. Transfer to ungreased baking tray.

3 Bake until calzones are heated through and golden brown, about 20 minutes. Cool on wire rack for 15 minutes. (To make calzones ahead, wrap unbaked pies in plastic wrap and store in the refrigerator for up to 3 days before baking.)

per calzone 166 calories, 8 g protein, 5 g fat (including 2 g saturated fat),
9 mg cholesterol, 23 g carbohydrates, 2 g fiber, 373 mg sodium

on the menu

For a substantial lunch, serve two Corned Beef & Cabbage Calzones per person with a crisp green salad on the side and ice cream or a fruit sorbet for dessert.

on the menu

*To make four servings for lunch, cut each wrap in half. To serve as finger food
at a party or for a snack, cut each wrap into six equal pieces.*

avocado-turkey wraps

Avocado is rich in heart-protective monounsaturated fats and vitamin E.

Makes 12 mini-wraps   QUICK RECIPE
Preparation 10 minutes

3 tablespoons light mayonnaise
1 tablespoon coarse-grained Dijon mustard
2 flour tortillas
1 medium ripe avocado, pitted, peeled and
    cut lengthways into thin slices
8 oz (250 g) thinly sliced cooked turkey breast
8 oz (250 g) jarred roasted red peppers, drained
    and cut into strips

1 Combine mayonnaise and mustard in a small bowl. Lay tortillas on a work surface. Spread mayonnaise mixture evenly over each one.

2 Place the avocado slices on top, leaving a small border around the edge. Top with turkey and pepper strips.

3 Roll up each tortilla tightly and place, seam side down, on a cutting board. Trim the ends of the wraps evenly with a serrated knife. Cut each wrap into 6 equal pieces and place, cut side down, on a serving platter.

per mini-wrap 99 calories, 7 g protein, 4 g fat (including 1 g saturated fat), 17 mg cholesterol, 9 g carbohydrates, 2 g fiber, 126 mg sodium

HINT helpful HINT HINTHINTHINT

Pita, lavash and other thin flatbreads all make good "containers" for wraps. While it may look better to layer the ingredients separately, it is often more practical to mix some together so that the filling is firmer and stays intact, making the wrap easier to eat. For example, instead of slicing the avocado for Avocado-Turkey Wraps, mash it with mayonnaise and mustard to make a spread that keeps all the ingredients in place.

herbed cheese bagels

Fresh parsley makes a healthy contribution of vitamin C.

Serves 4   QUICK RECIPE
Preparation 10 minutes   HEART HEALTHY

3½ oz (100 g) light cream cheese
2 scallions, thinly sliced
½ cup parsley, finely chopped
2 tablespoons chopped dill
1 tablespoon chopped tarragon
4 bagels
½ small cucumber, thinly sliced
3 medium tomatoes, thinly sliced
1 medium red onion, thinly sliced

1 Combine cream cheese, scallion, parsley, dill and tarragon in a bowl. Add salt and pepper, to taste.

2 Slice bagels in half horizontally. Spread cheese mixture on bagel bases. Layer on cucumber, tomato and onion slices and cover with tops of bagels. Serve immediately.

per bagel 280 calories, 11 g protein, 7 g fat (including 3 g saturated fat), 15 mg cholesterol, 50 g carbohydrates, 9 g fiber, 290 mg sodium

fresh ideas

For a milder herb flavor, reduce the parsley to 2 tbsp. Alternatively, for a peppery flavor, finely chop a handful of watercress, tough stalks removed, in place of the parsley.

roasted vegetable baguettes

Feta cheese can be high in fat and salt, but because it has such a strong flavor, a little goes a long way.

Serves 4 Preparation 45 minutes

2 medium red peppers, roasted, *(see page 291),*
    quartered lengthwise
4 short baguettes or rolls,
    each halved horizontally
1 medium red onion, cut into small wedges
2 large zucchini, thickly sliced diagonally
2 or 3 garlic cloves, finely chopped
leaves from 3 sprigs rosemary
1 tablespoon extra-virgin olive oil
6 oz (170 g) feta cheese

1 Preheat broiler. Use a grill pan to lightly toast the cut sides of the bread under the broiler; set aside.

2 Remove the grill rack and discard any crumbs from the bottom of the grill pan. Put onion, zucchini and garlic in the pan, sprinkle with rosemary leaves and drizzle with oil. Add salt and pepper, to taste. Cook, turning vegetables once, until browned on both sides, about 10 minutes.

3 Cut peppers into thick slices. Arrange pepper and the zucchini mixture on halves of toast, spooning over all the pan juices. Arrange, side by side, in the grill pan.

4 Crumble feta cheese over the top. Broil for 3 to 4 minutes or until cheese is slightly browned. Top with the remaining bread halves. Cut in half at an angle; serve immediately.

per serving 260 calories, 13 g protein, 12 g fat (including 5 g saturated fat), 15 mg cholesterol, 29 g carbohydrates, 5 g fiber, 730 mg sodium

HINT helpful HINT HINTHINTHINT

Baguettes, loved for their wonderful crusts and chewy texture, don't keep well because they are made without fat. Buy them fresh on your way home for dinner and use them right away. Fresh baguettes can be frozen for later use.

fresh ideas

Drizzle some balsamic vinegar over the grilled vegetables before adding feta. Fresh thyme can be used instead of rosemary. Use pita bread or thickly sliced rye bread in place of baguettes.

taco with homemade salsa & guacamole

This great recipe will tempt even the most ardent of meat lovers into enjoying a meal based on vegetables.

Serves 4 Preparation 10 minutes
Cooking 20 minutes

QUICK RECIPE

2 tablespoons extra-virgin olive oil
1 medium onion, finely chopped
1 eggplant, cubed
1 butternut squash (1½ pounds/750 g), halved, seeded, peeled and cubed
1 large zucchini (6 oz/170 g), cubed
¼ teaspoon chili powder
½ teaspoon ground cumin
1 garlic clove, crushed
14-oz (398 mL) can tomatoes
1 large ripe avocado
juice of ½ lime
3 medium ripe tomatoes, diced
½ medium red onion, finely chopped
¼ cup chopped cilantro
8 taco shells
1 cup low-fat plain yogurt
lime wedges and sprigs of cilantro

1 Heat oil in a large pot over medium-high heat. Add onion and eggplant; sauté, stirring frequently, until vegetables are lightly browned.

2 Add squash and zucchini. Stir in chili powder, cumin and garlic. Pour in canned tomatoes with their juice. Add salt and pepper, to taste. Heat to boiling, breaking up tomatoes with a wooden spoon. Cover and simmer 15 minutes, stirring occasionally, until pumpkin is just tender. Check occasionally, adding water, if needed, to prevent vegetables from sticking.

3 Preheat oven to 180°C. To make the guacamole, halve and pit the avocado, scoop flesh into a bowl and mash with lime juice. To make salsa, combine tomato, red onion and cilantro in a small bowl. Set guacamole and salsa aside.

4 Put taco shells on a baking tray; warm 3 to 4 minutes in the oven. Transfer shells to serving plates. Fill with eggplant mixture and top with guacamole, yogurt and salsa. Garnish with lime wedges and cilantro.

per serving 420 calories, 8 g protein, 21 g fat (including 3 g saturated fat),
0 mg cholesterol, 56 g carbohydrates, 15 g fiber, 150 mg sodium

DID YOU KNOW

...that when tomatoes were introduced into Europe, they were regarded with suspicion and thought to have aphrodisiac properties? Nutritionists now know that "love apples," as these fruits were called, do have benefits for the heart, but not in the romantic sense.

vegetable tart

Every slice is rich in fiber and vital nutrients such as vitamin C and beta-carotene.

Serves 6   Preparation 25 minutes
Cooking 45 minutes

MAKE AHEAD

1 unbaked 9-in. (23 cm) round pastry crust
1 small butternut squash, peeled
1 large zucchini, cut into ¼-in. (5 mm) slices
1 medium red onion, cut into ¼-in. (5 mm) slices
1 tablespoon plus 1 teaspoon olive oil
½ teaspoon salt
¼ cup grated Parmesan cheese
3 tablespoons chopped basil
6 oz (170 g) jarred roasted red peppers, drained,
    cut into strips

1   Heat oven to 400°F (200°C). Use a rolling pin to shape pastry crust into a square; place it in an 8-in. (20 cm) tart pan. Fold edges of pastry over and crimp to make a decorative edge. Prick bottom with a fork. Line pastry crust with aluminum foil; fill with uncooked rice or dried beans. Bake 15 minutes. Remove foil and rice and bake until golden, 5 to 10 minutes. Leave oven on.

2   Slice squash crosswise into ¼ in. (5 mm) thick rounds up to the seeded part. Scoop out seeds. Slice remaining squash into rings.

3   Place squash and onion in a single layer on a baking tray; drizzle with ½ tbsp oil and sprinkle with salt. Place zucchini on a second tray; drizzle with ½ tbsp oil and sprinkle with salt. Roast zucchini until tender, 10 to 12 minutes. Remove from baking tray. Continue roasting squash and onion just until tender, about 5 minutes. Reduce oven to 250°F (120°C).

4   Assemble tart just before serving. Sprinkle bottom of tart shell with 1 tbsp Parmesan. Top with an even layer of zucchini, half the onion, 1 tbsp Parmesan and 1 tbsp basil. Add a layer of squash, the remaining onion, 1 tbsp Parmesan and 1 tbsp basil. Arrange roasted pepper on top. Brush with remaining oil; sprinkle with the remaining Parmesan. Heat tart in oven for 10 minutes. Sprinkle with remaining basil and serve.

per serving 189 calories, 4 g protein, 11 g fat (including 3 g saturated fat), 3 mg cholesterol, 19 g carbohydrates, 3 g fiber, 561 mg sodium

cheese & spinach terrine with leeks

Vitamin C from the peppers helps your body absorb more iron from the spinach.

Serves 12 Preparation 30 minutes MAKE AHEAD
Cooking 1 hour 10 minutes

1 tablespoon olive oil
2 medium leeks cut into ½-in. (1 cm) pieces
    and rinsed
2 cloves garlic, minced
2 bunches spinach,
    stems removed
1 cup milk
2 medium red peppers, seeded
    and cut in ¼-in. (5 mm) pieces
1½ teaspoons salt
1 teaspoon curry powder
¾ teaspoon black pepper
1 cup coarsely grated light
    mozzarella cheese
5 large eggs

1 Preheat oven to 350°F (180°C). Lightly coat a 9 x 5-in. (23 x 13 cm) loaf pan with non-stick cooking spray. Line bottom of pan with wax paper. Coat paper with cooking spray.

2 Heat oil in a large non-stick frying pan over medium heat. Add leeks and garlic; sauté until softened, 7 minutes. Remove to large bowl.

3 Wash spinach, leaving some water clinging to leaves. Place in the frying pan over a medium-low heat. Cook, covered, until spinach wilts, 2 minutes. Add to leeks.

4 Place vegetable mixture in food processor with ¼ cup milk and whirl until smooth. Return mixture to bowl. Add peppers, salt, curry powder, black pepper and cheese.

5 Beat eggs lightly with remaining ¾ cup milk. Stir into the vegetable mixture. Pour into prepared loaf pan. Place pan in a larger baking dish half-filled with hot water.

6 Bake 1 hour. Remove loaf pan from water bath. Let terrine cool completely. Refrigerate until ready to serve.

7 To serve, unmold onto a platter and remove wax paper.

per serving 102 calories, 7 g protein, 6 g fat (including 2 g saturated fat),
97 mg cholesterol, 7 g carbohydrates, 2 g fiber, 361 mg sodium

on the menu

Spinach terrine is suitable as a first course or as part of a party buffet, where it can be served with crackers or rounds of baguette.

italian spinach pie

With vitamins A and C and folate, spinach is good for heart health.

Serves 6   Preparation 10 minutes
Cooking 40 minutes

MAKE AHEAD

1 tablespoon olive oil
2 medium leeks, white part only, halved
   lengthwise, thinly sliced, and rinsed
10 oz (300 g) frozen chopped spinach, thawed
   and squeezed dry
1 cup cooked long-grain white rice
3 large eggs
1 cup grated Parmesan cheese
½ teaspoon dried marjoram
½ teaspoon salt
¼ teaspoon black pepper

1 Heat oil in a medium non-stick frying pan. Add the leeks; sauté until softened, about 8 minutes. Set aside.

2 Preheat oven to 375°F (190°C). Lightly coat a 23 cm glass pie plate with non-stick cooking spray. Combine the leeks, spinach, rice, eggs, ¾ cup Parmesan, marjoram, salt and pepper in a medium bowl. Spoon mixture into the prepared pie plate, smooth the top and sprinkle with remaining Parmesan.

3 Bake until firm and browned, about 30 minutes. Serve warm or at room temperature, cut into wedges.

per serving 174 calories, 11 g protein, 9 g fat (including 4 g saturated fat),
117 mg cholesterol, 13g carbohydrates, 2 g fiber, 524 mg sodium

crustless quiche vegetable squares

Carrots are super-rich in the disease-fighting antioxidant beta-carotene, which your body uses to make vitamin A.

Makes 16 small squares   MAKE AHEAD
Preparation 15 minutes   Cooking 1 hour

1 teaspoon olive oil
1 large onion, finely chopped
1 large zucchini, cut into small cubes
½ teaspoon salt
2 large eggs
¼ cup milk
3 medium carrots, peeled, grated and
   blotted dry
1 cup coarsely grated cheddar cheese
1 tablespoon chopped dill

1 Heat oven to 375°F (190°C). Lightly coat an 8-in. (20 cm) square or round baking pan with non-stick cooking spray. Heat oil in a large non-stick frying pan over medium heat. Add onion; sauté until softened, 3 minutes. Stir in zucchini. Increase heat to medium-high; sauté until zucchini is soft and the liquid has evaporated, 7 to 10 minutes. Stir in ¼ tsp salt. Remove from heat.

2 In a large bowl, beat eggs, milk and remaining ¼ tsp salt. Add carrot, zucchini, cheese and dill. Spread in prepared pan.

3 Bake until quiche is just set in center, about 45 minutes. Transfer to a wire rack and cool for at least 10 minutes before cutting. Serve warm or at room temperature.

per square 54 calories, 3 g protein, 3 g fat (including 2 g saturated fat),
35 mg cholesterol, 3 g carbohydrates, 1 g fiber, 128 mg sodium

on the menu

Cut the Crustless Quiche Vegetable Squares into four portions instead of 16 to make a main course for lunch that is both nutritious and low in calories. Finish off the meal with a crisp baguette, a salad and a healthy dessert, such as Sweet & Spicy Carrot Pie with Nut Crust (page 249).

savory soups
soups savory s
ury soups sava
soups savory

savory soups

gazpacho

Lycopene, a cancer-fighting phytochemical is found in tomatoes and tomato products.

Serves 4   Preparation 25 minutes
Standing time 1 hour

4 cups (1 L) tomato juice
4 plum tomatoes, seeded and
    coarsely chopped
1 cucumber, peeled, seeded and
    coarsely chopped
1 small yellow pepper, seeded and
    coarsely chopped
3 scallions, finely chopped
¼ cup freshly squeezed lemon juice
¼ cup coarsely chopped basil
1 clove garlic, minced
¼ teaspoon salt
¼ teaspoon black pepper
¼ teaspoon Tabasco

Combine all the ingredients in a large jug. Refrigerate for at least 1 hour before serving. Gazpacho is always served cold.

per serving 76 calories, 3 g protein, 0 g fat (including 0 g saturated fat),
0 mg cholesterol, 15 g carbohydrates, 2 g fiber, 1,020 mg sodium

HINT **helpful HINT** HINTHINTHINT

Make a quick version of borscht using 8 cups of store-bought vegetable stock, canned beet and packaged shredded cabbage. Serve chilled.

summer borscht

Beets provide the B vitamin folate. Cabbage and onions boost the vitamin C content of this classic chilled soup.

Serves 6   Preparation 25 minutes
Cooking 50 minutes

8 cups (2 L) water
2 medium celery stalks, chopped
1 medium carrot, peeled and chopped
1 medium onion, quartered
3 cloves garlic, crushed
4 sprigs parsley
2 bay leaves
½ teaspoon salt
4 medium beets
1 small turnip
2 teaspoons olive oil
1 medium onion, very finely chopped
2 cups thinly sliced green cabbage
2 tablespoons finely chopped dill
1½ tablespoons freshly squeezed lemon juice
¼ cup light sour cream

1 Place water, celery, carrot, onion, garlic, parsley, bay leaves and salt in a large pan; bring to a boil. Reduce heat. Simmer, covered, for about 25 minutes, to make a stock. While the stock simmers, peel the beets and turnip, adding all the peel to the pan. Chop the beets and turnip into small pieces.

2 Heat oil in a large saucepan over medium heat. Add the chopped onion. Sauté until softened, about 5 minutes. Add the beet, turnip and cabbage. Strain the stock, discarding the vegetables. Add the stock to the beet mixture. Simmer, uncovered, until root vegetables are tender, about 20 minutes.

3 Remove from heat. Stir in dill and lemon juice. Cool to room temperature. Cover; refrigerate until cold. Whisk in sour cream just before serving.

per serving 71 calories, 2 g protein, 3 g fat (including 1 g saturated fat),
4 mg cholesterol, 11 g carbohydrates, 3 g fiber, 223 mg sodium

on the menu

Traditionally, warm boiled potatoes are eaten as an accompaniment to the borscht. They are served on a separate plate, sprinkled with chopped chives. Instead of mixing the sour cream into the soup, it is served in a bowl so that people can add it to both the soup and the potatoes, as they like.

carrot soup with dill

One bowl of this soup provides four times the daily requirement for vitamin A. It's also rich in vitamin C, potassium and fiber.

Serves 4   Preparation 10 minutes
Cooking 45 minutes

MAKE AHEAD
HEART HEALTHY

1 tablespoon canola oil
1 medium onion, coarsely chopped
1 clove garlic, crushed
3⅓ cups low-sodium chicken stock
4 cups peeled and coarsely
    chopped carrots
½ teaspoon dried thyme
¼ teaspoon salt
¼ teaspoon white pepper
¼ cup low-fat plain yogurt
1 tablespoon finely chopped dill

1 Heat oil in a medium saucepan over medium heat. Add onion and garlic; sauté until softened, 5 minutes. Add stock, carrot and thyme. Simmer, uncovered, until vegetables are very tender, about 40 minutes.

2 Purée soup in batches in a blender or food processor. Add salt and pepper. To serve hot, ladle into bowls and garnish with yogurt and dill. To serve cold, cool to room temperature. Cover and refrigerate until cold. Garnish just before serving.

per serving 135 calories, 6 g protein, 4 g fat (including 0 g saturated fat), 1 mg cholesterol, 20 g carbohydrates, 5 g fiber, 773 mg sodium

HINT helpful HINT HINTHINTHINT

An equal amount of any puréed winter squash, like turban, butternut or acorn, or puréed fresh pumpkin can replace canned pumpkin in just about any recipe. All of these orange-fleshed varieties, though distinct in flavor, are perfectly complemented by the same seasonings — herbs, spices, citrus juices and zest.

pumpkin soup

Pumpkin is a useful source of fiber and vitamins A and C.

Serves 4   Preparation 10 minutes
Cooking 45 minutes

MAKE AHEAD

1 tablespoon canola oil
1 small onion, finely chopped
2 medium carrots, peeled and finely chopped
2 medium celery stalks, finely chopped
¼ cup tomato paste
3⅓ cups low-sodium chicken stock
1 bay leaf
½ teaspoon dried thyme
15-oz (540 mL) can pumpkin purée
¼ cup light sour cream
¼ teaspoon salt
¼ teaspoon white pepper
lime slices and chopped cilantro,
    for garnish (optional)

1 Heat oil in a large saucepan over medium heat. Add onion, carrot and celery; sauté until softened, about 5 minutes. Stir in the tomato paste. Cook 1 minute. Add the stock, bay leaf and thyme; simmer, uncovered, until all the vegetables are tender, about 30 minutes.

2 Stir in pumpkin. Cook for 5 minutes. Remove bay leaf.

3 Purée soup in batches in a blender or food processor. Pour soup back into saucepan. Add sour cream. Bring to a simmer. Add salt and pepper. Add a little water if mixture is too thick. Garnish with lime and cilantro just before serving.

per serving 131 calories, 6 g protein, 6 g fat (including 1 g saturated fat), 6 mg cholesterol, 16 g carbohydrates, 6 g fiber, 725 mg sodium

asparagus soup

Asparagus is an excellent source of folate, a B vitamin that helps in preventing heart disease and birth defects.

Serves 6   Preparation 20 minutes   Cooking 50 minutes

1 pounds (1 kg) asparagus, trimmed
1 tablespoon canola oil
1 teaspoon butter
2 medium leeks, pale green and white parts only, rinsed and finely chopped
1 small onion, finely chopped
2 cloves garlic, crushed
3 tablespoons uncooked long-grain white rice
grated zest of 1 lemon
5 cups (1.25 L) low-sodium chicken stock
1/2 teaspoon salt
1/4 teaspoon black pepper
1/2 teaspoon dried tarragon
3 tablespoons plain yogurt

1 Slice the tips from the asparagus; blanch in boiling water for 1 minute. Drain. Coarsely chop remaining asparagus.

2 Heat oil and butter in a large saucepan over medium heat. Add leeks, onion and garlic; sauté until softened, 5 minutes. Add chopped asparagus. Cook, covered, 10 minutes.

3 Add rice, lemon zest, stock, salt and pepper. Partially cover; simmer for 30 minutes.

4 Purée soup in batches in a blender or food processor. Return to pan. Stir in tarragon and the reserved asparagus tips. Simmer 3 minutes. Remove from heat. Stir in yogurt and serve.

per serving 111 calories, 6 g protein, 4 g fat (including 1 g saturated fat), 2 mg cholesterol, 15 g carbohydrates, 2 g fiber, 757 mg sodium

on the menu

Both asparagus and cauliflower go well with the flavor of mustard, so if you want to serve either soup as part of a soup-and-sandwich combo, ham on rye with a generous dab of Dijon mustard is a perfect pairing for a sustaining lunch.

cauliflower soup with gruyère

Satisfy your daily vitamin C requirement with a single serving of this soup.

Serves 4   Preparation 15 minutes   [MAKE AHEAD]
Cooking 35 minutes

1 tablespoon canola oil
1 small leek, white part only, rinsed and coarsely chopped
1 medium onion, finely chopped
2 x 14 oz (398 mL) cans low-sodium chicken stock
1/2 large head of cauliflower, coarsely chopped
1/2 teaspoon dried thyme
1/2 teaspoon ground cumin
1/4 teaspoon white pepper
2/3 cup coarsely grated Gruyère cheese

1 Heat oil in a large saucepan over medium-high heat. Add leek and onion. Sauté until softened, about 5 minutes. Add the stock, cauliflower, thyme and cumin. Simmer, uncovered, until cauliflower is tender, about 30 minutes.

2 Add pepper. Ladle soup into individual bowls and sprinkle cheese over each serving.

per serving 162 calories, 11 g protein, 10 g fat (including 4 g saturated fat), 20 mg cholesterol, 10 g carbohydrates, 4 g fiber, 700 mg sodium

creamy greens soup

English spinach and Swiss chard add a rich amount of beta-carotene to every sip of this smooth, creamy soup.

Serves 8   Preparation 25 minutes
Cooking 1 hour

MAKE AHEAD
HEART HEALTHY

2 teaspoons olive oil
2 medium leeks, pale green and white parts only, rinsed and coarsely chopped
1 medium onion, coarsely chopped
2 cloves garlic, crushed
1 bunch collard greens, stemmed and coarsely chopped
1 bunch Swiss chard, stemmed and coarsely chopped
2 medium Yukon gold or all-purpose potatoes, unpeeled, coarsely chopped
1 medium carrot, peeled and coarsely chopped
2 x 14-oz (398 mL) cans low-sodium chicken stock
4 cups (1 L) water
½ teaspoon salt
½ cup light sour cream

1 Heat oil in a large saucepan over medium heat. Add leeks and onion; sauté until softened, about 5 minutes. Add garlic; sauté 2 minutes. Add collard greens, Swiss chard, potato and carrot. Stir in stock, water and salt. Simmer, partially covered, for 50 minutes.

2 Purée soup in batches in a blender or food processor. Return to pan. Stir in sour cream. Heat just until warmed.

per serving 124 calories, 5 g protein, 4 g fat (including 2 g saturated fat), 7 mg cholesterol, 20 g carbohydrates, 5 g fiber, 459 mg sodium

corn chowder with peppers

Peppers pump up the flavor and the vitamin C content of this soup.

Serves 6   Preparation 15 minutes
Cooking 50 minutes

MAKE AHEAD

3 slices turkey bacon
1 tablespoon olive oil
1 large onion, finely chopped
½ pound (250 g) potatoes, unpeeled and cubed
2 x 14 oz (398 mL) cans low-sodium chicken stock
14 oz (398 mL) can corn kernels, drained
1 medium green or yellow pepper, seeded and finely chopped
2 cups 2% milk
¼ teaspoon salt
3 mild green chili peppers, finely chopped

1 Cook bacon in a large pan until crisp, about 6 minutes. Drain on paper towels.

2 Heat oil in same pan over medium heat. Add onion; sauté until softened, 5 minutes. Add the potato and stock; simmer, partially covered, until potato is tender, about 20 minutes. Stir in corn. Simmer 5 minutes.

3 Place half the potato and corn with a little liquid in a food processor. Purée. Return to saucepan. Add chopped pepper, milk and salt. Cover and simmer for 10 minutes.

4 Finely chop the bacon. Stir into chowder with the chili peppers. Heat through and serve.

per serving 166 calories, 8 g protein, 6 g fat (including 2 g saturated fat), 13 mg cholesterol, 22 g carbohydrates, 3 g fiber, 849 mg sodium

fresh ideas

To make the Creamy Greens Soup for vegetarians, replace the chicken stock with vegetable stock. A low-sodium variety is best. Alternatively, omit salt from the recipe. This soup has plenty of flavor without it.

on the menu

Kick-start a barbecue or Tex-Mex-style meal with a cup of this satisfying corn chowder. For added flavor, top it with sprigs of coriander.

To turn Summer Garden Soup into a main dish for lunch or a light supper, stir in small pieces of ham or cooked chicken, turkey or lamb just before serving.

summer garden soup

A mixture of vegetables ensures a good variety of vitamins and minerals.

Serves 6 Preparation 25 minutes
Cooking 45 minutes

MAKE AHEAD
HEART HEALTHY

2 teaspoons olive oil
1 medium onion, finely chopped
1 large stalk celery, finely chopped
2 teaspoons peeled, finely chopped
    fresh ginger
¼ pound (125 g) green beans, cut into short pieces
2 medium potatoes, unpeeled, cut
    into small cubes
1 large carrot, peeled and cubed
1 medium yellow summer squash, quartered lengthwise,
    seeded and cubed
1 bay leaf
¾ teaspoon salt
¾ cup fresh or frozen green peas
2 plum tomatoes, seeded and coarsely chopped
2 tablespoons finely chopped basil leaves
1½ teaspoons finely chopped thyme leaves

1 Heat oil in a large pan over medium heat. Add onion, celery and ginger. Sauté until very tender, 10 minutes. Add green beans, potato, carrot, squash, 8 cups (2 L) water, bay leaf and salt. Simmer, covered, 20 minutes.

2 Uncover soup. Simmer 15 minutes. For the last 5 minutes, add peas, tomato, basil and thyme. Remove bay leaf. Serve.

per serving 88 calories, 3 g protein, 2 g fat (including 0 g saturated fat), 0 mg cholesterol, 17 g carbohydrates, 4 g fiber, 307 mg sodium

---

HINT **helpful HINT** HINTHINTHINT

The vegetables for Roasted Vegetable Soup can be cooked alongside a meat main dish. Meat needs a longer oven time, so the soup can be prepared while the meat finishes. Leave the meat to rest on top of the oven while you serve the soup.

roasted vegetable soup

Carrot juice in place of stock sweetens the soup and boosts the beta-carotene content.

Serves 4 Preparation 10 minutes
Cooking 40 minutes

MAKE AHEAD
HEART HEALTHY

1 tablespoon olive oil
5 cloves garlic, peeled
¾ pound (375 g) potatoes, unpeeled and cubed
2 medium green peppers, seeded
    and cut into small squares
½ teaspoon dried rosemary
1 medium yellow summer squash, quartered lengthwise,
    seeded and cubed
1 large red onion, cut into small cubes
1½ cups carrot juice or low-sodium vegetable stock
¾ pound (375 g) tomatoes, diced
1 teaspoon dried tarragon
¾ teaspoon salt

1 Preheat oven to 425°F (220°C). Combine oil and garlic in a large roasting pan; roast in oven 5 minutes. Add potato, capsicum and rosemary. Toss to coat. Roast until potato begins to soften, about 15 minutes.

2 Stir in squash and onion. Roast 15 minutes longer.

3 Combine the juice, tomato, tarragon and salt in a large saucepan. Bring to a boil over medium heat. Add vegetables.

4 Pour 1 cup water into roasting pan; scrape up any browned bits from bottom of pan. Pour the pan juices into the saucepan; simmer for 2 minutes and serve.

per serving 229 calories, 7 g protein, 5 g fat (including 1 g saturated fat), 0 mg cholesterol, 45 g carbohydrates, 7 g fiber, 833 mg sodium

greek spinach, egg & lemon soup

This traditional Greek soup is made healthier by using fewer egg yolks, reduced-fat stock and brown rice without compromising the rich taste and velvety texture.

Serves 4   Preparation 5 minutes
Cooking 10 minutes

QUICK RECIPE
HEART HEALTHY

3 cups low-sodium chicken stock
3 scallions, thinly sliced
3 cloves garlic, crushed
10-oz (310 g) package frozen chopped spinach
½ teaspoon dried oregano
1 cup cooked brown rice
1 teaspoon grated lemon zest
3 tablespoons freshly squeezed lemon juice
½ teaspoon salt
1 large egg plus 2 egg whites

1 Place ¼ cup stock, scallions and garlic in a medium saucepan. Cook over medium heat until the onion is tender, about 2 minutes.

2 Add remaining stock, the spinach and the oregano; bring to a boil. Reduce to a simmer. Cover; cook until spinach is tender, about 5 minutes.

3 Stir in rice, lemon zest, lemon juice and salt; return to a simmer. Whisk ½ cup of the hot liquid into the whole egg and egg whites in medium bowl. Whisking constantly, pour warmed egg mixture into the simmering soup. Serve.

per serving 114 calories, 8 g protein, 2 g fat (including 1 g saturated fat), 53 mg cholesterol, 17 g carbohydrates, 3 g fiber, 728 mg sodium

tomato egg drop soup

Garlic adds rich flavor and cancer-fighting power to this Cuban-style soup.

Serves 6   Preparation 10 minutes
Cooking 16 minutes

QUICK RECIPE

1 tablespoon olive oil
1 small onion, finely chopped
6 cloves garlic, minced
4 medium ripe tomatoes, seeded and finely chopped
2 x 14-oz (398 mL) cans low-sodium chicken stock
1 bay leaf
½ teaspoon salt
2 large eggs, lightly beaten
6 slices (about 1 in./2.5 cm thick) Italian bread, toasted
3 tablespoons coarsely chopped parsley

1 Heat oil in a large saucepan over medium heat. Add onion; sauté until softened, 5 minutes. Add garlic; sauté 30 seconds. Stir in tomato; sauté 1 minute.

2 Add stock, bay leaf and salt. Reduce heat to low. Simmer, uncovered, 10 minutes. Remove from heat. Discard bay leaf. Stir in eggs. Place a slice of bread in each serving bowl and ladle in hot soup. Sprinkle with parsley; serve immediately.

per serving 135 calories, 7 g protein, 5 g fat (including 1 g saturated fat), 71 mg cholesterol, 17 g carbohydrates, 2 g fiber, 897 mg sodium

HINT helpful HINT HINTHINTHINT

Egg yolks enrich and thicken soups, but they do add fat and cholesterol. If this is a problem for you, substitute 2 egg whites for every whole egg used in a soup recipe. Or, use 1 whole egg and substitute egg whites for a second or third egg.

on the menu

Tomato Egg Drop Soup is a perfect light start to a meal featuring roast meat and a starchy vegetable such as potatoes as the main dish. Serve a simple, palate-cleansing dessert of fruit sorbet or slices of fresh pineapple wedges.

on the menu

This soup serves six as a first course or four as a light main dish. If you are serving it as a main course, round out the meal with a salad of crisp lettuce leaves dressed with a herb-flavored vinaigrette. Serve fruit for dessert.

chicken-tomato soup with tortillas

This soup is a good source of vitamin C. Lime juice adds a punch to the flavor.

Serves 6   Preparation 20 minutes
Cooking 50 minutes

MAKE AHEAD
HEART HEALTHY

1 whole bone-in chicken breast,
    skin removed
6 cups (1.5 L) low-sodium chicken stock
2 cups water
3 cloves garlic
1 teaspoon black pepper
1 teaspoon dried oregano
1 tablespoon olive oil
5 scallions, coarsely chopped
3½ oz (100 g) drained, pickled green chili peppers
4 medium tomatoes, coarsely chopped
½ cup freshly squeezed lime juice
4 corn tortillas (6 in./15 cm), sliced into
    3 even strips, toasted
3 tablespoons chopped cilantro

1 Place chicken, stock, water, 2 cloves garlic, pepper and oregano in a medium saucepan. Simmer, uncovered, 25 minutes.

2 Remove chicken from pan. Discard bones. Cut chicken into large chunks. Strain and reserve stock.

3 Heat oil in a large saucepan over medium heat. Crush remaining garlic and add to pan with the scallions. Sauté until softened, 5 minutes. Add chili peppers, tomato and strained stock. Simmer, partially covered, 15 minutes. (Recipe can be made ahead up to this point.)

4 Add chicken, lime juice and toasted tortilla strips. Simmer 5 minutes. Garnish with cilantro.

per serving 200 calories, 25 g protein, 5 g fat (including 1 g saturated fat), 60 mg cholesterol, 11 g carbohydrates, 2 g fiber, 550 mg sodium

DID YOU KNOW

...that laboratory studies show that chicken soup slows the migration of neutrophils, which cause inflammation at the infection site, relieving sore throats and runny noses?

country-style chicken veggie soup with noodles

Root vegetables add earthy flavors and a mix of antioxidant nutrients that protect against chronic disease.

Serves 4   Preparation 15 minutes
Cooking 40 minutes

HEART HEALTHY

1 tablespoon canola oil
1 medium onion, coarsely chopped
3 medium carrots, peeled and diced
1 medium celery stalk, diced
2 x 14-oz (398 mL) cans low-sodium chicken stock
14-oz (398 mL) can diced tomatoes
½ pound (250 g) bone-in chicken breast, skin removed
1 small turnip or parsnip, peeled and diced
1 teaspoon dried basil
3½ oz (100 g) thin noodles
¼ teaspoon black pepper

1 Heat oil in a large saucepan over medium heat. Add onion, carrots and celery. Sauté until softened, 5 minutes. Add stock, tomato, chicken breast, turnip and basil. Simmer, uncovered, until chicken is cooked through, 30 minutes.

2 Remove chicken from pan. Discard bones. Coarsely chop chicken. Return to soup with the noodles. Cook until noodles are tender, 4 minutes. Add pepper.

per serving 283 calories, 19 g protein, 5 g fat (including 1 g saturated fat), 25 mg cholesterol, 41 g carbohydrates, 5 g fiber, 828 mg sodium

turkey, spinach & rice in roasted garlic broth

A combination of enriched rice, fresh spinach and lean turkey makes this a healthy source of the B vitamins needed to produce energy.

Serves 4   Preparation 15 minutes
Cooking 1 hour

MAKE AHEAD
HEART HEALTHY

2 medium whole heads garlic, unpeeled
2 tablespoons tomato paste
2 x 14-oz (398 mL) cans low-sodium chicken stock
1 cup cooked cubed turkey
1 cup cooked long-grain white rice
¾ pound (375 g) spinach, stemmed
    and coarsely chopped
¼ teaspoon black pepper
¼ teaspoon chili flakes, or to taste
1 tablespoon freshly squeezed lemon juice

1 Preheat oven to 400°F (200°C).

2 Cut top third off garlic heads and discard. Wrap each head in foil. Bake until very soft, about 50 minutes. Let cool. Remove foil. Squeeze out pulp into a small bowl.

3 Combine garlic pulp and tomato paste in a large saucepan. Stir in stock. Bring to a boil. Add the turkey, rice, spinach, pepper and chili flakes. Simmer, uncovered, 8 minutes. Just before serving, stir in lemon juice.

per serving 197 calories, 19 g protein, 4 g fat (including 1 g saturated fat), 30 mg cholesterol, 24 g carbohydrates, 3 g fiber, 208 mg sodium

white bean soup with sage & Parmesan

Spinach and beans provide folate for fighting heart disease and preventing birth defects in the early weeks of pregnancy.

Serves 4   Preparation 5 minutes
Cooking 25 minutes

QUICK RECIPE
MAKE AHEAD

1 tablespoon canola oil
4 small Italian-style turkey sausages,
    casings removed
2 cloves garlic, crushed
1 teaspoon dried sage
19-oz (796 mL) can white kidney or other white beans,
    drained and rinsed
14-oz (398 mL) can low-sodium chicken stock
4 cups (1 L) torn spinach leaves or
    5 oz (150 g) chopped frozen spinach
freshly ground black pepper, to taste
dash of Tabasco
2 tablespoons finely chopped parsley
1 tablespoon freshly squeezed lemon juice
¼ cup grated Parmesan cheese

1 Heat oil in a large non-stick saucepan over medium heat. Add sausages. Cook, stirring to break them up, until browned, 3 minutes. Drain on paper towel.

2 Cook garlic and sage in the pan for 30 seconds. Add the beans, stock and 1½ cups water. Simmer, uncovered, for 10 minutes.

3 Purée half the beans in a food processor, adding a few spoonfuls of the cooking liquid. Return bean mixture to pan. Add sausage, spinach, salt, pepper and Tabasco. Simmer, uncovered, 10 minutes. Stir in the parsley and lemon juice. Sprinkle with Parmesan.

per serving 173 calories, 12 g protein, 7 g fat (including 1 g saturated fat), 21 mg cholesterol, 15 g carbohydrates, 4 g fiber, 890 mg sodium

HINT **helpful HINT** HINTHINTHINT

Most soups will thicken if they are made ahead, refrigerated and reheated before serving. Should a soup get too thick, stir in enough extra stock or water to achieve the desired consistency.

on the menu

There are many types of gourmet sausage on the market, including veal, turkey, pork, chicken and a combination of meats or poultry, that will work just as well in this white bean soup recipe. Some range from mild to hot and spicy while others are seasoned with a variety of herbs. White bean varieties include white kidney, butter, navy and soy beans.

quick fish chowder with tomato & fennel

Aromatic fennel seeds can be used to make a refreshing tea that is thought to be helpful in alleviating intestinal problems.

Serves 4 Preparation 8 minutes
Cooking 25 minutes

QUICK RECIPE
HEART HEALTHY

1 tablespoon olive oil
1 medium onion, coarsely chopped
2 cloves garlic, crushed
1 teaspoon fennel seeds
2 cups fish stock
14 oz (398 mL) stewed tomatoes
½ cup (125 mL) dry white wine
½ pound (250 g) red potatoes,
    unpeeled, cut into small dice
1 pound (500 g) firm fish fillets, such as cod,
    cut into 8 even pieces
¼ cup coarsely chopped parsley

1 Heat oil in a large saucepan over medium-high heat. Add onion and garlic; sauté until softened, 5 minutes. Add fennel seeds; sauté 30 seconds. Add the stock, tomatoes, wine and potato. Simmer, uncovered, until potato is tender, 15 minutes.

2 Add fish and parsley. Bring to a gentle boil. Remove from heat and serve immediately.

per serving 215 calories, 26 g protein, 4 g fat (including 1 g saturated fat), 50 mg cholesterol, 16 g carbohydrates, 4 g fiber, 569 mg sodium

root vegetable chowder with bacon

This is a nutritious blend of sweet potatoes, carrots, onions, potatoes and other vitamin- and mineral-rich vegetables.

Serves 4 Preparation 25 minutes
Cooking 40 minutes

MAKE AHEAD
HEART HEALTHY

2 teaspoons olive oil
1 large onion, finely chopped
2 medium stalks celery, coarsely chopped
1¼ teaspoons dried thyme
2 medium carrots, peeled and
    coarsely chopped
1 large sweet potato, peeled
    and coarsely chopped
1 medium parsnip, peeled and
    coarsely chopped
1 large red potato, peeled and
    coarsely chopped
½ green pepper, seeded
    and coarsely chopped
1⅔ cups (420 mL) low-sodium chicken
    or vegetable stock
pinch of salt
1⅔ cups 2% milk
1 tablespoon balsamic vinegar
3 strips turkey bacon, cooked and
    coarsely chopped

1 Heat oil in a large saucepan over medium heat. Add the onion, celery and thyme; sauté until softened, 5 minutes. Add carrot, sweet potato, parsnip, potato, green pepper, stock and salt. Add just enough water to cover the ingredients. Simmer, covered, until vegetables are tender, 30 minutes.

2 Purée half the soup in a blender until smooth. Return the purée to the pan. Stir in milk and heat gently. Stir in vinegar. Sprinkle with bacon just before serving.

per serving 269 calories, 9 g protein, 7 g fat (including 2 g saturated fat), 21 mg cholesterol, 45 g carbohydrates, 7 g fiber, 774 mg sodium

fresh
ideas

Two or three slices of coarsely chopped hot salami or a little pancetta or prosciutto can be sprinkled on the soup in place of bacon.

chicken & turkey

A chef's salad can include any combination of meat, vegetables and cheese. You can substitute lean roast beef or turkey for some or all of the chicken and ham and add more salad vegetables to the mix, such as sliced cucumber and radishes. In place of goat cheese, try crumbled feta or cubes of Swiss or Havarti cheese.

chef's salad

A nutritional makeover updates this classic main-dish salad to include dark leafy greens, roasted peppers, lean chicken breast and creamy goat's cheese.

Serves 6   Preparation 15 minutes   QUICK RECIPE
Cooking 15 minutes

6 chicken tenderloins or 2 boneless skinless
    chicken breasts
3 cups romaine or other dark
    green lettuce
3 cups baby spinach leaves
6 oz (180 g) thinly sliced smoked lean ham,
    cut into strips
1 medium roasted yellow pepper (see
    page 291), cut lengthwise into thin strips
1 medium roasted orange pepper (see
    page 291), cut lengthwise into thin strips
18 grape or cherry tomatoes, halved
3 oz (90 g) goat cheese, crumbled
½ cup extra virgin olive oil
¼ cup balsamic vinegar
1 teaspoon Dijon mustard
1 clove garlic, crushed
¾ teaspoon dried tarragon
¼ teaspoon salt

1 In a medium saucepan, gently simmer chicken in lightly salted water, uncovered, until cooked — 10 minutes. Drain well.

2 Divide lettuce leaves evenly among serving plates. Top each serving with ½ cup spinach, mounding it in the center. Cut chicken lengthwise into thin strips. Place chicken, ham, pepper, tomato and goat cheese on each salad.

3 Whisk together oil, vinegar, mustard, garlic, tarragon and salt in a small bowl. Serve dressing in a jug with the salad.

per serving 331 calories, 18 g protein, 25 g fat (including 7 g saturated fat), 45 mg cholesterol, 12 g carbohydrates, 2 g fiber, 587 mg sodium

grilled chicken salad

This tangy mix of fresh fruit, lean chicken and salad vegetables is rich in antioxidants.

Serves 4   Preparation 15 minutes   Refrigerate 30 minutes
Cooking 6 minutes

¼ cup orange juice
3 tablespoons freshly squeezed lime juice
2 tablespoons olive oil
1 tablespoon white wine vinegar
½ teaspoon Dijon mustard
¾ teaspoon salt
freshly ground black pepper, to taste
¾ pound (375 g) boneless skinless chicken breasts
1 medium mango, peeled and cut
    into thin wedges
1 medium tomato, cored and cut into
    thin wedges
½ medium cucumber, seeded and thinly sliced
1 medium red onion, thinly sliced
4 cups mixed salad greens

1 Whisk orange juice, lime juice, oil, vinegar, mustard, salt and pepper in a small bowl. Transfer ¼ cup dressing to another small bowl, add chicken breasts and turn to coat. Refrigerate, covered, 1 hour. Reserve remaining dressing.

2 Preheat grill or barbecue to medium-hot. Grill chicken until browned on one side, or about 3 minutes. Baste with marinade from the bowl that held the chicken. Turn chicken and grill until cooked through, or 3 minutes. Transfer to a cutting board and let sit 5 minutes. Cut into thick slices.

3 Combine remaining dressing, mango, tomato, cucumber and onion in a large bowl. Add the grilled chicken. Serve over salad greens.

per serving 220 calories, 19 g protein, 17 g fat (including 9 g saturated fat), 47 mg cholesterol, 17 g carbohydrates, 3 g fiber, 512 mg sodium

teriyaki chicken & vegetable kebabs

Kebabs are a fun, easy way to include a variety of healthy vegetables in one meal.

Serves 4   Preparation 20 minutes   Refrigerate 30 minutes
Cooking 14 minutes

1 pound (500 g) skinless chicken thigh fillets,
    cut into 1 inch (2.5 cm) chunks
½ cup (125 mL) bottled teriyaki baste and glaze
1 medium zucchini, quartered lengthwise and
    cut crosswise into ¼ inch (5 mm)-thick pieces
1 large red pepper, cut into 1 inch (2.5 cm) squares
4 scallions, trimmed and cut
    crosswise in half
8 canned whole water chestnuts,
    drained and rinsed

1 Combine chicken and half the teriyaki baste in a small bowl. Refrigerate, covered, 30 minutes.

2 Preheat grill or barbecue to medium-hot. Thread chicken, zucchini, pepper, scallion and water chestnuts on eight 12 inch (30 cm) metal skewers, finishing with a water chestnut. Brush with a little of the remaining teriyaki baste.

3 Grill or barbecue kebabs 4 inches (10 cm) from heat, turning often and brushing with baste, until vegetables are crisp-tender and chicken is cooked through, 12 to 14 minutes.

per serving 212 calories, 23 g protein, 9 g fat (including 2 g saturated fat), 74 mg cholesterol, 10 g carbohydrates, 1 g fiber, 1,452 mg sodium

grilled chicken breast with corn & pepper relish

Black beans add heart-healthy soluble fiber and rich flavor to the Mexican-style relish.

Serves 4   Preparation 20 minutes   QUICK RECIPE
Cooking 8 minutes   HEART HEALTHY

2 cloves garlic, crushed
2 teaspoons chili powder
¼ teaspoon salt
3 tablespoons freshly squeezed
    lime juice
2 tablespoons canola oil
1½ pounds (750 g) boneless skinless chicken breasts,
    pounded ⅜ inch (1.25 cm) thick
¾ cup low-sodium chicken stock
1⅓ cups fresh drained canned or
    thawed frozen corn kernels
1 large roasted red pepper
    (see page 291), diced
⅔ cup drained canned black beans,
    rinsed
2 tablespoons coarsely chopped red onion
1 jalapeño pepper, seeded and finely chopped
¼ teaspoon salt
3 tablespoons chopped cilantro

1 Combine garlic, chili powder, salt, 2 tbsp lime juice and the oil in a medium bowl. Add chicken and rub with marinade. Let stand at room temperature for no more than 15 minutes.

2 Preheat grill or barbecue to medium-hot.

3 Grill chicken 2 inches (5 cm) from heat just until cooked through, or 3 to 4 minutes per side.

4 To make relish, heat stock in a large frying pan. Add corn kernels, pepper, black beans, onion, jalapeño and salt. Heat through. Just before serving, stir in cilantro and remaining lime juice. Serve chicken topped with relish.

per serving 375 calories, 40 g protein, 12 g fat (including 2 g saturated fat), 95 mg cholesterol, 29 g carbohydrates, 5 g fiber, 521 mg sodium

on the menu

To follow a main course featuring grilled chicken, sliced fresh strawberries topped with a purée of frozen raspberries make a refreshing, palate-cleansing dessert.

pan-fried chicken with carrots in orange sauce

Each serving satisfies your daily requirement for vitamin A, in the form of disease-fighting beta-carotene.

Serves 4 Preparation 10 minutes
Cooking 25 minutes

HEART HEALTHY

1 cup freshly squeezed orange juice
3 tablespoons balsamic vinegar
   or red wine vinegar
1 pound (500 g) boneless skinless chicken breasts
$\frac{1}{4}$ teaspoon salt
freshly ground black pepper, to taste
$\frac{1}{4}$ cup all-purpose flour
2 tablespoons canola oil
4 scallions, thinly sliced
$\frac{1}{2}$ teaspoon ground coriander
4 medium carrots, peeled and cut
   into $\frac{1}{4}$ inch (5 mm) thick slices
2 tablespoons chopped parsley

1 Combine orange juice and vinegar in a small bowl.

2 Season chicken with salt and pepper, and coat with flour. Heat oil in a large non-stick frying pan over medium heat. Add the chicken and cook until browned, or 3 minutes each side. Transfer to a plate.

3 Add scallions, coriander and $\frac{1}{4}$ cup juice mixture to the frying pan, scraping up any browned bits from the bottom of the pan. Cook 30 seconds. Add the remaining juice mixture, carrot and chicken. Bring to a boil. Tightly cover frying pan, lower heat and simmer until chicken is cooked through and carrot is tender, about 20 minutes.

4 Place a chicken breast each on 4 plates. Spoon carrot mixture and sauce over the top. Garnish with parsley.

per serving 447 calories, 55 g protein, 13 g fat (including 2 g saturated fat), 145 mg cholesterol, 23 g carbohydrates, 3 g fiber, 318 mg sodium

chicken stir-fry

Packets of pre-sliced vegetables from the supermarket make this a quick, easy dish.

Serves 4 Preparation 5 minutes
Cooking 12 minutes

QUICK RECIPE

2 tablespoons olive oil
1 pound (500 g) boneless skinless chicken breasts ,
   cut in $\frac{1}{2}$ inch (1 cm)-wide strips
$\frac{1}{2}$ teaspoon salt
$\frac{1}{4}$ teaspoon black pepper
$1\frac{1}{2}$ cups sliced, seeded red,
   green or yellow peppers
$1\frac{1}{2}$ cups sliced zucchini
2 cloves garlic, crushed
10 cherry tomatoes, each halved
$\frac{1}{2}$ teaspoon dried oregano
2 teaspoons balsamic vinegar

1 Heat oil in a large non-stick frying pan over medium-high heat. Add chicken. Sauté until barely cooked through, or about 4 minutes. Sprinkle on half the salt and all the pepper. Remove chicken from pan.

2 In the same pan, sauté pepper and zucchini just until tender, or 4 minutes. Sprinkle with remaining salt. Add garlic; sauté 30 seconds. Add tomato and oregano. Cook 1 minute. Return chicken to pan. Sprinkle with vinegar and heat through.

per serving 209 calories, 24 g protein, 10 g fat (including 2 g saturated fat), 63 mg cholesterol, 6 g carbohydrates, 2 g fiber, 352 mg sodium

fresh ideas

For the Chicken Stir-fry, many other fresh vegetables can be used, such as broccoli and green beans.

mediterranean chicken

Fennel, green beans and white kidney beans add folate, calcium and fiber to this earthy chicken dish.

Serves 4   Preparation 20 minutes   HEART HEALTHY
Cooking 1 hour

2 tablespoons olive oil
1 whole chicken (about 3½ pounds/1.75 kg), cut into 8 pieces, skin removed
¼ cup all-purpose flour
1 large fennel bulb, about 1½ pounds (750 g), trimmed and sliced
4 cloves garlic, cut into slivers
1 cup low-sodium chicken stock
2 tablespoons freshly squeezed lemon juice
½ teaspoon salt
¼ teaspoon each dried rosemary, thyme and pepper
19 oz (798 mL) can white kidney or other white beans, rinsed and drained
½ pound (250 g) green beans, cut into 2 inch (5 cm) lengths

1 Preheat oven to 350°F (180°C). In a heatproof casserole dish with a tight-fitting lid, heat oil over medium-high heat. Dredge the chicken in flour and sauté until golden, about 4 minutes per side. Transfer to a plate.

2 Add fennel to pan. Reduce heat to medium. Cook, stirring frequently, until fennel is golden, or 7 minutes. Add garlic; cook 1 minute. Add stock, lemon juice, salt, rosemary, thyme and pepper. Bring to a boil. Add chicken, cover and place in oven.

3 Cook until chicken is done, or about 35 minutes. Stir in the white beans and green beans. Bake a further 5 minutes.

per serving 780 calories, 95 g protein, 24 g fat (including 5 g saturated fat), 280 mg cholesterol, 42 g carbohydrates, 13 g fiber, 1,090 mg sodium

chicken baked with 40 cloves of garlic

Garlic has properties that could fight cancer, cholesterol and heart disease. Given the amount of garlic in this recipe, this is just about the healthiest dish you can eat.

Serves 8   Preparation 25 minutes   MAKE AHEAD
Cooking 1 hour 15 minutes

6 tablespoons olive oil
2 whole chickens (about 3½ pounds/1.75 kg each), each cut into 8 serving pieces, skin removed
⅓ cup all-purpose flour
40 cloves garlic, unpeeled
3 medium stalks celery, halved lengthwise and cut crosswise into 1 inch (2.5 cm) lengths
4 sprigs fresh rosemary or 1 teaspoon dried
3 sprigs fresh thyme or ½ teaspoon dried
1 cup dry vermouth or white wine
1 cup low-sodium chicken stock
1½ teaspoons salt

1 Preheat oven to 350°F (180°C). Heat 2 tbsp oil in a large frying pan over medium heat. Dredge chicken in flour, shaking off excess. Add a third of the chicken to the pan and sauté until golden brown, or about 4 minutes each side. Transfer to a 10 x 14 inch (25 x 35 cm) roasting pan. Sauté remaining chicken in two more batches, using 2 tbsp oil per batch, then transfer to the roasting pan.

2 Add garlic, celery, rosemary and thyme to the frying pan, and cook 1 minute. Add vermouth or wine. Increase heat to high, bring to a boil and cook 2 minutes so the alcohol evaporates. Add the stock and salt to the pan and bring to a boil. Remove from heat. Pour vegetables and cooking liquid over chicken in roasting pan. Cover pan with aluminum foil.

3 Bake until chicken is cooked and garlic is meltingly tender, or about 45 minutes. Serve chicken with a little of the garlic.

per serving 660 calories, 87 g protein, 23 g fat (including 5 g saturated fat), 280 mg cholesterol, 13 g carbohydrates, 1 g fiber, 700 mg sodium

DID YOU KNOW ...when garlic enjoys long, slow cooking — 45 minutes or more in the oven —it loses its characteristic bite and strong odor, and adds a very mellow flavor to whatever it has been cooked with?

To cut the amount of saturated fat in these dishes by half, remove the skin from the chicken pieces and Cornish hens after cooking and discard. To remove more fat from the stew, refrigerate it overnight and scoop off all the solidified fat the next day. Reheat the stew and serve.

chicken stew with butternut squash & white beans

This satisfying cold-weather comforter is rich in folate, fiber and flavor.

Serves 6   Preparation 15 minutes
Cooking 1 hour

MAKE AHEAD

1 tablespoon olive oil
3 pounds (1.5 kg) chicken parts
½ teaspoon salt
¼ teaspoon black pepper
1 medium onion, coarsely chopped
4 cloves garlic, peeled and each one halved
1 cup white wine
2 tablespoons tomato paste
2 bay leaves
½ teaspoon dried thyme
14 oz (398 mL) can white kidney or other white beans, drained and rinsed
1½ pounds (750 g) butternut squash, seeded, peeled, and cut into 2 inch (5 cm) pieces

1 Preheat oven to 350°F (180°C). Heat the oil in a large heatproof casserole over medium-high heat. Season chicken with half the salt and all the pepper. Brown chicken in batches in casserole, for about 6 minutes each. Transfer to a plate.

2 Lower heat to medium. Add onion and garlic. Sauté until slightly softened, or about 3 minutes. Add wine and scrape up any browned bits from the bottom of the dish. Stir in tomato paste, bay leaves, thyme and remaining salt. Add chicken. Bring to a boil. Cover.

3 Bake in the oven for 20 minutes. Stir in the beans and squash. Cover. Bake until chicken and squash are tender, or 20 to 30 minutes. Discard bay leaves and serve.

per serving 381 calories, 29 g protein, 21 g fat (including 5 g saturated fat), 75 mg cholesterol, 19 g carbohydrates, 5 g fiber, 330 mg sodium

cornish hens with honey-glazed vegetables

Fiber-rich sweet potatoes, parsnips and celeriac protect the digestive tract.

Serves 4   Preparation 15 minutes   Cooking 1 hour

2 large sweet potatoes, peeled and cut into 1 inch (2.5 cm) chunks
2 large parsnips, peeled and cut into 1 inch (2.5 cm) chunks
1 large celeriac, peeled and cut into 1 inch (2.5 cm) chunks
1 medium red onion, quartered
2 teaspoons fresh thyme or 1 teaspoon dried thyme
½ teaspoon salt
½ teaspoon black pepper
2 tablespoons olive oil
4 Cornish hens (about 1 pound/500 g each)
½ teaspoon paprika
2 tablespoons honey

1 Place oven rack in lowest position and preheat oven to 350°F (180°C).

2 In large roasting pan or 2 smaller pans, combine potatoes, parsnip, celeriac, onion, thyme, salt, pepper and oil. Place hens, breast-side up, in among the vegetables. Sprinkle with paprika.

3 Bake for 50 minutes, stirring vegetables occasionally. Stir honey into the vegetables. Bake until the hens are cooked through and vegetables are fork-tender, or 10 to 15 minutes. Cut each hen in half to serve.

per serving 630 calories, 45 g protein, 28 g fat (including 7 g saturated fat), 134 mg cholesterol, 50 g carbohydrates, 8 g fiber, 715 mg sodium

poached chicken with seasonal vegetables

Try different combinations of vegetables in this simple all-in-one supper dish.

Serves 4 Preparation 10 minutes
Cooking 25 minutes

HEART HEALTHY

4 boneless skinless chicken breasts (1¼ pounds/600 g)
3 cups low-sodium chicken stock
3 tablespoons dry sherry or
    dry white wine
1 bouquet garni (parsley, thyme
    and bay leaf)
1½ pounds (750 g) mixed vegetables, such as carrots,
    asparagus spears, baby corn, broccoli, cauliflower,
    leeks and savoy cabbage
chopped fresh parsley, to garnish

1 Combine the chicken breasts, stock, sherry or wine and the bouquet garni in a large heatproof casserole or deep frying pan. Bring to a boil. Lower heat and cover. Poach chicken for about 20 minutes, skimming off foam that forms as necessary.

2 Meanwhile, cut all the vegetables into bite-sized pieces.

3 After chicken has been poaching for 20 minutes, add all the vegetables to pan. Cover; cook until vegetables are tender and chicken juices run clear when breasts are pierced with the tip of a knife, about 6 minutes. Discard bouquet garni.

4 Spoon the pan juices and vegetables into large, shallow serving bowls. Top with chicken, whole or sliced, as you prefer. Sprinkle with parsley and serve.

per serving 340 calories, 32 g protein, 17 g fat (including 6 g saturated fat), 90 mg cholesterol, 14 g carbohydrates, 3 g fiber, 180 mg sodium

turkey cutlets with green beans & sweet onion sauce

Green beans have more than five times as much beta-carotene as the yellow variety.

Serves 4   Preparation 15 minutes
Cooking 13 minutes

2 tablespoons grated orange zest
½ cup freshly squeezed orange juice
2 teaspoons grated lemon zest
¼ cup freshly squeezed lemon juice
3 tablespoons honey
½ teaspoon freshly ground black pepper
4 skinless turkey breast cutlets (4 oz/125 g each)
½ teaspoon salt
1 pound (500 g) green beans
2 tablespoons unsalted butter
1 extra-large yellow onion, finely sliced
2 large shallots, sliced
2 large garlic cloves, minced

1 Whisk orange zest and juice, lemon zest and juice, honey and pepper in a small bowl. Set aside.

2 Place each cutlet between two sheets of plastic wrap and pound until about ½ inch (1.25 cm) thick. Sprinkle both sides with ¼ tsp salt.

3 Half-fill a medium saucepan with water. Add remaining salt and bring to a boil over medium-high heat. Add beans and cook just until they turn bright green, or about 3 minutes. Drain. Transfer to a platter and keep warm.

4 Meanwhile, melt butter in a large non-stick frying pan over medium-high heat. Add the onion, shallot and garlic. Sauté for 2 minutes, or just until the onion is transparent but not brown. Use a slotted spoon to transfer mixture to a plate.

5 Sauté turkey in same pan, for 3 minutes on each side. Arrange on top of the platter of beans. Keep hot. Pour the reserved juice mixture into the pan, add onion mixture and boil 2 minutes. Spoon over turkey and beans and serve.

per serving 315 calories, 29 g protein, 7 g fat (including 4 g saturated fat), 86 mg cholesterol, 37 g carbohydrates, 4 g fiber, 587 mg sodium

chicken breasts stuffed with spinach & cheese

The phytochemical-rich filling fights chronic disease and helps protect your eyesight.

Serves 6   Preparation 20 minutes   MAKE AHEAD
Cooking 35 minutes

6 skinless chicken breast fillet halves
    (about 1½ pounds/750 g)
¾ teaspoon salt
¼ teaspoon black pepper
½ teaspoon dried basil
½ pound (250 g) frozen spinach, thawed and squeezed dry
6 medium roasted red pepper halves
    (see page 291)
6 thin slices reduced-fat Jarlsberg or
    Swiss cheese (4 oz/115 g)
½ cup low-fat buttermilk
2 cups fresh whole wheat bread crumbs

1 Preheat oven to 425°F (220°C). Coat baking dish with non-stick cooking spray.

2 Place each chicken breast between 2 sheets plastic wrap; pound to ⅛ inch (3 mm) thick. Season one side with salt, pepper and basil. Top each breast evenly with spinach, pepper and cheese, leaving a ¼ inch (5 mm) border around the edge. Roll up the chicken breasts and secure with toothpicks.

3 Dip chicken in buttermilk, then coat evenly with bread crumbs. Place, seam-side down, on the baking dish.

4 Bake until chicken is cooked through and crumb coating is browned, about 35 minutes. Remove toothpicks and serve.

per serving 236 calories, 31 g protein, 8 g fat (including 4 g saturated fat),
76 mg cholesterol, 10 g carbohydrates, 2 g fiber, 518 mg sodium

chicken pot pie with chunky vegetables

This classic comfort food has a healthy, modern twist: It contains a higher ratio of vegetables to poultry.

Serves 6   Preparation 25 minutes   Cooking 45 minutes

2 tablespoons olive oil
3 medium leeks, rinsed, white and pale green parts
    coarsely chopped
2 medium celery stalks, coarsely chopped
2 large carrots, peeled and thickly sliced
1 large red potato, unpeeled and cut into
    bite-sized chunks
1 cup thickly sliced mushrooms
3 tablespoons plain flour
½ teaspoon dried thyme
¼ teaspoon salt
14 oz (398 mL) can low-sodium chicken stock
½ pound (250 g) bite-sized pieces cooked chicken
1 cup fresh or frozen green peas
Premade pastry for single-crust 9 inch (23 cm) pie
1 large egg beaten with 1 tablespoon
    milk, for glazing

1 Heat oil in a large saucepan over medium heat. Add leeks, celery, carrot and potato. Cook, stirring occasionally, 5 minutes. Add mushrooms. Cook, stirring occasionally, 5 minutes. Stir in flour, thyme and salt until blended. Stir in stock. Increase heat to medium-high. Cook, stirring, until thickened, or 2 minutes. Stir in chicken and peas. Transfer to 9 or 10 inch (23 cm or 25 cm)-deep pie plate. Let cool to room temperature.

2 Preheat oven to 400°F (200°C). Unfold pastry, checking its fit on top of pie plate. Brush underside of pastry with glaze and place over filling. Trim edge of pastry; crimp or mark decoratively with a fork, if desired. Brush top with glaze. Cut four 1 inch (2.5 cm) slits in the center to allow steam to escape.

3 Bake until filling is bubbling and pastry is golden brown, or 25 to 30 minutes. Let stand at least 10 minutes before serving.

per serving 393 calories, 22 g protein, 16 g fat (including 5 g saturated fat),
82 mg cholesterol, 39 g carbohydrates, 5 g fiber, 500 mg sodium

on the menu

*Start an autumn dinner with a creamy tomato soup, then follow with this
hearty pie and a crisp green salad. End the meal with a light lemon mousse.*

asian vegetable-packed turkey burgers

Grated carrot is the secret ingredient that boosts both the flavor and the antioxidant power of these low-fat, low-calorie burgers.

Makes 6 burgers **Preparation** 10 minutes QUICK RECIPE
Cooking 10 minutes

1½ pounds (750 g) lean ground turkey
2 medium carrots, peeled and finely shredded
3 scallions, finely chopped
2 tablespoons low-sodium soy sauce
2 teaspoons finely chopped, peeled fresh ginger
¼ teaspoon salt
¼ teaspoon black pepper

1 Preheat broiler. Combine turkey, carrot, scallions, soy sauce, ginger, salt and pepper in a medium bowl. Shape into 6 equal patties.

2 Broil burgers 4 inches (10 cm) from heat for 5 minutes. Turn over and grill just until no longer pink in the center, or about 4 to 5 minutes.

per burger 135 calories, 16 g protein, 6 g fat (including 2 g saturated fat), 67 mg cholesterol, 3 g carbohydrates, 1 g fiber, 498 mg sodium

on the menu

Place the burgers on bread rolls with lettuce and tomato, or serve on a bed of thin noodles with finely sliced pepper and scallions, and tossed with a few drops of dark sesame oil. Cucumber slices in rice vinegar make a refreshing side dish.

tex-mex turkey casserole

Spicy and hearty, this dish is rich in vitamins C, B$_6$, E and folate.

Serves 6   Preparation 15 minutes
Cooking 55 minutes

MAKE AHEAD
HEART HEALTHY

1 tablespoon canola oil
1 medium onion, coarsely chopped
1 tablespoon chili powder
$\frac{1}{2}$ teaspoon cinnamon
$\frac{1}{4}$ teaspoon salt
3 tablespoons plain flour
14 oz (398 mL) can diced tomatoes
1 mild green chili pepper, finely chopped
14 oz (398 mL) can low-sodium chicken stock
$\frac{1}{2}$ pound (250 g) piece of oven-roasted turkey (available
    from delicatessens and supermarkets), sliced $\frac{1}{2}$ inch
    (1 cm)-thick and cut into cubes
2 medium zucchini, cut into $\frac{1}{2}$ inch (1 cm) cubes
1 cup frozen corn kernels
1$\frac{1}{2}$ cups cooked long-grain white rice
1 cup coarsely grated reduced-fat
    cheddar cheese

1 Preheat oven to 350°F (180°C). Heat oil in a large saucepan over medium heat. Add onion and sauté until softened, or 5 minutes. Stir in the chili powder, cinnamon, salt and flour. Cook, stirring, 2 minutes. Stir in the tomato, chili and stock. Cook, stirring, until slightly thickened, about 2 minutes. Take off the heat and stir in the turkey, zucchini, corn and rice. Pour the mixture into an ungreased 9 x 9 x 2 inch (23 x 23 x 5 cm) baking dish. (This recipe can be prepared ahead up to this point.)

2 Bake until mixture is bubbling, about 40 minutes. Sprinkle with cheese. Bake until cheese has melted, or about 5 minutes. Let stand 5 minutes before serving.

per serving 264 calories, 20 g protein, 8 g fat (including 3 g saturated fat),
47 mg cholesterol, 29 g carbohydrates, 3 g fiber, 831 mg sodium

DID YOU KNOW

...cooking corn releases beneficial nutrients that can substantially reduce the risk of heart disease and cancer? Research indicates that the longer the corn is cooked, the higher the level of antioxidants.

lamb & pork
pork beef lam
& pork beef
ef lamb & por

on the menu

A full niçoise salad has all the elements needed for a healthy main course. Start the meal with a bowl of hot consommé. For dessert, serve two or three soft cheeses with a baguette and fresh pears.

beef salad niçoise

Slices of iron-rich rump steak top a mixture of vitamin-packed vegetables.

Serves 4   Preparation 15 minutes
Cooking 20 minutes   HEART HEALTHY

1 thick-cut lean rump steak (12 oz/350 g), trimmed
¼ teaspoon dried herbes de Provence,
    or to taste
pinch each of salt and pepper
1 pound (500 g) small new potatoes, scrubbed
½ pound (250 g) green beans, trimmed
½ pound (250 g) frozen fava beans, thawed
½ pound (250 g) cherry tomatoes, halved
½ cup mixed pitted black and
    green olives
2 tablespoons snipped chives
3 tablespoons chopped parsley
2 tablespoons extra virgin olive oil
1 tablespoon red wine vinegar
2 teaspoons Dijon mustard
5 oz (150 g) baby spinach leaves
4 cups torn lettuce leaves

1 Pat steak dry with paper towel. Season on both sides with herbes de Provence and salt and pepper. Set aside.

2 Cook potatoes in a large pan of boiling water, 10 minutes. Add green and fava beans. Cook until all vegetables are just tender, about 5 minutes. Drain and rinse in cold water to cool.

3 Combine potatoes, beans, tomatoes, olives, chives and parsley in a large bowl. Set aside.

4 Heat ridged cast-iron grill pan or non-stick frying pan over medium-high heat until hot. Grill steak 3 minutes each side or until cooked as liked. Remove to plate; let stand 5 minutes.

5 Combine oil, vinegar, mustard and 2 tbsp water in a screw-top jar. Season with salt and pepper. Shake to combine.

6 Slice steak thinly. Add to vegetables. Pour any juices that have collected on the plate into the dressing. Pour dressing over meat and vegetables, and toss well. Place spinach and lettuce leaves in a large bowl. Spoon steak salad over the top.

per serving 500 calories, 35 g protein, 19 g fat (including 3 g saturated fat),
50 mg cholesterol, 51 g carbohydrates, 17 g fiber, 890 mg sodium

beef & green salad

The more deeply colored salad greens are, the more vitamins and minerals they contain.

Serves 4   Preparation 20 minutes
Cooking 2 minutes   QUICK RECIPE

1 cup parsley leaves
1 tablespoon capers, drained
1 tablespoon Dijon mustard
1 tablespoon white wine vinegar
1 clove garlic, peeled
3 tablespoons olive oil
2 tablespoons low-sodium chicken stock
1 tablespoon vegetable oil
1 pound (500 g) beef round steak, cut into
    wide, thin strips
1 medium romaine lettuce, torn into bite-sized pieces
1 large red pepper, seeded and cut into strips
½ medium red onion, thinly sliced

1 Combine parsley, capers, mustard, vinegar, garlic, olive oil and stock in a food processor or blender. Process until smooth to make a dressing.

2 Heat oil in a medium non-stick frying pan over high heat. Add beef and sauté just until pink, or about 2 minutes. Transfer to a plate. Let cool.

3 Combine lettuce, pepper and onion on a serving platter. Top with beef strips. Serve with dressing.

per serving 339 calories, 27 g protein, 23 g fat (including 5 g saturated fat),
65 mg cholesterol, 8 g carbohydrates, 4 g fiber, 187 mg sodium

stir-fried beef

Mushrooms supply selenium and potassium that help reduce the risk of strokes.

Serves 4   Preparation 20 minutes
Marinating 20 minutes   Cooking 13 minutes

3 tablespoons low-sodium soy sauce
2 teaspoons dark brown sugar
1 pound (500 g) beef round steak, cut across the grain
    into ⅛ inch (3 mm)-thick strips
1 small head broccoli,
    cut into 4 inch (10 cm)-long florets
2 tablespoons vegetable oil
2 cups sliced shiitake mushroom caps
1 medium red pepper, seeded and thinly sliced
5 oz (150 g) snow peas, stems and strings removed
4 scallions, finely sliced diagonally
1 tablespoon crushed garlic
1 tablespoon peeled, finely chopped fresh ginger
pinch of chili flakes
⅓ cup low-sodium chicken stock
1 tablespoon balsamic vinegar
2 teaspoons cornstarch

1 Mix 1 tbsp soy sauce and all the brown sugar in a medium bowl. Add beef and toss to coat. Marinate at room temperature for 20 minutes. Steam broccoli until crisp-tender, or 3 to 4 minutes. Cool under cold running water and drain.

2 Heat oil in a large non-stick frying pan over a high heat. Add meat. Stir-fry just until pink, 2 minutes. Remove from pan.

3 Add mushrooms, pepper, snow peas, scallions, garlic, ginger and chili flakes to pan. Stir-fry until snow peas are crisp-tender, or 3 to 4 minutes.

4 Combine the stock, remaining soy sauce, vinegar and cornstarch in a small bowl until smooth. Add to pan. Bring to a boil. (Mixture will be thick.) Add broccoli. Cook just until heated through, or about 2 minutes.

5 Drain beef. Add to pan. Heat through for about 30 seconds. Serve immediately.

per serving 301 calories, 30 g protein, 12 g fat (including 2 g saturated fat), 66 mg cholesterol, 21 g carbohydrates, 4 g fiber, 838 mg sodium

fresh ideas

A beef stir-fry is an adaptable dish that is easily varied to make use of seasonal vegetables and a range of seasonings. Try a combination of sugar snap peas, asparagus spears and radishes with onions and lemon zest. Go for a mix of red, yellow and green peppers with fresh basil and garlic. Green or lima beans, baby corn and zucchini with scallions and dill taste good, too.

thai-style beef sandwich

Vitamin-packed coleslaw enriches a simple beef sandwich.

HEART HEALTHY

Serves 4 Preparation 10 minutes
Marinating 30 minutes Cooking 10 minutes

2 tablespoons tomato paste
½ cup freshly squeezed lime juice
    (about 3 limes)
1½ teaspoons ground coriander
1 pound (500 g) well-trimmed sirloin steak
1 teaspoon sugar
1 teaspoon salt
1 teaspoon chili flakes
3 cups shredded green cabbage
2 medium carrots, coarsely grated
1 large red pepper, cut into matchsticks
½ cup chopped cilantro
⅓ cup chopped mint
4 hard rolls, halved crosswise

1 Mix tomato paste, half the lime juice and all the ground coriander in a shallow dish. Add the steak, turning to coat. Refrigerate for 30 minutes.

2 Whisk the remaining lime juice, the sugar, salt and chili flakes in a large bowl. Add the cabbage, carrot, pepper, cilantro and mint; toss thoroughly to combine. Refrigerate coleslaw until serving time.

3 Preheat broiler. Remove steak from marinade. Cook 6 inches (15 cm) from heat for 4 minutes per side for medium-rare, brushing any remaining marinade over steak halfway through the cooking time. Let stand for 10 minutes. Cut steak diagonally across the grain into thin slices. (Steak can also be cooked on a barbecue.)

4 To serve, fill rolls with coleslaw and top with steak.

per serving 420 calories, 32 g protein, 13 g fat (including 5 g saturated fat), 55 mg cholesterol, 47 g carbohydrates, 7 g fiber, 890 mg sodium

You can substitute baby carrots or chunks of pumpkin for the sweet potatoes in Moroccan Beef Stew without significantly changing its flavor or nutritional value.

moroccan beef stew with chickpeas

Chickpeas add low-fat protein to this dish. Dried apricots and raisins give it a sweetness that complements the warmth of the spices.

Serves 6   Preparation 15 minutes
Cooking 1 hour 50 minutes

MAKE AHEAD

1 tablespoon vegetable oil
1 pound (500 g) beef round steak,
    cut into 1 inch (2.5 cm) cubes
1 medium onion, finely chopped
4 cloves garlic, crushed
1/2 teaspoon each ground ginger,
    cinnamon, nutmeg and turmeric
1/2 teaspoon salt
1/4 teaspoon black pepper
1/2 cup chopped dried apricots
1/4 cup sultanas or seeded raisins
2 medium sweet potatoes, peeled and cut
    into 1 inch (2.5 cm) chunks
3 cups (750 mL) low-sodium chicken stock
1 15 oz (540 mL) can chickpeas, drained and rinsed
thinly sliced strips of scallion
thin strips of orange peel

1 Heat oil in a large non-stick saucepan over medium-high heat. Cook beef in batches, browning meat on all sides, 3 to 4 minutes per batch. Transfer the meat to a plate as it browns. Add onion to saucepan. Cook until softened, about 5 minutes. Add a spoonful of water, if needed, to prevent sticking.

2 Add garlic, ginger, cinnamon, nutmeg, turmeric, salt and pepper. Cook 1 minute. Add the apricots, raisins, sweet potato, reserved beef and stock. Cover and simmer until meat is very tender, or about 1 hour 30 minutes.

3 Stir in chickpeas. Heat through. Garnish with scallion strips and orange peel.

per serving 330 calories, 18 g protein, 12 g fat (including 4 g saturated fat), 48 mg cholesterol, 37 g carbohydrates, 5 g fiber, 812 mg sodium

veal stew with beer

This heart-healthy main dish is low in saturated fat and high in fiber.

Serves 4   Preparation 15 minutes
Cooking 1 hour 30 minutes

MAKE AHEAD
HEART HEALTHY

1 pound (500 g) stewing veal, cut into 1 inch (2.5 cm)
    cubes
3/4 teaspoon salt
1/4 teaspoon black pepper
2 tablespoons vegetable oil
2 portobello mushrooms, stems removed
    and caps cut into 1 inch (2.5 cm) slices
8 large shallots (or 1 medium onion),
    finely chopped
2 tablespoons all-purpose flour
1 1/2 cups (375 mL) dark beer such as Guinness
1 tablespoon white wine vinegar
1/2 teaspoon dried thyme
1 pound (500 g) large carrots, peeled and
    cut into 2 inch (5 cm) lengths

1 Pat veal pieces dry with paper towel. Season with 1/4 tsp salt and the pepper. Heat oil in a large heatproof casserole over high heat. Working in batches, add veal and brown on all sides, about 4 minutes per batch. Transfer veal to a plate.

2 Lower heat to medium. Add mushrooms and shallots to casserole. Sauté until shallots are just golden, about 5 minutes. Stir in flour. Add veal, beer, vinegar, thyme and the remaining salt. Bring to a boil. Add carrot and cover. Lower the heat and simmer until veal is tender, or about 1 hour 15 minutes.

3 Transfer veal, carrot and mushrooms to serving dish. Boil sauce until reduced to about 1 1/4 cups. Pour over veal.

per serving 310 calories, 26 g protein, 11 g fat (including 2 g saturated fat), 95 mg cholesterol, 21 g carbohydrates, 3 g fiber, 490 mg sodium

grilled steak with portobello mushrooms

Round out the nutritional profile of an iron-rich steak with vitamin-rich vegetables.

Serves 4 Preparation 15 minutes
Cooking 15 minutes

QUICK RECIPE

2 teaspoons olive oil
2 cloves garlic, minced
4 thin slices red onion
4 large portobello mushrooms,
    stems removed
non-stick olive-oil cooking spray
2 boneless rib-eye steaks (12 oz/375 g each)
½ teaspoon salt
¼ teaspoon black pepper
3 ripe tomatoes
fresh chives or parsley, finely chopped

1 Heat grill or barbecue until hot. Heat oil in a small frying pan over medium heat. Add garlic and sauté 2 minutes. Transfer oil and garlic to a large bowl.

2 Coat onion slices and mushroom caps thoroughly with cooking spray.

3 Grill onion and mushrooms just until browned, for about 2 minutes each side. Cut mushrooms into thick slices. Add mushrooms and onion to garlic oil. Toss to coat.

4 Cut steaks crosswise into two equal pieces. Pat meat dry with paper towel. Season with salt and pepper and coat lightly with cooking spray.

5 Grill steaks until seared and browned grill marks appear, for about 4 minutes. Turn steaks. Grill 2 to 3 minutes for medium-rare, or until cooked as liked.

6 To serve, cut each tomato into 4 slices. Place 3 slices on top of each cooked steak. Top with the mushroom mixture. Sprinkle with chives or parsley.

per serving 305 calories, 23 g protein, 20 g fat (including 7 g saturated fat), 67 mg cholesterol, 8 g carbohydrates, 2 g fiber, 159 mg sodium

DID YOU KNOW

...cooked fresh mushrooms have almost three times the niacin and potassium, twice the iron and 15 times the riboflavin of a comparable amount of canned mushrooms?

beef, onion & pepper fajitas

A fajita is a tortilla wrapped around meat and an assortment of vegetables, which means it's naturally loaded with vitamins, minerals and phytochemicals.

Makes 8 fajitas   Preparation 15 minutes
Marinating 1 to 2 hours   Cooking 12 minutes

1 pound (500 g) sirloin steak, in one piece
1 medium red onion, sliced
1 small red pepper, seeded
    and cut into thin strips
1 small green pepper, seeded
    and cut into thin strips
1 small yellow pepper, seeded
    and cut into thin strips
4 cloves garlic, crushed
½ cup freshly squeezed lime juice
2 tablespoons olive oil
2 tablespoons balsamic vinegar
1 teaspoon ground cumin
½ teaspoon salt
¼ teaspoon black pepper
1 serrano or jalapeño pepper, seeded
    and finely chopped
8 medium flour tortillas (6 inches/15 cm), warmed
    following package directions
4 oz (125 g) cheddar cheese, coarsely grated

1 Combine steak, onion and pepper in a shallow baking dish. Whisk together garlic, lime juice, oil, vinegar, cumin, salt, pepper and chili in a small bowl. Pour over steak mixture; toss to coat. Refrigerate, covered, for 1 to 2 hours.

2 Preheat grill. Cook steak about 4 inches (10 cm) from heat, for 2 minutes each side. Add the onion and pepper. Spoon any remaining marinade over steak and vegetables. Grill, turning meat and vegetables occasionally, until the meat is cooked as liked and vegetables are crisp-tender, about a further 7 minutes. Leave meat to stand 5 minutes.

3 Cut meat diagonally across grain into thin slices. Divide meat, onion and pepper evenly between warmed tortillas. Top with cheese. Place under grill just until the cheese melts, about 30 seconds. Fold tortillas over filling and serve.

per fajita 293 calories, 18 g protein, 14 g fat (including 6 g saturated fat), 40 mg cholesterol, 24 g carbohydrates, 2 g fiber, 411 mg sodium

on the menu

Other flatbreads, such as lavash and pita bread, can also be used for this recipe. Warm them lightly in the oven, under the grill or in the microwave. You can vary the cut of beef used depending on your taste and budget.

peppers stuffed with sausages & rice

Bell peppers are full of vitamin C and other nutrients that boost the immune system and fight chronic disease.

Serves 4   Preparation 15 minutes   MAKE AHEAD
Cooking 40 minutes

4 large peppers (any colors)
10 oz (300 g) mild Italian sausages
1 teaspoon dried oregano, crumbled
1½ cups cooked white rice
1 medium carrot, peeled and grated
½ cup coarsely grated cheddar cheese
1½ cups tomato pasta sauce, warmed (optional)

1 Cut peppers in half through the stem end. Scrape out membranes and seeds. Steam peppers for 5 minutes to soften slightly. Finely chop usable part of pepper tops.

2 Heat a large non-stick frying pan over medium heat. Take sausage meat out of casings; crumble into pan. Add chopped pepper tops and oregano. Cook sausage, breaking it up with a wooden spoon, until it is browned and cooked through, about 3 minutes. Remove pan from heat. Add rice, carrot and cheese.

3 Preheat oven to 375°F (190°C). Place peppers in 9-inch (23 cm)-square baking dish. Using a small spoon, fill each pepper with rice mixture. Cover with aluminium foil.

4 Bake until peppers are tender, or 25 to 30 minutes. Serve with tomato pasta sauce, if desired.

per serving 306 calories, 14 g protein, 15 g fat (including 6 g saturated fat), 43 mg cholesterol, 31 g carbohydrates, 4 g fiber, 435 mg sodium

cider-braised ham with sweet potato

High-fiber sweet potatoes and lean pork are combined in this tasty low-fat dish.

Serves 4   Preparation 15 minutes   HEART HEALTHY
Cooking 30 minutes

1 cup plus 1 tablespoon apple cider
1 tablespoon Dijon mustard
1 tablespoon peeled, finely chopped fresh ginger
½ teaspoon ground cloves
1 medium sweet potato, peeled and thinly sliced
1 pound (500 g) extra lean ham steak
1 Granny Smith apple, peeled, cored and cut into 12 wedges
1 tablespoon cornstarch
½ cup diagonally sliced green part of scallions

1 Combine 1 cup of the cider, the mustard, ginger and cloves in a large frying pan. Bring to a simmer. Add the sweet potato. Cover tightly and simmer until partially tender, or 15 minutes.

2 Add ham steak. Cover with sweet potato slices. Arrange apple wedges over the top. Cover and simmer until apples and potato are tender and ham is heated through, 10 to 15 minutes.

3 Using a slotted spoon, transfer ham, potato and apple to plate. Cover with aluminium foil to keep warm.

4 Blend cornstarch and 1 tbsp cider in a small bowl. Stir a little of the hot pan liquid into the mixture until smooth. Add cornstarch mixture to pan. Cook over medium heat, stirring, until slightly thickened, about 1 minute.

5 Divide ham, sweet potato and apple between four plates. Spoon on sauce from the pan. Garnish with scallions.

per serving 211 calories, 18 g protein, 4 g fat (including 1 g saturated fat), 38 mg cholesterol, 25 g carbohydrates, 2 g fiber, 1,188 mg sodium

fresh ideas

Adding fresh fruit to a meat dish is an easy way to include more vitamins and fiber. Sliced pears, halved kumquats, orange segments or pineapple chunks could be used with the Cider-Braised Ham in place of the apple.

stir-fried pork with bok choy

Bok choy supplies the same disease-fighting antioxidants as other cabbages, as well as considerably higher amounts of calcium and beta-carotene.

Serves 4 Preparation 15 minutes
Marinating 15 minutes Cooking 10 minutes

3 tablespoons dry sherry or rice wine
2 tablespoons soy sauce
1 tablespoon cornstarch
1 teaspoon dark sesame oil
1 teaspoon brown sugar
1/4 teaspoon black pepper
1 pound (500 g) pork tenderloin, cut into
    1/8 inch (3 mm)-thick slices
2 tablespoons vegetable oil
5 cups coarsely chopped bok choy
2 cloves garlic, minced

1 Stir together half the sherry and all the soy sauce, cornstarch, sesame oil, sugar and pepper in a small bowl. Add pork. Toss to coat. Marinate, room temperature, for 15 minutes.

2 Heat 1 tbsp oil in large non-stick frying pan or wok over high heat. Add bok choy. Stir-fry 2 minutes. Cover. Cook until wilted, or about 2 minutes. Transfer bok choy to a plate. Discard liquid left in frying pan.

3 Add remaining oil to pan. Add garlic and sauté 15 seconds. Add the pork mixture and stir-fry until the meat is just cooked through, or 3 to 4 minutes. Add bok choy and remaining sherry. Cook until heated through. Serve immediately.

per serving 267 calories, 25 g protein, 16 g fat (including 4 g saturated fat), 64 mg cholesterol, 5 g carbohydrates, 2 g fiber, 536 mg sodium

pork & bean chili

If you can't find pork shoulder, choose another cut that's suitable for stewing.

Serves 6 Preparation 20 minutes | MAKE AHEAD
Cooking 2 hours

1 1/2 pounds (750 g) stewing pork, cut into 1/2 inch
    (1 cm) cubes
1/2 cup all-purpose flour
2 tablespoons vegetable oil
1 large onion, finely chopped
1 medium green pepper, seeded
    and coarsely chopped
1 jalapeño pepper, seeded and finely chopped
3 cloves garlic, crushed
28 oz (796 mL) can Italian tomatoes
    with juice, coarsely chopped
1 cup low-sodium chicken stock
3 tablespoons chili powder
1/4 teaspoon salt
2 x 15 oz (540 mL) cans pinto beans,
    drained and rinsed

1 Coat pork with flour and shake off any excess. Heat oil in a large non-stick saucepan over medium-high heat. Working in batches, add pork and brown on all sides, about 5 minutes per batch. Transfer pork to a plate as it browns.

2 Lower heat to medium. Add the onion, pepper, chopped chili and garlic. Cook until onion is softened, about 5 minutes. Return pork to pan. Add the tomatoes, stock, chili powder and salt. Simmer 1 hour, stirring occasionally. Stir in beans. Simmer until meat is tender and sauce is thickened, about 40 minutes.

per serving 298 calories, 25 g protein, 11 g fat (including 3 g saturated fat), 56 mg cholesterol, 24 g carbohydrates, 7 g fiber, 583 mg sodium

roast pork tenderloin with carrots & apples

Pork tenderloin and sweet vegetables such as sweet potatoes and carrots—heart-savers that are high in fiber—make a good team.

Serves 4 Preparation 20 minutes
Marinating 2 hours Cooking 45 minutes

½ cup orange juice
    concentrate
1 teaspoon honey
½ teaspoon ground cumin
¼ teaspoon cinnamon
¼ teaspoon chili powder
1¼ pounds (625 g) boned pork loin roast, trimmed
1 tablespoon vegetable oil
2 medium sweet potatoes, peeled and
    cut into ¾ inch (1.5 cm) pieces
1 medium onion, cut into ¾ inch (1.5 cm) pieces
2 medium carrots, peeled and
    cut into ¾ inch (1.5 cm) pieces
2 medium apples, cored, peeled and
    cut into 1¾ inch (3 cm) pieces
½ teaspoon salt
½ cup dry white wine
1 tablespoon butter

1 Combine juice concentrate, honey, cumin, cinnamon and chili powder in a large bowl. Add pork and turn to coat. Cover and refrigerate for at least 2 hours or up to 24 hours, turning pork occasionally.

2 Preheat oven to 350°F (180°C). Heat oil in a very large baking dish over medium-high heat. Add pork. Brown on all sides for about 5 minutes. Transfer to a plate. Wipe dish clean.

3 Place sweet potato, onion, carrot, apple, salt and wine in baking dish. Place pork on top of vegetables and brush with marinade. Cover with aluminium foil.

4 Roast pork until instant-read meat thermometer inserted in the center registers 167°F (75°C), after about 40 minutes. The juices should run clear when a skewer is inserted into the pork.

5 Place pork on a cutting board and let stand 5 minutes. Stir butter into vegetables. Slice pork and serve with vegetables.

per serving 397 calories, 33 g protein, 14 g fat (including 5 g saturated fat), 103 mg cholesterol, 36 g carbohydrates, 4 g fiber, 654 mg sodium

on the menu

Calcium-rich mustard greens would be a good foil for the sweet fruits and vegetables that are cooked around this pork roast. A slice of watermelon would make a refreshing dessert, too.

pork chops with fresh sauerkraut

When you make sauerkraut yourself, cabbage retains its fresh flavor and much more of its nutritional power.

Serves 4 Preparation 15 minutes Cooking 55 minutes

1 tablespoon vegetable oil
4 pork chops (about 6 oz/175 g each)
¾ teaspoon salt
¼ teaspoon black pepper
1 medium onion, thinly sliced
1 cup peeled, coarsely chopped carrot
2 cloves garlic, sliced
1 cup white wine
6 cups shredded savoy cabbage
   (1 small head)
1 bay leaf
3 whole cloves
2 tablespoon white wine vinegar
1 teaspoon sugar

1 Heat oil in a large non-stick frying pan over medium-high heat. Season chops with a little of the salt and all the pepper. Add the chops to pan. Sauté until well browned on both sides, or about 3 minutes per side. Transfer chops to a plate.

2 Lower heat to medium. Add onion, carrot and garlic to pan and sauté until onion is softened, for about 5 minutes. Add the wine and bring to a boil. Stir in cabbage, bay leaf and cloves. Cover and simmer over medium-low heat until the cabbage is tender, or 20 to 30 minutes.

3 Stir vinegar, sugar and remaining salt into the cabbage mixture. Add the pork chops. Cover. Simmer until pork is just cooked through, or about 10 minutes.

per serving 275 calories, 29 g protein, 12 g fat (including 3 g saturated fat), 73 mg cholesterol, 13 g carbohydrates, 5 g fiber, 524 mg sodium

DID YOU KNOW

...cabbage is one of the oldest cultivated vegetables? The grandfather of the brassica family—with cauliflower, broccoli, brussels sprouts and kale—it probably originated along the coasts of temperate northern Europe.

irish stew

This classic gets a nutrition update: The ratio of vegetables to meat has been increased.

Serves 6   Preparation 20 minutes
Cooking 1 hour 30 minutes

MAKE AHEAD
HEART HEALTHY

2 teaspoons vegetable oil
1 pound (500 g) boneless lamb shoulder,
    cut into 1 inch (2.5 cm) chunks
4 red potatoes, unpeeled and
    coarsely chopped
3 medium carrots, peeled and
    cut into bite-sized chunks
2 medium onions, coarsely chopped
2 leeks, rinsed, white and pale green
    parts coarsely chopped
1 large turnip, peeled and coarsely chopped
2 tablespoons all-purpose flour
1 bay leaf
½ teaspoon dried rosemary
1 teaspoon salt
¼ teaspoon black pepper
1 cup green peas, fresh or frozen

1 Heat oil in a large heatproof casserole or non-stick deep frying pan over medium-high heat. Add meat in batches and brown on all sides, about 5 minutes per batch. Place in a bowl.

2 Add the potatoes, carrots, onions, leeks and turnip to pan. Cook 10 minutes, stirring occasionally. Stir in flour. Add 3 cups water, bay leaf, rosemary, salt and pepper. Bring to a boil. Reduce heat. Add meat. Simmer uncovered until meat is tender, 50 to 60 minutes. Add peas. Simmer 5 minutes. Serve.

per serving 270 calories, 18 g protein, 9 g fat (including 3 g saturated fat), 45 mg cholesterol, 30 g carbohydrates, 6 g fiber, 510 mg sodium

country lamb cobbler

This British classic is topped with delicious pastry. Here, it goes low-fat.

Serves 4   Preparation 20 minutes
Cooking 1 hour

HEART HEALTHY

1 pound (500 g) lean lamb steak,
    trimmed and cut into 1 inch
    (2.5 cm) cubes
1 pound (500 g) carrots, thickly sliced
4 large stalks celery, thickly sliced
1 pound (500 g) leeks, thickly sliced
1½ cups strong dry cider
2 cups low-sodium chicken stock
2 cups frozen peas, thawed
sprigs rosemary, sage and thyme, tied
    together to make a bouquet garni
1 cup white self-raising flour, sifted
¼ cup chopped fresh parsley and sage
    combined
½ teaspoon salt
freshly ground black pepper, to taste
½ cup light sour cream
1 to 2 teaspoons 1% milk (optional)

1 Dry-fry lamb over medium-high heat in a large flameproof casserole until lightly browned for 6 to 8 minutes, stirring frequently. Add carrots, celery and leeks. Cook 4 minutes, stirring occasionally.

2 Add cider and stock. Bring to a boil. Reduce heat to low, cover and simmer until vegetables are tender, 20 to 25 minutes.

3 Meanwhile, heat oven to 400°F (200°C). To make pastry topping, combine the flour, parsley, sage, salt and pepper in a medium bowl. Stir in sour cream and mix to make a firm dough. If dough is too dry, add 1 or 2 tsp milk. Roll out to ¾ inch (1.5 cm) thick. Cut into 16 triangles.

4 Add peas and bouquet garni to casserole. Arrange pastry triangles on top, covering the surface.

5 Bake until pastry topping is well risen and golden brown, or 25 to 30 minutes.

per serving 530 calories, 35 g protein, 12 g fat (including 5 g saturated fat), 90 mg cholesterol, 73 g carbohydrates, 9 g fiber, 750 mg sodium

on the menu

With all the vegetables, meat and pastry in the Country Lamb Cobbler, you'll need to add very little to make it a full meal. You might start with a cream of pumpkin or spinach soup, and finish with fresh fruit and a selection of your favorite cheeses.

fish & seafood

tex-mex grilled shrimp salad

Avocado, shrimp and olive oil are all rich in heart-protecting vitamin E.

Serves 4 Preparation 15 minutes
Cooking 6 minutes   QUICK RECIPE

1 pound (500 g) medium raw shrimp, peeled and deveined
¼ teaspoon salt
¼ teaspoon black pepper
non-stick olive-oil cooking spray
⅔ cup cooked corn kernels (either fresh, drained canned or thawed frozen)
1 avocado, stoned, peeled and sliced
12 grape tomatoes, each halved
¼ cup finely chopped red onion
2 tablespoons coarsely chopped, bottled pickled jalapeño peppers
2 tablespoons pickled jalapeño liquid
¾ teaspoon ground cumin
1 tablespoon olive oil
16 bite-sized tortilla chips
2 tablespoons chopped cilantro
¼ cup light sour cream

1 Preheat broiler. Season shrimp with salt and pepper. Coat with cooking spray.

2 Grill shrimp 4 inches (10 cm) from heat until curled and bright pink, 2 to 3 minutes each side. Let cool slightly.

3 Combine corn, avocado, tomato, onion, pickled jalapeños and liquid, cumin and oil in a large bowl. Let stand 5 minutes. Fold in shrimp, tortilla chips and cilantro.

4 Divide salad between 4 serving plates. Top each one with sour cream. Serve immediately.

per serving 238 calories, 17 g protein, 13 g fat (including 3 g saturated fat), 130 mg cholesterol, 17 g carbohydrates, 6 g fiber, 437 mg sodium

fresh ideas
Pickled jalapeños give this salad its hot punch. The pickling liquid can also spice up homemade salsas.

stir-fried shrimp & snow peas

The vitamin E in shrimp and vitamin C in snow peas are a winning combination for boosting immunity.

Serves 4 Preparation 10 minutes
Cooking 8 minutes   QUICK RECIPE

1 tablespoon plus 2 teaspoons canola oil
4 oz (125 g) snow peas
1 small red pepper, seeded and very thinly sliced
¼ teaspoon salt
1 pound (500 g) medium raw shrimp, peeled and deveined
3 scallions, finely chopped
½ teaspoon chili flakes
2 cloves garlic, crushed
1 tablespoon peeled, finely chopped fresh ginger
2 tablespoons low-sodium soy sauce
1 tablespoon freshly squeezed lemon juice
1 tablespoon grated lemon zest

1 Heat the 2 tsp oil in a large non-stick frying pan or wok over medium heat. Add snow peas, pepper and salt. Stir-fry until crisp-tender, or about 3 minutes. Transfer to a plate.

2 Heat remaining oil in the same pan. Add shrimp, scallions and chili flakes. Stir-fry 1½ minutes. Add garlic and ginger. Stir-fry 1 minute. Add soy sauce and lemon juice. Stir-fry until shrimp are curled, bright pink and cooked through, or about 1 minute.

3 Add snow peas and pepper to pan. Stir-fry just long enough to heat through, or about 30 seconds. Stir in lemon zest and serve immediately.

per serving 169 calories, 20 g protein, 7 g fat (including 1 g saturated fat), 168 mg cholesterol, 6 g carbohydrates, 2 g fiber, 795 mg sodium

scallops florentine

"Florentine" tells us that this recipe contains spinach—in other words, it's rich in the vitamins, minerals and phytochemicals that make leafy green vegetables good for you.

Serves 4   Preparation 10 minutes   QUICK RECIPE
Cooking 12 minutes

12 oz (350 g) English spinach
2 tablespoons olive oil
1½ pounds (750 g) scallops
2 cloves garlic, crushed
1 teaspoon grated lemon zest
1 cup low-sodium chicken stock
1 cup frozen peas, thawed
1 tablespoon freshly squeezed lemon juice
¼ teaspoon salt
¼ teaspoon black pepper

1 Steam spinach until just wilted, for about 3 minutes. Cool under cold running water. Squeeze dry.

2 Heat oil in a large non-stick frying pan over high heat. Add scallops. Sauté until still slightly uncooked in center, or 2 minutes per side. Transfer to a plate.

3 Lower heat to medium. Add garlic and lemon zest to pan and cook 30 seconds. Add stock and peas; simmer 3 minutes. Add spinach, scallops, lemon juice, salt and pepper. Cook just until heated through. Serve in shallow bowls or on plates.

per serving 286 calories, 31 g protein, 13 g fat (including 2 g saturated fat), 52 mg cholesterol, 13 g carbohydrates, 4 g fiber, 550 mg sodium

shrimp with fennel

The vitamin B_{12} content of shrimp matches the vitamin C in fennel, tomatoes and onion.

Serves 4   Preparation 15 minutes   HEART HEALTHY
Cooking 25 minutes

1 tablespoon extra virgin olive oil
1 large onion, chopped
1 bulb fennel, trimmed and chopped
1 garlic clove, crushed
15 oz (540 mL) can tomatoes in juice, chopped
½ cup fish stock
½ tablespoon fennel seeds
pinch each of salt and pepper
finely grated zest and juice of ½ orange
1 cup long-grain rice
pinch of saffron threads
1 pound (500 g) raw jumbo shrimp, peeled and deveined

1 Heat oil in a large non-stick frying pan over medium heat. Add onion, fennel and garlic. Cook, stirring occasionally, until vegetables are soft, or 5 minutes. Add tomatoes with their juice, fish stock, fennel seeds, and orange zest and juice. Season with salt and pepper. Bring to a boil, stirring. Reduce heat to low and partially cover pan. Simmer 12 minutes.

2 Meanwhile, cook rice according to package directions; and add crushed saffron to the boiling water.

3 Bring tomato sauce back to a boil. Place shrimp on top of sauce. Cover pan tightly and cook over low heat until shrimp are done, or 3 to 4 minutes.

4 Divide rice among serving bowls. Top with shrimp and tomato sauce. Sprinkle with basil leaves, if desired.

per serving 380 calories, 30 g protein, 7 g fat (including 1 g saturated fat), 175 mg cholesterol, 49 g carbohydrates, 5 g fiber, 400 mg sodium

DID YOU KNOW

...scallops contain about twice as much omega-3 fatty acids as water-packed light tuna? Omega-3 fatty acids help to suppress inflammatory compounds in the body and improve cardiovascular health.

on the menu

*Serve over—or with—steaming hot rice that's been cooked in chicken stock.
Sliced ripe tomatoes make a good side dish. Serve fresh fruit for dessert.*

crab gumbo

The fibrous gums and pectins found in okra help lower cholesterol and provide protection against stomach ulcers.

Serves 4 **Preparation** 10 minutes
Cooking 35 minutes

2 tablespoons canola oil
½ pound (250 g) okra, cut into ½ inch (1 cm) slices
1 medium onion, coarsely chopped
1 medium red pepper, seeded and diced
1 medium green pepper, seeded and diced
¾ cup diced baked ham
2 cloves garlic, minced
15 oz (540 mL) can crushed tomatoes
2 cups low-sodium chicken stock
1 pound (500 g) cooked crabmeat
¼ teaspoon Tabasco
¼ teaspoon salt
¼ teaspoon black pepper

1 Heat oil in a large saucepan over medium-high heat. Add the okra, onion, pepper and ham. Sauté until okra is tender and no longer sticky, or about 10 minutes.

2 Add garlic and sauté 1 minute. Add tomatoes and chicken stock mixture. Simmer, uncovered, 20 minutes.

3 Stir in crab, Tabasco, salt and pepper. Gently heat through.

per serving 293 calories, 31 g protein, 11 g fat (including 1 g saturated fat), 126 mg cholesterol, 18 g carbohydrates, 5 g fiber, 1,006 mg sodium

DID YOU KNOW

...that gumbo got its name from a Bantu word meaning 'okra'? What goes into a gumbo is pretty much up to the individual cook. However, okra is usually an ingredient in this spicy stew which is considered a classic in the American South.

scallop & cherry tomato sauté

Sizzling, protein-rich scallops and tiny tomatoes packed with vitamin C go from the pan to the dining table in minutes.

Serves 4 Preparation 5 minutes
Cooking 10 minutes

QUICK RECIPE
HEART HEALTHY

1 pound (500 g) scallops
4 teaspoons cornstarch
2 teaspoons olive oil
3 cloves garlic, minced
1 pound (500 g) cherry tomatoes
²/₃ cup dry vermouth,
    white wine or chicken stock
½ teaspoon salt
⅓ cup chopped basil
1 tablespoon cold water

1 Dredge scallops in 3 tsp of the cornstarch, shaking off the excess. Heat oil in a large non-stick frying pan over medium heat. Add scallops and sauté until golden brown and cooked through, for about 3 minutes. Using a slotted spoon, transfer the scallops to a bowl.

2 Add garlic to pan and cook 1 minute. Add tomatoes and cook until they begin to collapse, or about 4 minutes. Add vermouth, wine or stock, salt and basil. Bring to a boil and cook for about 1 minute.

3 Blend remaining cornstarch and cold water in a small bowl. Add mixture to pan and cook, stirring, until sauce is slightly thickened, or about 1 minute.

4 Return scallops to pan. Reduce to a simmer and cook just until heated through, about 1 minute.

per serving 176 calories, 20 g protein, 4 g fat (including 1 g saturated fat), 37 mg cholesterol, 10 g carbohydrates, 1 g fiber, 483 mg sodium

Almost any dish made with shellfish can also be made with a firm-fleshed fish. Fillet of monkfish, cut into bite-sized chunks, is a great substitute for shrimp, scallops, lobster or crabmeat because it has a taste similar to that of shellfish. Mahimahi, salmon, swordfish and tuna can all be used as substitutes in recipes calling for shellfish.

asian steamed fish

Low-fat fish and vitamin-packed vegetables are cooked using one of the healthiest of all cooking techniques: steaming.

Serves 4   Preparation 15 minutes
Cooking 12 minutes

QUICK RECIPE
HEART HEALTHY

1½ pounds (750 g) firm-fleshed
    whitefish fillets, in 4 pieces
2 tablespoons soy sauce
2 tablespoons white wine or sake
1 thin slice fresh ginger, peeled and
    cut into thin sticks
2 medium carrots, peeled and
    cut into ¼ inch (5 mm) sticks lengthwise
2 oz (60 g) snow peas, cut in half lengthwise
½ medium yellow pepper, seeded
    and cut into thin sticks

1 Place fish in a baking dish that fits inside a large steamer basket or on a rack that will fit into a large frying pan. Combine the soy sauce and white wine or sake and pour over the fish. Top with ginger and carrot.

2 Fill pan with water to a depth of 1 inch (2.5 cm). Bring to a simmer. Place steamer basket or wire rack in pan. Place baking dish in the basket or on the rack. Cover pan or basket. Steam fish for 5 to 6 minutes. Add snow peas and pepper to baking dish. Cover. Steam until fish flakes when touched with the tip of a knife and vegetables are crisp-tender, or about 5 minutes.

per serving 175 calories, 32 g protein, 3 g fat (including 0 g saturated fat), 45 mg cholesterol, 7 g carbohydrates, 2 g fiber, 558 mg sodium

DID YOU KNOW

...shellfish have an unjustified bad rap for their cholesterol? Mussels and scallops are actually both lower in cholesterol than a lean turkey breast. Shrimp are the highest in cholesterol among shellfish, but they are still a low-fat source of protein.

caribbean curry

Ginger, curry powder, chilies and allspice contain health-protecting phytochemicals.

Serves 4   Preparation 30 minutes
Cooking 30 minutes

MAKE AHEAD

2 teaspoons olive oil
6 thin scallions, finely chopped
1 medium yellow pepper, seeded
    and coarsely chopped
1 tablespoon peeled, finely chopped,
    fresh ginger
1½ teaspoons curry powder
¼ teaspoon chili flakes, or to taste
¼ teaspoon ground allspice
2 tablespoons low-sodium soy sauce
1½ tablespoons brown sugar
¼ teaspoon salt
14 oz (398 mL) can reduced-fat coconut milk
3 plum tomatoes, quartered lengthwise
    and seeded
½ pound (250 g) halibut steaks,
    skin removed, cut into 2 inch (5 cm) chunks
½ pound (250 g) medium shrimp, peeled and deveined
2 tablespoons chopped cilantro
1 tablespoon freshly squeezed lime juice

1 Heat oil in a large heatproof casserole over medium heat. Add scallion, pepper and ginger. Sauté until softened, or 5 minutes. Add curry powder, chili flakes and allspice. Sauté 2 minutes. Stir in soy sauce, brown sugar, salt, coconut milk and tomato. Simmer gently, uncovered, for 15 minutes.

2 Add fish and shrimp to mixture. Simmer gently, uncovered, just until fish is cooked through, or 5 to 8 minutes. Add cilantro and lime juice. Serve immediately.

per serving 223 calories, 22 g protein, 9 g fat (including 4 g saturated fat), 99 mg cholesterol, 17 g carbohydrates, 2 g fiber, 605 mg sodium

salmon on a bed of greens

Kale is rich in calcium and makes a bone-building base for a fish fillet.

Serves 4   Preparation 15 minutes
Refrigerate 30 minutes   Cooking 16 minutes

¼ cup grapefruit juice
1½ tablespoons Dijon mustard
1½ tablespoons honey
¼ teaspoon chili flakes
4 salmon fillets
1½ pounds (750 g) kale, large stems removed
    and leaves chopped
3 tablespoons olive oil
½ medium red pepper, seeded
    and finely chopped
½ medium yellow pepper, seeded
    and finely chopped

1 In a baking dish large enough to hold fish fillets in a single layer, combine the juice, mustard, honey and chili flakes. Place salmon in dish, turning to coat both sides with the marinade. Refrigerate, covered, for 30 minutes.

2 Preheat grill. Bring a large saucepan of water to a boil, and add kale. Return water to a boil and cook 5 minutes. Drain well, and squeeze out excess water.

3 Heat olive oil in a large frying pan over medium heat. Add all the pepper. Sauté 1 minute. Add kale, and sauté until pepper and kale are tender, or about 3 minutes. Remove pan from heat and keep mixture warm.

4 Remove salmon from marinade. Place skin side down on a rack in a foil-lined grill pan. Reserve marinade.

5 Grill salmon 4 inches (10 cm) from heat for 3 minutes. Brush with marinade. Grill until fish is opaque and flakes when touched with the point of a knife, or 3 to 4 minutes. (If fish is browning too much, move it to a lower rack.) Serve on a bed of vegetables.

per serving 402 calories, 41 g protein, 18 g fat (including 3 g saturated fat), 97 mg cholesterol, 21 g carbohydrates, 3 g fiber, 233 mg sodium

baked cod casserole with potatoes, tomatoes & arugula

A one-dish meal, tailor-made for the health of your heart, that combines lean fish and lots of vitamin-rich vegetables.

Serves 4 Preparation 20 minutes HEART HEALTHY
Cooking 38 minutes

1 pound (500 g) red potatoes, unpeeled and
    cut in ½ inch (1.5 cm)-thick slices
1 medium onion, thinly sliced
1 tablespoon olive oil
½ teaspoon salt
4 plum tomatoes, seeded and
    coarsely chopped
3 cloves garlic, minced
½ teaspoon dried oregano,
    crumbled
1½ cups arugula leaves
1 pound (500 g) cod, halibut or
    other thick, firm-fleshed whitefish
    steaks, cut into 2 inch (5 cm) chunks

1 Preheat oven to 350°F (180°C). Combine potato, onion, oil and half the salt in a medium baking dish.

2 Bake for 20 minutes, stirring mixture once.

3 Stir tomato, garlic and oregano into potato mixture. Spread the arugula over the top in an even layer. Top with fish steaks. Sprinkle with remaining salt.

4 Bake, covered with aluminum foil, until fish is just cooked through, or 15 to 18 minutes. Transfer fish and vegetable mixture to serving plates. Spoon pan juices over each serving.

per serving 213 calories, 22 g protein, 5 g fat (including 1 g saturated fat), 43 mg cholesterol, 21 g carbohydrates, 4 g fiber, 363 mg sodium

HINT **helpful HINT** HINTHINTHINT

Almost any baked fish will release some liquid during cooking, so don't be surprised if you find a puddle at the bottom of your casserole dish. Simply spoon these juices over the fish for extra flavor and moisture.

roast trout & potatoes

A bed of watercress adds vitamins and a slightly peppery flavor to this dish.

Serves 4 Preparation 20 minutes
Cooking 50 minutes

HEART HEALTHY

1½ pounds (750 g) potatoes, quartered
1 tablespoon olive oil
4 medium trout, cleaned
sprigs of fresh tarragon
pinch each of salt and black pepper
1 orange, cut into 16 half slices
1 lemon, cut into 16 half slices
¼ cup freshly squeezed orange juice
1 English cucumber, peeled
6 oz (175 g) low-fat plain yogurt
2 tablespoons chopped mint
5 oz (150 g) watercress, washed and trimmed

1 Preheat oven to 400°F (200°C). Place potatoes in a large saucepan with enough water to cover. Bring to a boil. Reduce heat and simmer 5 minutes. Drain and return potatoes to pan. Drizzle with oil and toss to coat, then lay out on a baking sheet. Roast until tender, turning several times, for about 25 minutes.

2 Season inside of trout with tarragon, salt and pepper. Cut four 12 inch (30 cm) squares of aluminum foil. Divide half the citrus slices among foil squares, lay fish on top and cover with remaining slices. Sprinkle orange juice over the top.

3 Wrap fish in foil and seal packets. Lay packets on second baking sheet and bake for 20 minutes. Meanwhile, coarsely grate the cucumber into a sieve and press out excess water. Combine cucumber, yogurt and mint in a small bowl.

4 Arrange the fish and potatoes on serving plates. Spoon on cucumber sauce and garnish with watercress and citrus slices.

per serving 430 calories, 40 g protein, 12 g fat (including 3 g saturated fat), 165 mg cholesterol, 43 g carbohydrates, 6 g fiber, 160 mg sodium

grilled tuna steaks with corn & tomato

Together, the tuna and vegetables provide a complete collection of anti-oxidant vitamins A, C and E. Tuna is high in omega-3 fatty acids, which are thought to protect against heart disease.

Serves 4 Preparation 20 minutes
Cooking 10 minutes

QUICK RECIPE
HEART HEALTHY

1¼ pounds (600 g) tuna steaks (1 inch/2.5 cm thick)
½ teaspoon salt
¼ teaspoon black pepper
¼ cup apricot jam
1 tablespoon Dijon mustard
1 ear of corn, husked and cut into
    8 equal pieces
2 medium tomatoes, cored and each
    cut into 8 equal wedges
2 medium zucchini, each quartered lengthwise
    and cut crosswise into ¼ inch (5 mm)-thick slices
2 cloves garlic, minced
2 serrano peppers, seeded and finely chopped
4 teaspoons olive oil

1 Preheat barbecue to medium-hot or preheat broiler. Season tuna steaks with half the salt and pepper. Combine jam and mustard in a small cup and spread one side of the tuna steaks with half of the jam mixture.

2 Place the corn, tomato and zucchini in the center of each of four 12 inch (30 cm) squares of aluminum foil, dividing them equally. Sprinkle the vegetables evenly with the garlic, remaining salt and pepper, chilies and oil. Fold edges of foil over to form tightly sealed packets.

3 Broil or barbecue the tuna and vegetable packets 4 inches (10 cm) from heat for 4 minutes. Turn tuna over and spread with remaining jam mixture. Cook until tuna is opaque in the center and flakes when touched with the tip of a fork, or 4 to 6 minutes. Open the vegetable packets carefully to avoid the steam that will escape from them. Serve with the tuna steaks.

per serving 302 calories, 35 g protein, 7 g fat (including 1 g saturated fat), 62 mg cholesterol, 27 g carbohydrates, 3 g fiber, 458 mg sodium

on the menu

A crisp salad containing peppery watercress, sliced red cabbage and mixed green leaves makes a good accompaniment to Grilled Tuna Steaks.

fresh ideas

You can try any combination of vegetables and herbs you want for a pasta sauce. Sauté them in a little olive oil, add stock for liquid and sprinkle with parmesan. Try the following combinations: arugula, leeks, broccoli and tarragon; eggplant, rapini, garlic and thyme; or green beans, sugar snap peas, fennel and parsley.

pasta primavera

This simple recipe delivers seven healthy vegetables in just one dish.

Serves 4   Preparation 15 minutes
Cooking 25 minutes

HEART HEALTHY

2 tablespoons olive oil
4 plum tomatoes, coarsely chopped
1 medium carrot, peeled and cut into
    thin slices
2 cloves garlic, thinly sliced
1 cup sliced mushrooms
¾ cup low-sodium chicken or vegetable stock
1 pound (500 g) asparagus, trimmed and blanched
    in boiling water
1 cup frozen peas, thawed
1 medium yellow summer squash cut into ½ inch
    (1.25 cm)-thick slices
¼ cup finely chopped basil
¼ cup grated parmesan cheese
½ pound (250 g) fettuccine

1 Heat oil in a medium non-stick saucepan over medium heat. Add tomato, carrot and garlic. Cook 10 minutes. Add mushroom and stock. Cook 10 minutes. Add asparagus, peas and squash. Cook until all the vegetables are tender, or about 2 minutes. Add basil and parmesan. Cover and set aside.

2 While sauce is cooking, cook pasta in a large saucepan of lightly salted boiling water until al dente, following package instructions. Drain. Place in a serving bowl. Add vegetable sauce and toss to combine.

per serving 386 calories, 16 g protein, 11 g fat (including 3 g saturated fat),
5 mg cholesterol, 60 g carbohydrates, 8 g fiber, 542 mg sodium

DID YOU KNOW

...almost any dish that is made with fresh vegetables can be called primavera? The word means "springtime" in Italian.

pasta with no-cook vegetable sauce

When a sauce is made from finely chopped raw vegetables, it retains the vitamin C and B that can be lost during lengthy cooking.

Serves 4   Preparation 15 minutes
Cooking 12 minutes

QUICK RECIPE
HEART HEALTHY

½ pound (250 g) fusilli
1 medium zucchini, cut into ¼ inch (5 mm) dice
1 medium yellow pepper, seeded
    and cut into ¼ inch (5 mm) dice
2 large tomatoes, cut into ¼ inch (5 mm) dice
2 tablespoons olive oil
¼ cup chopped basil
¾ teaspoon salt
½ teaspoon black pepper
2 tablespoons grated parmesan cheese

1 Cook pasta in a large saucepan of lightly salted boiling water until al dente, following package instructions.

2 Combine the zucchini, pepper, tomato, oil, basil, salt, pepper and parmesan in a large serving bowl.

3 Drain pasta. Add to vegetables in bowl. Toss to combine.

per serving 303 calories, 10 g protein, 9 g fat (including 2 g saturated fat),
2 mg cholesterol, 47 g carbohydrates, 5 g fiber, 772 mg sodium

sausage & pepper medley pasta

Peppers contain phytochemicals that protect against heart disease, strokes and cancer, while also boosting the immune system.

Serves 4   Preparation 10 minutes   QUICK RECIPE
Cooking 15 minutes

2 tablespoons olive oil
½ pound (250 g) chicken sausages, sliced
2 medium onions, thinly sliced
2 large red or orange peppers,
    seeded and thinly sliced
1 large green pepper,
    seeded and thinly sliced
2 cloves garlic, minced
1 teaspoon dried basil
½ cup pitted black olives
1 tablespoon balsamic vinegar
¼ teaspoon salt
¼ teaspoon black pepper
½ pound (250 g) fusilli or farfalle (bow ties)
¼ cup grated parmesan cheese

1 Heat oil in a large non-stick frying pan over medium-high heat. Add sausage and onion. Sauté until onion is softened and light golden, or about 5 minutes. Add pepper, garlic and basil. Sauté until pepper is very tender, or 10 minutes. Remove from heat. Stir in olives, vinegar, salt and pepper.

2 Meanwhile, cook pasta in a large saucepan of lightly salted boiling water until al dente, following package instructions. Drain, reserving ¼ cup of the cooking water. Toss pasta with sausage mixture and reserved water. Serve with parmesan.

per serving 443 calories, 19 g protein, 16 g fat (including 3 g saturated fat), 35 mg cholesterol, 57 g carbohydrates, 3 g fiber, 933 mg sodium

Fusilli with pan-roasted vegetables

One serving supplies more than one-third of your daily recommended fiber.

Serves 4   Preparation 20 minutes   HEART HEALTHY
Cooking 25 minutes

2 tablespoons olive oil
1 large red onion, cut into thin wedges
1 medium yellow pepper, seeded and chopped
1 small butternut squash (1¼ pounds/625 g), peeled,
    seeded and cut into 1 inch (2.5 cm) chunks
¼ teaspoon salt
¼ cup finely chopped basil
5 cloves garlic, crushed
1 cup grape or cherry tomatoes, each cut in half
4 cups baby spinach leaves, tough stems removed
4 cups low-sodium chicken stock
½ pound (250 g) fusilli

1 Heat 1 tbsp oil in a large non-stick frying pan over medium heat. Add onion and pepper. Sauté until softened, or about 5 minutes. Add squash, half the salt, basil and half the garlic. Cover and cook, stirring occasionally, 8 minutes. Increase heat to high. Cook, uncovered, stirring occasionally, until the vegetables brown slightly and squash is just tender, or about 7 minutes. Transfer mixture to a large bowl. Add tomato.

2 Heat remaining oil in the pan over medium heat. Add the remaining garlic and salt and all of the spinach. Cook, stirring occasionally, until spinach wilts, or about 2 minutes. Add spinach to the mixture in the bowl.

3 Meanwhile, bring the stock and 2 cups water to a boil in a large saucepan. Add pasta. Cook until al dente, following package instructions. Reserve ½ cup of the cooking liquid. Drain pasta and combine with vegetable mixture and reserved cooking liquid.

per serving 372 calories, 12 g protein, 9 g fat (including 1 g saturated fat), 1 mg cholesterol, 66 g carbohydrates, 9 g fiber, 485 mg sodium

on the menu

Creamy Farfalle with Green Peas & Sun-dried Tomatoes doesn't require much more than a simple salad of mixed greens in a tangy vinaigrette and a chilled fruit salad for dessert to make a satisfying—and healthy—meal.

creamy farfalle with green peas & sun-dried tomatoes

Peas add muscle-building protein to this dish and B vitamins for energy production.

Serves 4 Preparation 10 minutes
Cooking 15 minutes

QUICK RECIPE
HEART HEALTHY

½ pound (250 g) farfalle
1 tablespoon olive oil
1 tablespoon butter or margarine
1 cup finely chopped onion
3 cloves garlic, crushed
½ teaspoon dried oregano
¼ teaspoon dried marjoram
1½ tablespoons all-purpose flour
1 cup low-sodium chicken
    or vegetable stock
1 cup fresh or frozen green peas
⅔ cup sun-dried tomato halves,
    thinly sliced
⅓ cup grated parmesan cheese

1 Cook pasta in a large saucepan of lightly salted boiling water until al dente, following package instructions.

2 Heat the oil and butter in a large non-stick frying pan over medium heat. Add onion, garlic, oregano and marjoram. Sauté until the onion is softened, or about 5 minutes. Stir in flour until thoroughly combined. Whisk in the stock. Heat, stirring, until thickened, or 2 to 3 minutes. Stir in peas and sun-dried tomato. Cook just until peas are tender, or about 5 minutes. Remove from heat. Stir in 3 tbsp parmesan.

3 Drain pasta, reserving ½ cup of the cooking water. Toss pasta with vegetable mixture and reserved water. Sprinkle with the remaining parmesan.

per serving 380 calories, 16 g protein, 10 g fat (including 4 g saturated fat), 13 mg cholesterol, 60 g carbohydrates, 6 g fiber, 647 mg sodium

linguine with spinach pesto

A sauce made with spinach contains phytochemicals that add extra protection against age-related blindness.

Serves 8 Preparation 15 minutes
Cooking 12 minutes

QUICK RECIPE
HEART HEALTHY

1 pound (500 g) linguine
3 cups baby spinach leaves, tough stems
    removed
½ cup basil leaves
3 cloves garlic
3 tablespoons walnuts
3 tablespoons olive oil
⅓ cup freshly squeezed lemon juice
¾ teaspoon salt
½ teaspoon black pepper
2 medium red peppers, seeded and diced
4 plum tomatoes, diced
¼ cup grated parmesan cheese

1 Cook pasta in a large saucepan of lightly salted boiling water until al dente, following package instructions.

2 For the pesto, combine spinach, basil, garlic and walnuts in a food processor. Process until finely chopped. With the machine running, add olive oil, lemon juice, salt and pepper. Process until smooth.

3 Drain pasta. Transfer to a large serving bowl. Add spinach pesto, pepper and tomato. Toss gently to combine. Sprinkle with the parmesan.

per serving 300 calories, 10 g protein, 8 g fat (including 2 g saturated fat), 2 mg cholesterol, 48 g carbohydrates, 3 g fiber, 420 mg sodium

rigatoni with rapini

The plentiful vitamin C in this combination of vegetables boosts the immune system to help your body fight infection.

Serves 4   Preparation 10 minutes
Cooking 12 minutes

12 oz (350 g) rigatoni
2 small bunches rapini,
    tough stems removed and leaves cut
    crosswise into 1 inch (2.5 cm)-wide pieces
1 tablespoon olive oil
1 medium red onion, halved and thinly
    sliced crosswise
1 medium yellow pepper, seeded and
    cut lengthwise into thin strips
2 scallions, thinly sliced on the diagonal
½ cup golden raisins
¼ teaspoon red pepper flakes
¼ teaspoon salt
8 cloves roasted garlic *(see page 277)*
12 cherry tomatoes, each cut in half
pinch of ground nutmeg
¼ teaspoon black pepper
¼ cup grated parmesan cheese

1 Cook pasta in a large saucepan of lightly salted boiling water until al dente, following package instructions. Add the rapini to the pot for the last 5 minutes of cooking time. Drain pasta and rapini.

2 Heat oil in a large non-stick frying pan over medium-high heat. Add onion, pepper, scallion, raisins, red pepper flakes and salt. Sauté until vegetables are crisp-tender, or 4 minutes. Add roasted garlic. Sauté for 1 minute, then remove from heat.

3 Return pasta and rapini to the pan. Add pepper mixture, tomato and nutmeg. Sprinkle with the black pepper and parmesan.

per serving 514 calories, 21 g protein, 7 g fat (including 2 g saturated fat), 4 mg cholesterol, 4 g carbohydrates, 6 g fiber, 506 mg sodium

DID YOU KNOW

...grapes are around 80 per cent water? Raisins, or dried grapes, contain only about a fifth as much water and are, therefore, a more concentrated source of fiber, potassium, iron and calories.

penne with grilled eggplant

First salting and then grilling, instead of frying, keeps eggplant from absorbing too much oil and reduces the total fat.

Serves 4   Preparation 15 minutes
Standing time 30 minutes   Cooking 25 minutes

HEART HEALTHY

1 pound (500 g) eggplant, cut lengthwise into
   1 inch (2.5 cm)-thick slices
½ teaspoon salt
2 tablespoons olive oil
4 cloves garlic, thinly sliced
1 ½ pounds (750 g) ripe plum tomatoes, halved, seeded
   and coarsely chopped
1 teaspoon chopped fresh oregano or
   ½ teaspoon dried, crumbled
2 teaspoons balsamic vinegar
½ teaspoon sugar
non-stick olive-oil cooking spray
½ pound (250 g) penne
¼ cup shaved or shredded
   parmesan cheese

1 Sprinkle eggplant slices with half the salt. Leave salted, on a plate, for a least 30 minutes to draw out liquid.

2 Heat oil in a large non-stick frying pan over medium-low heat. Add garlic. Cook, stirring, 1 minute.

3 Add tomato, oregano and remaining salt. Increase heat to medium. Cook just until tomato is softened, or about 6 minutes. Stir in vinegar and sugar. Cook a further 30 seconds.

4 Preheat broiler or barbecue. Rinse eggplant slices and pat dry. Lightly coat both sides of eggplant with cooking spray.

5 Broil or barbecue eggplant 4 inches (10 cm) from heat until softened and, if barbecuing, dark grill marks score the surface—about 5 minutes each side. Set aside to cool slightly.

6 Meanwhile, cook the pasta in a large pot of lightly salted boiling water until al dente, following package instructions. Drain. Toss with the tomato mixture. Coarsely chop eggplant and add to pasta mixture. Stir in parmesan. Serve hot.

per serving 362 calories, 13 g protein, 10 g fat (including 2 g saturated fat),
4 mg cholesterol, 59 g carbohydrates, 7 g fiber, 406 mg sodium

on the menu

Serve with sliced smoked mozzarella cheese (available from specialty cheese stores) and Italian bread toasted and topped with roasted garlic (see page 277).

pasta with shrimp & cherry tomatoes

In addition to their great flavor, cherry tomatoes add plenty of vitamin C plus vitamin A in the form of beta carotene.

Serves 4 Preparation 10 minutes
Cooking 12 minutes

½ pound (250 g) medium pasta shells
2 tablespoons olive oil
1 pound (500 g) medium green shrimp, cleaned
3 cloves garlic, minced
4 flat canned anchovy fillets
½ teaspoon red pepper flakes, or to taste
4 cups red cherry or grape tomatoes,
    each cut in half
3 tablespoons fresh oregano leaves or
    1 teaspoon dried, crumbled
½ cup pitted green olives
2 tablespoons drained capers
¼ teaspoon black pepper

1 Cook pasta shells in a large saucepan of lightly salted boiling water until al dente, following package instructions.

2 Heat half the oil in a large non-stick frying pan over medium-high heat. Add shrimps and one-third of the garlic. Sauté until shrimps just turn pink and curl, or 2 to 3 minutes. Transfer to a plate.

3 Heat remaining oil in the same pan. Add remaining garlic, the anchovies and red pepper flakes. Sauté until garlic has softened, or about 30 seconds. Do not let it brown. Add the tomato and oregano. Sauté until tomato is softened, or 3 to 4 minutes. Add cooked shrimp, olives and capers.

4 Drain pasta well. Toss with shrimp and tomato mixture. Sprinkle with black pepper.

per serving 419 calories, 21 g protein, 14 g fat (including 2 g saturated fat), 129 mg cholesterol, 53 g carbohydrates, 3 g fiber, 1,141 mg sodium

pasta salad with arugula & mozzarella

Like all dark green, leafy vegetables, arugula can help lower your risk of having a stroke.

Serves 4 Preparation 15 minutes
Cooking 10 minutes

½ pound (250 g) penne or rotelle
12 oz (375 g) cherry tomatoes, each cut in half
½ small red onion, thinly sliced
4 oz (125 g) arugula leaves, chopped
3 oz (100 g) mozzarella cheese, cut into
    ½ inch (1 cm) cubes
2 tablespoons sun-dried tomatoes, finely chopped
    and soaked in boiling water for 10 minutes
2 tablespoons chopped pitted black olives
1 tablespoon olive oil
1 tablespoon balsamic vinegar
½ teaspoon salt
¼ teaspoon black pepper

1 Cook pasta in a large saucepan of lightly salted boiling water until al dente, following package instructions. Drain and rinse under cold running water.

2 Combine the cherry tomatoes, onion, arugula, mozzarella, sun-dried tomatoes, olives and pasta in a large bowl.

3 Whisk the olive oil, balsamic vinegar, salt and pepper in a small bowl. Add to pasta mixture and toss well.

per serving 368 calories, 15 g protein, 13 g fat (including 5 g saturated fat), 23 mg cholesterol, 50 g carbohydrates, 4 g fiber, 573 mg sodium

on the menu

To round out the meal, serve a salad of mixed greens with the dressing of your choice and a crisp baguette. Serve a variety of sliced apples and cheeses for dessert.

The tomatoes, pepper and white wine in Angel Hair with Clams & Roasted Pepper are classic foils for many **types of seafood**. You can substitute any firm-fleshed **whitefish** for the scallops or use crab instead of the clams.

angel hair with clams & roasted pepper

Peppers are rich in cancer-fighting anti-oxidants and a good amount of parsley adds more beta-carotene and vitamin C to the mix.

Serves 4 **Preparation** 10 minutes
Cooking 25 minutes

HEART HEALTHY

2 tablespoons olive oil
½ pound (250 g) scallops
2 cloves garlic
½ cup dry white wine
pinch of red pepper flakes
1 pound (500 g) clams, scrubbed
14 oz (540 mL) can diced tomatoes
1 large roasted red pepper, sliced
    (see page 291)
⅓ cup coarsely chopped flat-leaf parsley
12 oz (375 g) angel hair pasta

1 Heat oil in a large non-stick saucepan over medium-high heat. Add scallops. Cook until almost cooked through, or about 4 minutes. Transfer to a plate.

2 Add garlic to pan. Cook 15 seconds. Add wine, red pepper flakes and clams. Cover. Reduce heat to medium. Cook until clams have all opened, or about 8 minutes. Transfer clams with slotted spoon to bowl. Discard any that have not opened.

3 Add tomatoes with their liquid to the pan. Simmer until reduced and thickened, about 15 minutes. Stir in the roasted pepper, clams, scallops and parsley.

4 Cook angel hair pasta in a large saucepan of lightly salted boiling water until al dente, following package instructions. Drain well. Add to sauce in pan and serve immediately.

per serving 526 calories, 32 g protein, 9 g fat (including 1 g saturated fat), 55 mg cholesterol, 76 g carbohydrates, 5 g fiber, 638 mg sodium

linguine with shiitake mushrooms

Mushrooms are good at helping to keep your blood pressure on an even keel.

Serves 6 **Preparation** 10 minutes
Cooking 18 minutes

QUICK RECIPE
HEART HEALTHY

2 tablespoons olive oil
1 medium yellow pepper, trimmed, seeded
    and cut into small dice
½ pound (250 g) shiitake mushroom caps, cut
    into thin strips
4 oz (125 g) lean ham, finely chopped
2 cloves garlic, minced
28 oz (796 mL) can whole tomatoes, drained and
    chopped
½ teaspoon dried basil
¼ teaspoon salt
¼ teaspoon black pepper
12 oz (375 g) linguine
grated parmesan cheese *(optional)*

1 Heat oil in a large non-stick saucepan over medium-high heat. Add pepper, mushrooms, ham and garlic. Sauté until mushrooms are tender, 6 to 8 minutes. Add tomato and basil. Cook until thickened, about 10 minutes. Add salt and pepper.

2 Meanwhile, cook pasta in a large saucepan of lightly salted boiling water until al dente, following the package instructions. Drain. Add to sauce in pan. Serve with parmesan, if liked.

per serving 309 calories, 13 g protein, 6 g fat (including 1 g saturated fat), 9 mg cholesterol, 49 g carbohydrates, 3 g fiber, 638 mg sodium

asian noodle salad

A Thai-style seasoning of fresh basil, mint and cilantro adds vitamin C and carotenoids to a dish already packed with vitamins, minerals, fiber and phytochemicals.

Serves 6   Preparation 15 minutes
Cooking 10 minutes

QUICK RECIPE
MAKE AHEAD

12 oz (375 g) whole-wheat linguine
½ pound (250 g) snow peas, halved lengthwise
3 medium carrots, peeled, cut into 2 inch (5 cm) lengths, and thinly sliced lengthwise
2 cups firmly packed basil leaves
½ cup firmly packed mint leaves
¼ cup firmly packed cilantro
2 cloves garlic
2 tablespoons dark sesame oil
1 tablespoon vegetable oil
¼ teaspoon red pepper flakes
½ teaspoon salt
1 medium red pepper, seeded and thinly sliced
3 scallions, finely chopped
2 tablespoons chopped unsalted dry-roasted peanuts

1 Cook linguine in a large saucepan of lightly salted boiling water until al dente, following package instructions. Add snow peas and carrot for the last 2 minutes of cooking. Drain in a colander. Rinse under cold running water and drain again.

2 Place basil, mint, cilantro, garlic, sesame oil, vegetable oil, red pepper flakes and half the salt in a food processor and blend to form a paste.

3 Combine linguine, snow peas, carrots, pepper, scallions, herb paste and remaining salt in a large bowl. Serve at room temperature or chilled. Garnish with peanuts.

per serving 321 calories, 12 g protein, 10 g fat (including 1 g saturated fat), 0 mg cholesterol, 52 g carbohydrates, 11 g fiber, 355 mg sodium

tagliatelle with blue cheese

Broccoli and cauliflower add flavor, texture and—most importantly—a generous amount of nutrients to this quick dish.

Serves 4   Preparation 10 minutes
Cooking 15 minutes

QUICK RECIPE

½ pound (250 g) spinach tagliatelle
½ pound (250 g) broccoli florets, cut up
½ pound (250 g) cauliflower florets, cut up
6 oz (175 g) blue cheese, rind removed, diced
freshly grated nutmeg
pinch each of salt and black pepper

1 Cook pasta in large saucepan of lightly salted boiling water until al dente, following package instructions. Add broccoli and cauliflower for the last 3 minutes of cooking time. Drain pasta and vegetables in a large colander.

2 Rinse pan and return to a low heat. Add blue cheese. Cook, stirring often, until cheese melts into a smooth sauce.

3 Add pasta and vegetables. Stir gently to coat well and heat through. Season to taste with nutmeg, salt and black pepper.

per serving 490 calories, 26 g protein, 18 g fat (including 10 g saturated fat), 110 mg cholesterol, 58 g carbohydrates, 7 g fiber, 850 mg sodium

on the menu

This Asian Noodle Salad stands alone as a lunch dish or even a light supper dish. For a more substantial salad, add shredded cooked chicken, pork or beef. This salad also makes a good side dish for roasted or grilled meat or poultry.

tortellini with squash & ricotta

This warming, hearty dish is good to serve during the colder months.

Serves 4   Preparation 15 minutes   Cooking 30 minutes

1 tablespoon olive oil
1 medium onion, finely chopped
1½ pounds (750 g) butternut squash, seeded, peeled and
    cut into 1-inch (2 cm) cubes (about 5 cups)
½ cup salt-reduced chicken
    or vegetable stock
1 teaspoon ground sage
½ teaspoon salt
pinch of black pepper
12 oz (375 g) cheese tortellini
½ cup reduced-fat ricotta cheese
⅓ cup grated romano cheese
1 tablespoon finely chopped flat-leaf parsley

1 Heat oil in a large non-stick saucepan over medium heat. Add onion. Cook until golden, or about 10 minutes. Add squash, stock, sage, salt and pepper. Cook, covered, just until squash is tender, about 20 minutes.

2 Meanwhile, cook tortellini in a large saucepan of lightly salted water until al dente, following package instructions. Drain. Toss with ricotta in a large bowl.

3 Add squash, romano and parsley to tortellini mixture. Toss gently to combine.

per serving 305 calories, 15 g protein, 12 g fat (including 3 g saturated fat), 27 mg cholesterol, 36 g carbohydrates, 5 g fiber, 945 mg sodium

HINT helpful HINT HINTHINTHINT

Romano is an Italian hard cheese suitable for grating. Made from sheep's milk, its flavor is sharper than that of parmesan, a hard cheese made from cow's milk. The two cheeses are interchangeable, or you can combine them. Asiago is another Italian hard cheese for grating. Made from cow's milk, its flavor is somewhere between that of parmesan and romano.

meat tortellini with red pepper sauce

Convenience food can be a healthy option when you make smart choices. For example, roasted peppers in jars provide significant amounts of beta carotene and vitamin C.

Serves 4   Preparation 5 minutes
Cooking 10 minutes

QUICK RECIPE

12 oz (375 g) meat-filled tortellini
1 jar (270 g) roasted red peppers
2 cloves garlic
2 tablespoons olive oil
1 tablespoon low-sodium soy sauce
1 tablespoon cold butter, cut into
    small pieces
3 tablespoons shredded basil leaves

1 Meanwhile, cook tortellini in a large pan of lightly salted boiling water until al dente, following package instructions.

2 Purée peppers and their liquid, garlic, oil and soy sauce in a food processor. Transfer to a medium saucepan. Simmer over low heat for 10 minutes.

3 Drain tortellini. Just before serving, whisk cold butter into the purée and stir in the basil. Add tortellini. Toss to combine.

per serving 285 calories, 12 g protein, 17 g fat (including 6 g saturated fat), 116 mg cholesterol, 21 g carbohydrates, 1 g fiber, 657 mg sodium

on the menu

Serve Meat Tortellini with Red Pepper Sauce with a dish of lightly sautéed rapini. Finish the meal with chocolate sorbet. Please add one more ligne here Please add one more ligne here

manicotti with spinach & mushrooms

Here's a flavorsome one-dish meal that scores high in good nutrition.

Serves 4 Preparation 25 minutes **MAKE AHEAD**
Cooking 40 minutes

8 manicotti or cannelloni shells
2 teaspoons olive oil
1 small onion, finely chopped
½ pound (250 g) frozen chopped spinach, thawed
1 cup reduced-fat ricotta cheese
1 cup coarsely grated reduced-fat mozzarella cheese
¼ cup grated parmesan cheese
1 teaspoon dried basil
¼ teaspoon garlic powder
¼ teaspoon salt
1¼ cups prepared tomato sauce
10 oz (300 g) mushrooms, sliced

1 Cook manicotti in a large saucepan of lightly salted boiling water for 8 minutes. Drain. Let cool slightly.

2 Heat half the oil in a medium non-stick frying pan over medium heat. Add onion. Sauté until softened, or 5 minutes.

3 Briefly drain spinach in a colander; retain some liquid on the leaves. Combine spinach, ricotta, mozzarella, parmesan, basil, garlic powder and salt in a large bowl.

4 Preheat oven to 350°F (180°C). Spread ¼ cup tomato sauce over the bottom of a 13 x 9 x 2 inch (32 x 22 x 5 cm) baking dish. Fill each manicotti shell from both ends with spinach mixture. Arrange manicotti in baking dish in a single layer. Top with the remaining tomato sauce. Cover with aluminium foil. Bake until heated through, or about 30 minutes.

5 About 5 minutes before the end of the baking time, heat the remaining oil in a frying pan over medium heat. Add the mushrooms and sauté just until slightly softened, or 2 minutes. Serve manicotti topped with mushrooms.

per serving 382 calories, 26 g protein, 14 g fat (including 7 g saturated fat), 37 mg cholesterol, 40 g carbohydrates, 5 g fiber, 1,111 mg sodium

stuffed pasta shells

A creamy classic that's packed with vitamins and minerals.

Serves 4 Preparation 45 minutes **MAKE AHEAD**
Cooking 40 minutes

1 pound (500 g) spinach, trimmed and rinsed
3 zucchini, thinly sliced
4 cloves garlic, finely chopped
1⅔ cups low-sodium vegetable stock
1 cup ricotta cheese
3½ oz (100 g) coarsely chopped walnuts
¼ cup grated parmesan cheese
3 tablespoons each chopped marjoram, chives and basil
1 medium egg, lightly beaten
12 giant pasta shells, cooked al dente
2 oz (60 g) Edam cheese, grated

1 Place spinach with rinsing water still clinging to the leaves in a large saucepan. Cover and cook over high heat for 3 minutes. Shake the pan often. Drain and set aside to cool.

2 Combine zucchini, half the garlic and all the stock in the same pan. Bring to a boil; cook just until tender, 3 minutes. Pour mixture from pan, half the ricotta, the walnuts, 2 tbsp parmesan and salt and pepper to taste into a food processor. Purée until smooth.

3 Squeeze spinach dry and chop coarsely. Mix spinach with marjoram, chives, basil, the remaining garlic, ricotta and egg in a medium bowl.

4 Preheat oven to 375°F (190°C). Stuff pasta with spinach mixture. Arrange in baking dish. Pour zucchini sauce over the top and sprinkle with remaining parmesan. Cover. Bake for 30 minutes. Sprinkle on Edam. Let stand 5 minutes, then serve.

per serving 750 calories, 43 g protein, 30 g fat (including 11 g saturated fat), 95 mg cholesterol, 83 g carbohydrates, 8.5 g fiber, 450 mg sodium

baked pasta with garlic & greens

Here's an easy way to include more garlic in your diet and give your immune system a helping hand.

Serves 8   Preparation 15 minutes
Cooking 45 minutes

MAKE AHEAD
HEART HEALTHY

1 pound (500 g) penne or rigatoni pasta
1 tablespoon olive oil
6 cloves garlic, thinly sliced
½ pound (250 g) frozen chopped spinach, thawed
    and squeezed dry
3 cups prepared tomato sauce
1 cup reduced-fat ricotta cheese
1 cup shredded reduced-fat
    mozzarella cheese
kalamata olives, for garnish

1 Preheat oven to 350°F (180°C). Lightly coat a large baking dish with non-stick cooking spray.

2 Cook penne in a large saucepan of lightly salted boiling water until tender, following package instructions.

3 Heat oil in a medium non-stick frying pan over medium-low heat. Add garlic. Sauté until golden, about 5 minutes. Add spinach and heat through for about 5 minutes. Transfer to a large bowl. Stir in tomato sauce and ricotta.

4 Drain penne and add to bowl. Combine well. Transfer to baking dish. Top with mozzarella. Cover with aluminium foil.

5 Bake for 25 minutes. Remove foil. Bake until lightly golden, or about 10 minutes. Garnish with olives.

per serving 341 calories, 17 g protein, 8 g fat (including 4 g saturated fat), 18 mg cholesterol, 53 g carbohydrates, 4 g fiber, 810 mg sodium

creamy macaroni and cheese with tomatoes

Old-fashioned comfort food gets a flavor and vitamin boost from grated carrots and sliced tomatoes.

Serves 8   Preparation 15 minutes
Cooking 30 minutes

MAKE AHEAD

1 pound (500 g) elbow macaroni
3 tablespoons vegetable oil
4 scallions, coarsely chopped
¼ teaspoon salt
¼ cup all-purpose flour
4 cups low-fat (1%) milk, warmed
2 tablespoons Dijon mustard
3 cups coarsely grated reduced-fat
    sharp cheddar cheese
½ cup grated parmesan cheese
1 medium carrot, peeled and coarsely grated
2 medium tomatoes, cored and sliced
1 cup fresh whole wheat breadcrumbs

1 Cook macaroni in a large saucepan of lightly salted boiling water until al dente, following package instructions. Drain well, then return to pot.

2 Heat oil in a large non-stick saucepan over medium heat. Add the scallions and salt. Cook, stirring occasionally, for 3 minutes. Gradually stir in flour. Cook 1 minute. Gradually stir in 1 cup milk until thoroughly blended, then gradually mix in the remaining milk. Bring to a boil. Lower heat and simmer, stirring, until lightly thickened, or 2 to 3 minutes. Remove from heat. Stir in mustard, cheddar and half the parmesan.

3 Preheat oven to 375°F (190°C). Lightly coat a 13 x 9 x 2 inch (33 x 22 x 5 cm) baking dish with non-stick cooking spray.

4 Fold sauce into the macaroni. Transfer mixture to baking dish. Place the tomatoes in single layer over the top. Combine remaining parmesan and breadcrumbs; sprinkle over tomatoes.

5 Bake until the filling is bubbling and the topping is lightly browned, or about 20 minutes. Let stand 10 minutes and serve.

per serving 502 calories, 26 g protein, 19 g fat (including 9 g saturated fat), 39 mg cholesterol, 60 g carbohydrates, 3 g fiber, 862 mg sodium

fresh ideas

*Use any short to medium stubby pasta shape in this macaroni cheese recipe; radiatore, rotelle, short fusilli, **ziti**, **penne** or farfalle are suitable. For children, use fun shapes such as alphabet letters and stars.*

vegetables, legumes & grains

on the menu

These high-protein stuffed zucchini can be the centerpiece of a lunch or dinner with the addition of whole wheat rolls and a salad of red and yellow cherry tomatoes.

stuffed zucchini gratin

These zucchini "boats" filled with ricotta and gruyère cheese are a good source of bone-saving calcium.

Serves 4 Preparation 15 minutes
Cooking 23 minutes   HEART HEALTHY

4 medium zucchini
1 cup reduced-fat ricotta cheese
1 large egg, lightly beaten
¼ cup coarsely grated gruyère cheese
1 teaspoon all-purpose flour
½ teaspoon dried thyme
¼ teaspoon salt
¼ teaspoon black pepper
15 oz (540 mL) can corn kernels, drained and rinsed
2 teaspoons canola oil
4 scallions, thinly sliced
1 plum tomato, seeded and coarsely chopped

1 Preheat broiler. Cover a baking tray with aluminum foil.

2 Cook zucchini in a large saucepan of lightly salted boiling water until softened, or about 5 minutes. Drain and rinse under cold running water.

3 Halve zucchini lengthwise. Scoop out centers, leaving a shell about 1/3-inch (8 mm) thick. Coarsely chop the removed flesh. Place zucchini shells on baking tray.

4 Combine ricotta, egg, cheese, flour, thyme, salt, pepper and corn in a medium bowl.

5 Heat oil in a medium non-stick frying pan over medium-high heat. Add chopped zucchini, scallion and tomato. Sauté until light golden and mixture is dry, or about 8 minutes. Leave to cool slightly. Stir into the ricotta mixture. Spoon into zucchini halves.

6 Broil 6 inches (15 cm) from heat until heated through and the filling is lightly browned, or about 10 minutes. Allow to stand 10 minutes before serving.

per serving 329 caories, 15 g protein, 10 g fat (including 6 g saturated fat), 23 mg cholesterol, 49 g carbohydrates, 10 g fiber, 743 mg sodium

couscous-stuffed peppers

Chickpeas and couscous combine to give this low-calorie dish a high protein score.

Serves 6 Preparation 20 minutes
Cooking 30 minutes   MAKE AHEAD

6 large red, yellow, orange or green peppers
1 tablespoon canola oil
1 small zucchini, finely chopped
2 cloves garlic, crushed
1 tablespoon freshly squeezed lemon juice
2 cups cooked couscous
15 oz (540 mL) can chickpeas, drained and rinsed
1 medium ripe tomato, seeded and finely chopped
1 teaspoon dried oregano
½ teaspoon salt
¼ teaspoon black pepper
½ cup crumbled feta cheese

1 Slice tops off peppers to make lids. Scoop out seeds and membranes; discard. Simmer the peppers and lids in a large saucepan of lightly salted boiling water, covered, for 5 minutes. Drain and set aside.

2 Preheat oven to 350°F (180°C). Heat oil in a medium saucepan over medium heat. Add zucchini and garlic. Sauté 2 minutes. Stir in juice. Cook 1 minute and remove from heat. Stir in the couscous, chickpeas, tomato, oregano, salt, pepper and feta.

3 Fill each pepper with couscous mixture. Place upright in a shallow baking dish. Cover with pepper lids. Bake just until filling is heated through, or about 20 minutes.

per serving 207 calories, 8 g protein, 4 g fat (including 1 g saturated fat), 3 mg cholesterol, 36 g carbohydrates, 7 g fiber, 307 mg sodium

barley risotto with asparagus & mushrooms

To reduce saturated fat, olive oil replaces the butter usually used in this Italian-style dish.

Serves 4   Preparation 15 minutes   Cooking 40 minutes

3⅓ cups salt-reduced chicken stock
2 tablespoons olive oil
1 medium onion, finely chopped
½ pound (250 g) mushrooms, preferably a variety
    of types, coarsely chopped
2 cloves garlic, crushed
1 cup pearl barley
½ pound (250 g) asparagus, trimmed and cut into
    bite-sized pieces, leaving tips whole
½ cup grated parmesan cheese

1 Heat the stock and 2 cups water in a medium saucepan until almost simmering. Cover and keep at a simmer.

2 Heat oil in a large, deep, non-stick frying pan over medium heat. Sauté onion until slightly softened, about 3 minutes. Add chopped mushrooms and garlic. Sauté until mushrooms soften, 5 minutes. Add the barley. Stir in 2 cups hot stock mixture. Simmer, covered, 15 minutes.

3 Blanch asparagus tips in the stock liquid in the saucepan for 2 minutes. Transfer to a plate with a slotted spoon.

4 Add more hot stock to the barley mixture, ½ cup at a time, stirring frequently. Each addition of liquid must be fully absorbed before any more is added. When adding the last of the stock, stir in asparagus stems and parmesan. Serve the risotto topped with asparagus tips.

per serving 329 calories, 15 g protein, 10 g fat (including 2 g saturated fat), 23 mg cholesterol, 49 g carbohydrates, 10 g fiber, 743 mg sodium

vegetable pot pie

This flavorsome, vitamin-packed pie is enriched with cheddar cheese.

Serves 6   Preparation 20 minutes   MAKE AHEAD
Cooking 55 minutes

2 tablespoons butter
2 medium celery stalks, coarsely chopped
1 medium yellow onion, coarsely chopped
1 large carrot, peeled and cut
    into small chunks
1 small red pepper, seeded and
    coarsely chopped
¾ teaspoon dried thyme
3 tablespoons all-purpose flour
1 cup salt-reduced vegetable stock
1 cup broccoli florets
1 cup cauliflower florets
6 baby white onions or scallion bulbs
2 oz (60 g) cheddar cheese, cut into small cubes
premade shortcrust pastry
    to top 9-inch (23 cm) pie plate

1 Melt butter in a large non-stick saucepan over medium heat. Add celery, onion, carrot, pepper and thyme. Sauté until vegetables are tender, or 10 minutes.

2 Stir in the flour until thoroughly combined. Stir in stock. Increase heat to medium-high and add broccoli, cauliflower and onion. Bring to a boil. Lower heat and simmer, uncovered, for 15 minutes. Remove pan from heat. (If making filling ahead, let cool to room temperature, cover and refrigerate.)

3 Preheat oven to 400°C (200°C). Spread the vegetable mixture in a 9 inch (3 cm) glass or ceramic pie plate. Top with cheddar. Cover with pastry (see Helpful Hint, at right). Trim edges. (If the crust is not a lattice, cut 6 long slits in it to let the steam escape.) Place the plate on a baking tray.

4 Bake until pastry is golden and filling is bubbling, or 25 to 30 minutes. Let stand 10 minutes before serving.

per serving 296 calories, 7 g protein, 17 g fat (including 8 g saturated fat), 27 mg cholesterol, 32 g carbohydrates, 4 g fiber, 408 mg sodium

To make a lattice pie crust, roll out dough 6 inches (15 cm) wide and longer than the pie plate by 2 inches (5 cm). Cut into thin strips. Starting at the edge of the plate, weave the strips over the pie, lifting up the strips going the other way where necessary so you can weave the strips through-. Neatly trim the ends.

carrot-zucchini soufflé

This is one of the most sophisticated ways to get antioxidants into your diet.

Serves 8   Preparation 15 minutes
Cooking 1 hour 5 minutes

1 pound (500 g) carrots, peeled and cut into
   ½ inch (1.25 cm)-thick slices
2 tablespoons canola oil
1 small onion, coarsely chopped
2 tablespoons all-purpose flour
½ cup 1% milk
4 large eggs, separated
1 medium zucchini, grated
½ teaspoon salt
¼ teaspoon black pepper
¼ teaspoon ground nutmeg

1 Steam carrots until tender in a medium saucepan over simmering water, about 20 minutes. Purée in food processor.

2 Preheat oven to 400°F (200°C). Coat an eight-cup soufflé dish with non-stick cooking spray.

3 Heat oil in a small saucepan over medium heat. Add onion and sauté until softened, or 5 minutes. Stir in the flour. Cook, stirring occasionally, 1 minute. Add milk and bring to a boil, stirring constantly. Transfer to a large bowl. Stir in carrot and egg yolks, fold in zucchini and stir in salt, pepper and nutmeg.

4 Beat egg whites in a medium bowl until soft peaks form. Fold whites, a third at a time, into vegetable mixture. Spoon into the prepared dish. Bake until puffed and golden, or 30 to 40 minutes. Serve immediately.

per serving 116 calories, 5 g protein, 6 g fat (including 2 g saturated fat), 109 mg cholesterol, 10 g carbohydrates, 2 g fiber, 215 mg sodium

HINT **helpful HINT** HINTHINTHINT

The slightest amount of fat from butter, oil or egg yolk will prevent egg whites from forming soft peaks when whipped. To avoid this, make sure the bowl is clean and the egg whites are carefully separated, with not a speck of yolk.

vegetable tart provençale

A thyme-flavored pastry case is a container for nutrition-packed vegetables: tomatoes, onions and zucchini with vitamin C, as well as antioxidants beta-carotene and lycopene to fight cancer and heart disease.

Serves 4 Preparation 20 minutes
Cooking 45 minutes

MAKE AHEAD
HEART HEALTHY

2 large sweet Vidalia onions, sliced
1½ cups all-purpose flour
1½ teaspoons thyme leaves, chopped
½ teaspoon salt
⅓ cup iced water
2 tablespoons olive oil
2 large zucchini (8 oz/250 g each)
4 medium tomatoes, thinly sliced
2 tablespoons grated parmesan cheese

1 Coat a large non-stick frying pan with non-stick cooking spray and set over medium-high heat until hot. Reduce heat to medium-low. Add onion and sauté until very soft and golden, or 20 minutes. Transfer to a plate.

2 Preheat oven to 400°F (200°C). Mix flour, thyme and half the salt in a large bowl. Mix in water and oil until a soft dough forms. Lightly sprinkle work surface with flour and pat out dough into a 16 x 10 inch (40 x 25 cm) rectangle or 13 inch (33 cm) round. Fold in half and transfer to 12 x 9 inch (32 x 22 cm) tart pan or 9 inch (23 cm) round tart pan with removable base. Trim the edges.

3 Cut zucchini diagonally into long, 1 inch (2.5 cm)-thick slices. Coat frying pan again with cooking spray and set over medium heat. Add zucchini and sauté until golden, or 5 to 7 minutes.

4 Arrange zucchini, tomato and onion in rows on the pastry base, standing them up and overlapping them slightly. Sprinkle with remaining salt and all the parmesan. Bake until crust is golden, or about 20 minutes. Serve warm or room temperature.

per serving 305 calories, 9 g protein, 9 g fat (including 2 g saturated fat), 2 mg cholesterol, 49 g carbohydrates, 5 g fiber, 354 mg sodium

DID YOU KNOW

..."Provençale" is a term that refers to Provence, an area of southern France on the Mediterranean? In this region, olives, onions, tomatoes, garlic and dozens of herbs such as rosemary, thyme and marjoram grow in great profusion. They form the basis of a robust cuisine that is loved around the world.

fried rice with tofu & vegetables

Incorporate high-quality vegetable protein from tofu into your diet with this dish.

Serves 4 Preparation 20 minutes   HEART HEALTHY
Marinating 1 hour Cooking 20 minutes

1 cup dry white wine or chicken stock
¼ cup salt-reduced soy sauce
2 tablespoons honey
1 tablespoon peeled and grated fresh ginger
12 oz (375 g) extra-firm tofu, cut into 1 inch (2.5 cm) cubes
1 cup long-grain white rice
2 garlic cloves, crushed
1 package (1 pound/500 g) frozen mixed stir-fry vegetables, slightly thawed
5 scallions, cut into 2 inch (5 cm) pieces
¼ teaspoon pepper
1 large egg, lightly beaten

1 Combine wine, 1 tbsp soy sauce, honey and 1 tsp ginger in a large sealable plastic bag. Add tofu. Press out excess air, seal bag and shake gently to coat tofu with marinade. Marinate in refrigerator 1 hour, turning occasionally.

2 Meanwhile, cook the rice according to package instructions and keep warm. Lightly coat a large, deep frying pan with non-stick cooking spray. Set over high heat until hot but not smoking.

3 Stir-fry garlic and remaining ginger until fragrant, for about 1 minute. Add mixed vegetables, half the scallions, rice, the remaining soy sauce and pepper. Stir-fry until mixed vegetables are heated through, or about 4 minutes. Push ingredients to one side of wok, then pour in beaten egg. Cook until almost set. Cut into strips with heatproof spatula.

4 Pour marinade into a small saucepan. Boil over high heat for 2 minutes. Add tofu and marinade to wok. Stir-fry until tofu is heated through, or about 4 minutes. Sprinkle with remaining scallions.

per serving 442 calories, 21 g protein, 9 g fat (including 2 g saturated fat), 63 mg cholesterol, 61 g carbohydrates, 3 g fiber, 668 mg sodium

thai-style stir-fry

Ginger, chili peppers, garlic and scallions provide powerful antioxidant protection against chronic disease.

Serves 4 Preparation 15 minutes   QUICK RECIPE
Cooking 6 minutes

½ cup salt-reduced vegetable stock
¼ cup freshly squeezed lime juice
2 tablespoons salt-reduced soy sauce
2 teaspoons sugar
2 teaspoons cornstarch
2 tablespoons canola oil
4 cloves garlic, crushed
1 tablespoon peeled and finely chopped fresh ginger
2 serrano or jalapeño peppers, seeded and finely chopped
1 medium red bell pepper, seeded and cut into small squares
4 scallions, thinly sliced
1 medium zucchini, diced
12 canned or bottled baby corn
4 oz (125 g) Chinese or napa cabbage, shredded
1 pound (500 g) firm tofu, cut into ½-inch (1.25 cm) cubes

1 Whisk the stock, juice, soy sauce, sugar and cornstarch in a small bowl until smooth.

2 Heat 2 tsp oil in a large non-stick frying pan or wok over medium-high heat. Add garlic, ginger and jalapeños. Stir-fry 30 seconds and add to stock mixture.

3 Heat remaining oil in frying pan. Add pepper, scallion and zucchini. Stir-fry until crisp-tender, or 2 to 3 minutes. Add corn and cabbage. Stir-fry 1 minute. Add tofu and stock mixture. Cover and simmer 2 minutes. Serve at once.

per serving 196 calories, 11 g protein, 10 g fat (including 1 g saturated fat), 0 mg cholesterol, 16 g carbohydrates, 2.4 g fiber, 502 mg sodium

four-bean chili bake with polenta topping

Polenta (cornmeal) and beans contain plenty of fiber, while the vegetables add disease-fighting vitamins, folate and antioxidants.

Serves 6   Preparation 15 minutes   MAKE AHEAD
Cooking 50 minutes

1 tablespoon canola oil
1 medium onion, finely chopped
1 medium red bell pepper, seeded and coarsely chopped
3 cloves garlic, crushed
2 medium carrots, peeled and diced
2 small zucchini, halved lengthwise and cut crosswise into thin slices
2 tablespoons chili powder
2 teaspoons cumin
28 oz (796 mL) can crushed tomatoes
15 oz (540 mL) can black beans, drained and rinsed
15 oz (540 mL) can red kidney beans, drained and rinsed
15 oz (540 mL) can pinto beans, drained and rinsed
15 oz (540 mL) can chickpeas, drained and rinsed
5 cups water
1½ cups polenta
½ teaspoon salt
1½ cups coarsely grated reduced-fat cheddar cheese

1 Heat oil in a large non-stick saucepan over medium heat. Add onion and pepper and cook until softened, or 5 minutes. Stir in garlic; cook 30 seconds. Add carrot, cover and cook 2 minutes. Add zucchini, chili powder and cumin. Cook 1 minute. Stir in tomatoes. Bring to a boil, lower heat and simmer, partially covered, for 15 minutes, stirring occasionally.

2 Stir in the three types of beans and chickpeas. Heat through. Remove half the bean mixture; refrigerate or freeze in an airtight container to use for another meal.

3 Preheat oven to 400°F (200°C). Bring 4 cups of the water to a boil in a medium saucepan. Combine remaining water, the polenta and salt in a medium bowl. Gradually stir the polenta mixture into the boiling water. Simmer gently, stirring constantly, until polenta is no longer gritty, or 5 minutes.

4 Spread half the polenta over the bottom of a 8 x 8 x 2 inch (20 x 20 x 5 cm) baking dish. Spoon the remaining chili mixture over polenta. Reserve 2 tbsp cheddar. Sprinkle the rest over the chili. Spread remaining polenta on top and cover with the reserved cheddar.

5 Bake until filling is bubbling and the top is golden brown, or about 20 minutes. Let stand 15 minutes. Cut into rectangles.

per serving 436 calories, 24 g protein, 7 g fat (including 2 g saturated fat), 6 mg cholesterol, 71 g carbohydrates, 17 g fiber, 942 mg sodium

chili with beans, tomatoes & corn

Clear your arteries with the fiber in beans, the vitamin C in carrots and the vitamins C, B$_6$ and folate in peppers.

Serves 6   Preparation 15 minutes
Cooking 45 minutes

2 tablespoons canola oil
1 large onion, finely chopped
1 medium red pepper, seeded
    and coarsely chopped
1 small carrot, peeled and diced
1 small celery stalk, diced
4 cloves garlic, crushed
3 tablespoons chili powder
2 tablespoons sweet paprika
2 teaspoons dried oregano
1 teaspoon ground cumin
28 oz (796 mL) can whole tomatoes with
    their liquid, chopped
2 x 15 oz (540 mL) cans cannellini beans,
    drained and rinsed
15 oz (540 mL) can black beans,
    drained and rinsed
1 cup water
¼ cup salt-reduced soy sauce
2 cups frozen corn kernels

1 Heat oil in a large non-stick saucepan over medium-high heat. Add onion, pepper, carrot, celery and garlic. Cook until vegetables are softened, or about 5 minutes. Stir in chili powder, paprika, oregano and cumin. Cook 1 minute.

2 Add tomatoes, beans, water and soy sauce to saucepan. Simmer, uncovered, for 30 minutes, stirring occasionally. Stir in corn. Simmer a further 10 minutes, then serve hot.

fresh ideas

While black beans, white beans and yellow corn are a hearty foundation for this protein-rich vegetarian chili, any bean will do. You can also substitute an equal amount of canned (or cooked from dry) lentils for the beans used in this recipe. If you use lentils, add them with the corn near the end of cooking and simmer just the final 10 minutes.

per serving 274 calories, 15 g protein, 7 g fat (including 1 g saturated fat), 0 mg cholesterol, 48 g carbohydrates, 13 g fiber, 856 mg sodium

open-face grilled vegetable sandwich

Asparagus and mushrooms provide a wide range of B vitamins that your body needs for maximum energy production.

Serves 4 Preparation 15 minutes
Cooking 14 minutes

2 tablespoons olive oil
1 tablespoon balsamic vinegar
¼ teaspoon salt
pinch of black pepper
4 portobello mushrooms, stems removed
1 small bunch asparagus, trimmed and
    cut in half
1 large red pepper, halved and seeded
4 large slices Italian bread, such as ciabatta
3½ oz (100 g) goat cheese

1 Preheat broiler. Whisk olive oil, balsamic vinegar, salt and pepper in a small bowl. Brush mushrooms, asparagus and pepper with the mixture.

2 Broil vegetables 4 inches (10 cm) from the heat, turning once, until tender. Allow about 10 minutes for asparagus and pepper and about 12 minutes for mushrooms. Peel and slice pepper when it is cool enough to handle.

3 Turn off broiler. Place bread on grill rack or grill until warm, or about 2 minutes.

4 Spread bread with goat cheese. Place mushrooms on each slice. Top with pepper and asparagus. Serve warm.

per serving 274 calories, 11 g protein, 15 g fat (including 6 g saturated fat), 17 mg cholesterol, 26 g carbohydrates, 4 g fiber, 443 mg sodium

mixed salad greens pizza

Instead of serving pizza with a salad on the side, combine the two to create a light and healthy one-dish meal.

Serves 4 Preparation 20 minutes
Cooking 20 minutes

2 tablespoons cornmeal
1 large premade pizza crust,
    thawed if frozen
¼ cup grated parmesan cheese
2 tablespoons balsamic vinegar
1 tablespoon Dijon mustard
1 teaspoon brown sugar
¼ teaspoon salt
12 oz (350 g) plum tomatoes, cut into
    thin wedges
1 medium red onion, halved and thinly sliced
2 cups coarsely grated reduced-fat
    mozzarella
6 cups mixed salad greens

1 Preheat oven to 425°F (220°C). Sprinkle a large baking tray with polenta and place pizza crust on top. Sprinkle parmesan over the top. Bake until parmesan starts to brown and pizza begins to puff, or about 15 minutes.

2 Whisk vinegar, mustard, brown sugar and salt in a large bowl. Add tomato and onion and toss to combine. Set aside.

3 Top pizza with mozzarella and return to oven. Bake until cheese has melted and pizza crust is crisp, or about 5 minutes.

4 Add salad greens to tomato mixture and toss to coat. Scatter salad over hot pizza and serve.

per serving 330 calories, 22 g protein, 4 g fat (including 1 g saturated fat), 10 mg cholesterol, 49 g carbohydrates, 3 g fiber, 1,040 mg sodium

on the menu

Pizza needs little, if any, accompaniment and is a sustaining meal in itself. Serve with homemade lemonade flavored with chopped mint leaves.

side dishes v
egetable side
shes vegetabl
able side dis

vegetable side dishes

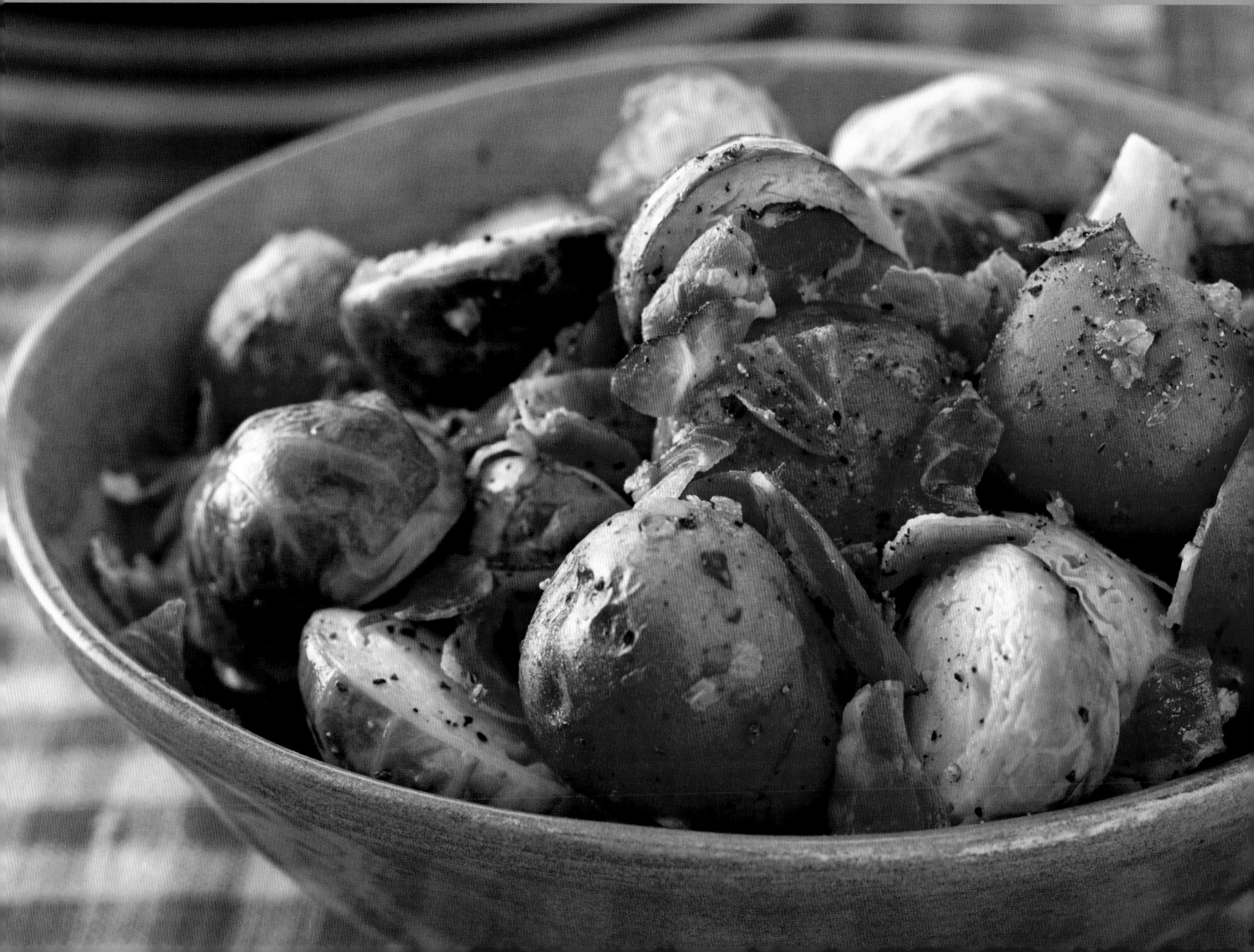

roasted asparagus with parmesan

Store fresh asparagus in the refrigerator or it will lose half its vitamin C—and a lot of its flavor—in just two or three days.

Serves 4   Preparation 10 minutes   QUICK RECIPE
Cooking 12 minutes

- 1 pound (500 g) asparagus, trimmed and bottom half of stalks thinly peeled
- 1 medium red pepper, seeded and cut lengthwise into thin strips
- 1 tablespoon olive oil
- 1 tablespoon balsamic vinegar
- 1 oz (30 g) Parmesan cheese, in one piece
- ¼ teaspoon black pepper

1 Preheat oven to 500°F (240°C). Place asparagus and pepper strips in a large shallow baking dish. Drizzle with the oil and toss to coat.

2 Roast until crisp-tender, or 10 to 12 minutes, turning occasionally. Transfer to a serving dish.

3 Sprinkle with vinegar. Toss to coat. Using a vegetable peeler, shave cheese into thin curls over vegetables. Season with pepper.

per serving 86 calories, 5 g protein, 6 g fat (including 2 g saturated fat), 6 mg cholesterol, 5 g carbohydrates, 2 g fiber, 140 mg sodium

HINT helpful HINT HINTHINTHINT

Roasted vegetables are an ideal accompaniment for roasted meat or poultry. When the roast goes into the oven, prepare the vegetables and place them in a roasting pan with oil and seasonings. When the roast comes out of the oven, turn up the heat and put in the vegetables. They'll have enough time to cook while the roast poultry or meat rests before carving. Turn the vegetables once or twice to brown them evenly.

stir-fried asparagus & snow peas

This green vegetable medley is loaded with nutrients that both prevent birth defects in newborns and ward off age-related diseases.

Serves 4   Preparation 10 minutes   QUICK RECIPE
Cooking 4 minutes

- 1 tablespoon olive oil
- 1 pound (500 g) asparagus, trimmed, bottom half of stalks peeled, stalks cut diagonally into 1 inch (2.5 cm) lengths, leaving tips about 2 inches (5 cm) long
- 4 oz (125 g) snow peas
- 4 scallions, thinly sliced
- ¼ teaspoon salt
- pinch of black pepper
- 1 small clove garlic, crushed
- 1 teaspoon grated lemon zest
- 2 tablespoons finely chopped parsley

Heat oil in a large non-stick frying pan or wok over medium-high heat. Add asparagus, snow peas, scallions, salt and pepper. Stir-fry until vegetables are almost crisp-tender, or 2 to 3 minutes. Add garlic, zest and parsley. Stir-fry 1 minute.

per serving 42 calories, 2 g protein, 3 g fat (including 0 g saturated fat), 0 mg cholesterol, 4 g carbohydrates, 1 g fiber, 104 mg sodium

broccoli & cauliflower with cream sauce

Carrot juice is an antioxidant-rich ingredient that makes the sauce for this dish every bit as healthy as the vegetables.

Serves 4   Preparation 10 minutes
Cooking 15 minutes   QUICK RECIPE

½ cup carrot juice
3 tablespoons light sour cream
2 cups broccoli florets
2 cups cauliflower florets

1 Bring the carrot juice to a boil in a small saucepan over high heat. Let it boil until reduced by about half, or about 8 minutes. Remove from heat. Whisk in sour cream.

2 Steam broccoli and cauliflower until crisp-tender, or about 5 minutes. Transfer to a serving dish. Serve with the sour cream sauce.

per serving 44 calories, 3 g protein, 2 g fat (including 1 g saturated fat),
4 mg cholesterol, 6 g carbohydrates, 2 g fiber, 45 mg sodium

balsamic beets with toasted pecans

High in natural sugars, beets boost energy like no other vegetable.

Serves 4   Preparation 5 minutes
Cooking 10 minutes   QUICK RECIPE

3 tablespoons chopped pecans
2 tablespoons balsamic vinegar
1 teaspoon sugar
2 teaspoons butter or margarine
3 medium beets, steamed, peeled,
    and sliced, or 1 jar (15 oz/540 mL)
    sliced beets, drained

1 Toast the pecans in a medium non-stick frying pan over medium heat, stirring often, until browned, or about 4 minutes. Take care not to burn. Transfer to a plate.

2 Heat the vinegar, sugar and butter in the same pan over medium-low heat. Add the beets. Cook, stirring often, until beets are heated through and all the liquid is absorbed, or about 5 minutes. Top with pecans. Serve at once.

per serving 86 calories, 1 g protein, 6 g fat (including 2 g saturated fat),
5 mg cholesterol, 8 g carbohydrates, 2 g fiber, 140 mg sodium

HINT **helpful HINT** HINTHINTHINT

Beet stains are all but impossible to remove from cutting boards. To save your work surfaces, peel steamed beets by first cutting off both ends over the sink and then holding the beets under cold running water while you peel off the skins. Coat the cutting board lightly with non-stick cooking spray before slicing. This may not prevent staining altogether, but it will help.

on the menu

Drizzle broccoli and cauliflower with the creamy carrot sauce, or serve the sauce separately in a small bowl to be used as a dip.

stir-fried bok choy with sugar snap peas

Bok choy has more of the disease-fighting antioxidant beta-carotene than other types of cabbage. It is low in calories, has no fat and is a rich source of fiber and vitamin C.

Serves 4 Preparation 10 minutes
Cooking 10 minutes

QUICK RECIPE
HEART HEALTHY

2 teaspoons olive oil
1 medium carrot, cut into matchsticks
2 tablespoons slivered fresh ginger
1 pound (500 g) bok choy, cut into very thin slices
½ pound (250 g) sugar snap peas, trimmed
3 tablespoons orange juice concentrate
1 tablespoon brown sugar
1 tablespoon low-sodium soy sauce
½ teaspoon salt
1 teaspoon cornstarch blended with
    1 tablespoon water

1 Heat ¼ cup water and the oil in a large non-stick frying pan over medium heat. Add carrot and ginger. Cook, stirring frequently, until carrot is crisp-tender, or about 3 minutes.

2 Add bok choy, sugar snap peas, orange juice concentrate, brown sugar, soy sauce and salt. Cover and cook 3 minutes, or until bok choy begins to wilt.

3 Uncover and cook, stirring frequently, until bok choy is crisp-tender, or about 2 minutes. Stir in the cornstarch mixture and cook, stirring constantly, until vegetables are evenly coated, or about 1 minute.

per serving 109 calories, 4 g protein, 2.5 g fat (including 0.5 g saturated fat), 0 mg cholesterol, 19 g carbohydrates, 3 g fiber, 630 mg sodium

fresh ideas

When you're cooking a member of the cabbage family—and that includes brussels sprouts, broccoli, bok choy and cauliflower—you can always use the seasoning from one dish to flavor another one. For example, any of these vegetables can be lightly steamed and served with the simple mustard sauce that accompanies the brussels sprouts and new potato recipe (at right).

mustard-glazed brussels sprouts & new potatoes

Cancer-fighting phytochemicals are in plentiful supply in this dish.

Serves 4 Preparation 10 minutes
Cooking 15 minutes

10 oz (300 g) brussels sprouts,
    halved if large
12 oz (375 g) red or white new potatoes,
    unpeeled and halved if large
1 tablespoon olive oil
1 tablespoon finely chopped shallots or onion
2 oz (60 g) lean ham or prosciutto,
    trimmed and chopped
2 teaspoons Dijon mustard
¼ teaspoon salt
pinch of black pepper

1 Steam brussels sprouts and new potatoes until tender, or 8 to 10 minutes. Drain.

2 Heat oil in large non-stick frying pan over medium-high heat. Add shallots. Sauté until softened, or 2 to 3 minutes. Stir in ham and mustard. Add brussels sprouts, potatoes, salt and pepper. Heat through for about 2 minutes. Serve at once.

per serving 133 calories, 7 g protein, 5 g fat (including 1 g saturated fat), 7 mg cholesterol, 18 g carbohydrates, 4 g fiber, 413 mg sodium

on the menu

Mustard-Glazed Brussels Sprouts & New Potatoes makes a good accompaniment to roast turkey or duck. A mixed green salad will lighten it up. Serve grapes or slices of melon for dessert.

*Most apples are suitable both for **cooking and eating**, but some varieties work better in recipes than others. Apples that are suitable for cooking, such as Granny Smith and Braeburn, are generally **firmer and tarter** than other varieties—they can withstand longer cooking times without disintegrating. This matters when you're **baking apples** or using them in a pie, but it is not so important when adding apples to a quick sauté.*

braised cabbage with apple & caraway

The protective phytochemicals in cabbage are particularly effective against hormone-related diseases such as breast cancer.

Serves 4 Preparation 15 minutes
Cooking 15 minutes

QUICK RECIPE
HEART HEALTHY

2 teaspoons canola oil
1 small onion, finely chopped
¾ teaspoon caraway seeds
1 pound (500 g) green cabbage, cored and
    thinly sliced (about 6 cups)
1 tablespoon rice wine vinegar or
    cider vinegar
½ teaspoon salt
2 small crisp red apples such as Gala or Empire, cored
    and cut into small cubes
1 teaspoon honey
2 tablespoons chopped walnuts,
    toasted (optional)

1 Heat oil in large non-stick frying pan over medium heat. Add onion and caraway seeds. Sauté until onion is softened, or about 5 minutes.

2 Stir in cabbage, vinegar and salt. Cover. Cook just until cabbage wilts, or about 4 minutes. Uncover. Increase heat to high. Add apple and honey. Cook, stirring frequently, until apple is crisp-tender and most of the liquid has evaporated, or 4 to 6 minutes. Transfer to a serving plate. Top with walnuts, if using, and serve.

per serving 67 calories, 2 g protein, 2 g fat (including 0 g saturated fat),
0 mg cholesterol, 13 g carbohydrates, 4 g fiber, 212 mg sodium

HINT helpful HINT HINTHINTHINT

One secret to successful stir-frying is to get the wok or frying pan very hot before adding the oil. This helps to prevent food from sticking. Stir-fry vegetables in small batches rather than piling them into the pan. If they're crowded, they will start to steam and lose the crisp-tender texture that is characteristic of a stir-fry.

chinese cabbage with ginger

Fresh ginger and crunchy peanuts add a tasty kick to napa cabbage.

Serves 4 Preparation 10 minutes
Cooking 6 minutes

QUICK RECIPE

1 tablespoon canola oil
1 tablespoon peeled, finely chopped
    fresh ginger
6 cups coarsely chopped Chinese (napa) cabbage or bok
    choy
¼ teaspoon salt
¼ cup low-sodium chicken or vegetable stock
1 tablespoon chopped roasted peanuts

1 Heat a large non-stick frying pan or wok over high heat. Add oil and ginger and cook 30 seconds. Add cabbage. Stir-fry 2 minutes. Add salt and stock, cover and cook until almost wilted, or about 2 minutes.

2 Remove pan from heat. Let sit, covered, 1 minute. Sprinkle with peanuts and serve.

per serving 70 calories, 2 g protein, 5 g fat (including 1 g saturated fat),
0 mg cholesterol, 4 g carbohydrates, 2 g fiber, 240 mg sodium

roasted carrots with rosemary

Eating carrots can reduce cholesterol levels, in turn decreasing the risk of heart disease.

Serves 6   Preparation 10 minutes
Cooking 20 minutes

1 pound (500 g) large carrots, peeled and cut
  into 2 x ¼ inch (5 cm x 5 mm) matchsticks
¼ teaspoon salt
1½ teaspoons olive oil
1 teaspoon finely chopped fresh rosemary leaves
  or ½ teaspoon dried

1 Preheat oven to 400°F (200°C). Mound carrot sticks on a baking tray. Sprinkle with salt and drizzle with oil. Toss gently to coat. Spread out on tray in a single layer.

2 Roast 10 minutes. Stir in rosemary. Roast until crisp-tender and lightly browned in spots, or 7 to 10 minutes.

per serving 44 calories, 1 g protein, 1 g fat (including 0 g saturated fat),
0 mg cholesterol, 8 g carbohydrates, 2 g fiber, 136 mg sodium

carrots parmesan

There's plenty of vitamin A in every serving, in the protective form of beta carotene.

Serves 6   Preparation 6 minutes   Cooking 30 minutes

2 tablespoons olive oil
1 pound (500 g) carrots, peeled and cut diagonally
  into thin slices
¼ teaspoon salt
¼ teaspoon black pepper
2 tablespoons grated Parmesan cheese

1 Heat oil in a medium non-stick saucepan over medium-low heat. Add carrot and cover. Cook just until carrot is tender, or about 15 minutes.

2 Increase heat to medium. Cook, uncovered, until lightly browned, stirring occasionally, about 15 minutes. Season with salt and pepper. Sprinkle with Parmesan just before serving.

per serving 82 calories, 2 g protein, 5 g fat (including 0 g saturated fat),
1 mg cholesterol, 10 g carbohydrates, 3 g fiber, 177 mg sodium

on the menu

Carrots Parmesan is a simple yet sophisticated dish. Serve with baked ham, dill on new potatoes, and strawberries and fresh pineapple for dessert.

braised carrot, celery & fennel

Celery is low in calories and a great source of fiber and potassium.

Serves 4   Preparation 10 minutes
Cooking 18 minutes

QUICK RECIPE
HEART HEALTHY

4 large carrots, peeled, halved lengthwise
    and cut into 2 x ¼ inch (5 cm x 5 mm)-long pieces
3 celery stalks, peeled and cut into 2 x ¼ inch
    (5 cm x 5 mm)-long pieces
1 small red onion, thinly sliced
½ fennel bulb, cored and thinly sliced
1⅔ cups low-sodium chicken stock
pinch each of salt and pepper
2 teaspoons butter

1 In a large saucepan over medium-high heat, gently simmer carrot, celery, onion and fennel in the stock, covered, until the vegetables are tender, or about 15 minutes.

2 Uncover saucepan. Boil until liquid has reduced slightly, or 2 to 3 minutes. Season to taste with salt and pepper. Stir in the butter and serve.

per serving 77 calories, 3 g protein, 2 g fat (including 1 g saturated fat), 5 mg cholesterol, 13 g carbohydrates, 4 g fiber, 616 mg sodium

HINT helpful HINT HINTHINTHINT

Combining vegetables can make a simple side dish into something much more exciting. Make sure you choose vegetables that will cook in the same amount of time. Try parsnips and carrots, for example, or zucchini and tomatoes. Others can be matched if you parboil the one needing more cooking, such as a potato, before combining it with one that cooks faster, such as leeks. Use seasonings that suit both vegetables.

carrot & parsnip purée

When buying parsnips, select ones the same size as a medium carrot for the best flavor.

Serves 4   Preparation 10 minutes
Cooking 20 minutes

QUICK RECIPE
MAKE AHEAD

3 large carrots, peeled and chopped
1 large parsnip, peeled and chopped
½ teaspoon salt
1 tablespoon butter or canola oil
1 teaspoon grated orange zest

1 Combine carrot, parsnip and salt in a medium saucepan with enough water to barely cover the vegetables. Simmer, uncovered, until vegetables are very tender and most of the liquid has evaporated, or about 20 minutes.

2 Drain vegetables. Transfer to food processor or blender. Add butter and orange zest and process to a smooth purée.

per serving 82 calories, 1 g protein, 3 g fat (including 2 g saturated fat), 8 mg cholesterol, 13 g carbohydrates, 3 g fiber, 408 mg sodium

braised baby vegetables

Slowly braising whole baby vegetables will preserve their nutrients and intensify their flavors. Reducing the cooking juices in the final stages creates a healthy, glossy sauce.

Serves 4   Preparation 15 minutes   Cooking 20–25 minutes

2 tablespoons butter or olive oil
4 baby leeks (½ pound/250 g), trimmed, halved lengthwise and washed thoroughly
½ pound (250 g) baby parsnips, trimmed and halved lengthwise
½ pound (250 g) baby carrots, trimmed
8 small white onions or shallots, trimmed and peeled
½ cup (125 mL) vegetable stock
1 teaspoon sugar
1 bay leaf
pinch of black pepper

1 Melt butter in a large saucepan or heatproof casserole dish over medium heat. Add leek, parsnip, carrots and onions or shallots. Stir in stock, sugar, bay leaf and pepper. Bring to a boil, cover and reduce heat to low.

2 Cook for 10 minutes or until vegetables are barely tender. Remove lid and boil liquid for 2 to 3 minutes, or until bubbling and reduced to a thick syrup-like glaze. Toss vegetables in the glaze. Discard bay leaf and serve immediately.

per serving 180 calories, 3 g protein, 7 g fat (including 1 g saturated fat), 0 mg cholesterol, 128 g carbohydrates, 5 g fiber, 42 mg sodium

fresh ideas

When baby vegetables are unavailable, use standard-sized vegetables and cut them into even chunks. Add the grated zest and juice of an orange at the same time as the stock to enrich the flavor.

...baby vegetables can either be fully ripe miniature varieties of a vegetable, or immature vegetables picked before they are fully grown? All are nutritious, and most are tender, more delicate versions of their full-sized relatives. About 45 types of baby vegetables are sold in North American groceries.

irish mashed potatoes with cabbage & leeks

Add cabbage and leeks to simple mashed potatoes to boost their flavor and nutrients.

Serves 8   Preparation 15 minutes
Cooking 50 minutes   HEART HEALTHY

2 pounds (1 kg) Yukon Gold potatoes, unpeeled and
    quartered
3⅓ cups low-sodium chicken stock,
    plus cold water as needed
1 pound (500 g) leeks, trimmed, thinly sliced,
    and rinsed
1 cup low-fat (1%) milk
3 cloves garlic, crushed
1 bay leaf
1 pound (500 g) green cabbage, cored and
    thinly sliced
¼ cup cold water
¼ teaspoon ground nutmeg
¼ teaspoon salt
¼ teaspoon ground white pepper
2 tablespoons unsalted butter
¼ cup finely chopped chives

1 Place potato in a large saucepan. Add stock and water as needed to cover. Boil potato until tender, or 20 to 25 minutes.

2 Place leek, milk, garlic and bay leaf in a large saucepan. Cover. Bring to a boil and simmer until leek is softened, or 20 minutes. Drain and reserve leek, milk and garlic liquid separately. Discard bay leaf.

3 In the same saucepan, place cabbage and ¼ cup water, then cover. Boil gently until tender, or 10 to 15 minutes. Drain. Squeeze cabbage dry and chop finely.

4 Drain potato and transfer to a large bowl. Add milk and garlic and mash well. Stir in leek, cabbage, nutmeg, salt, pepper and butter. Top with chives.

per serving 168 calories, 6 g protein, 4 g fat (including 2 g saturated fat),
9 mg cholesterol, 29 g carbohydrates, 3 g fiber, 379 mg sodium

HINT **helpful HINT** HINTHINTHINT

When a recipe calls for white pepper rather than black, it may be as much for its appearance as for its flavor. Chefs often use white pepper on pale-colored foods. A white peppercorn is a ripened black peppercorn with a milder flavor.

potato & pumpkin gratin

This dish supplies good amounts of fiber and a mixture of vitamins, including vitamin C from the potatoes, tomatoes and onion and vitamin A from the pumpkin. The cheese is an excellent source of calcium and protein.

Serves 4   Preparation 45 minutes   MAKE AHEAD
Cooking 35 minutes

1 pound (500 g) small potatoes, halved
1½ pounds (750 g) pumpkin or squash, chopped
½ cup apple cider
10 fl. oz (300 mL) low-sodium vegetable stock
1 small sprig of rosemary
1 large red onion, halved and thinly sliced
3 beefsteak or other large tomatoes, thickly sliced
2 sprigs of oregano, stalks discarded
2 cups grated Parmesan cheese
1 cup fresh white bread crumbs
pinch each of salt and pepper

1 Preheat oven to 350°F (180°C). Place potato with water to cover in a medium saucepan. Bring to a boil and cook for 15 minutes or until just tender. Drain.

2 Place pumpkin, cider, stock and rosemary in a large pan. Bring to a boil. Partially cover the pan and simmer 15 minutes. Add onion and continue to cook for 10 minutes. Discard the rosemary and add half the salt and pepper.

3 Slice potatoes and arrange half of them over the bottom of a large ovenproof baking dish. Lay half the tomato slices over the potato; scatter half the oregano leaves on top. Season with remaining salt and pepper. Sprinkle with half the Parmesan.

4 Spoon the cooked pumpkin on top, adding all the cooking liquid. Top with remaining potato, tomato slices and oregano. Combine the remaining Parmesan with the bread crumbs and sprinkle over the vegetables.

5 Bake for 35 to 40 minutes or until topping is crisp and golden brown. Serve hot.

per serving 480 calories, 30 g protein, 18 g fat (including 11 g saturated fat), 45 mg cholesterol, 53 g carbohydrates, 6 g fiber, 370 mg sodium

fresh ideas

*Substitute 8 oz (250 g) mushrooms for the pumpkin. Omit cider, stock, rosemary and onion. Slice the mushrooms and mix with chopped scallions. Layer with the **vegetables** in a baking dish. Cook 45 minutes.*

ginger candied sweet potatoes

There is twice the daily requirement for vitamin A in one serving of this spiced dish.

Serves 4   Preparation 10 minutes   Cooking 25 minutes

2 tablespoons honey
1½ tablespoons canola oil
1 pound (500 g) orange sweet potatoes, peeled and cut into about 1 inch (2.5 cm) pieces
½ teaspoon grated lemon zest
½ teaspoon peeled and grated fresh ginger
¼ teaspoon salt

1 Heat honey and oil in a medium non-stick saucepan over medium heat until bubbling, about 1 minute. Add the sweet potato. Cover. Cook over low heat until sweet potato begins to give off liquid, about 5 minutes. Add zest and ginger. Cook, covered, just until potato is tender, a further 10 to 15 minutes. Be sure not to overcook.

2 Uncover saucepan. Add salt. Boil over medium-high heat until potato is thickly glazed, or about 5 minutes.

per serving 752 kilojoules, 2 g protein, 7 g fat (including 1 g saturated fat), 0 mg cholesterol, 28 g carbohydrates, 3 g fiber, 165 mg sodium

mashed sweet potatoes with maple & cinnamon

This subtly spiced side dish is a phenomenal source of beta-carotene, which helps lower the risk of heart disease, strokes and cancer.

Serves 6   Preparation 10 minutes   Cooking 20 minutes

QUICK RECIPE
MAKE AHEAD
HEART HEALTHY

2 pounds (1 kg) orange sweet potatoes, peeled and chopped
½ teaspoon salt
1 cinnamon stick
2 tablespoons maple syrup
1½ tablespoons butter or canola oil

1 Combine sweet potato, salt and cinnamon in a medium saucepan with just enough water to cover. Boil, uncovered, stirring occasionally, until potato is tender, or about 20 minutes. Drain. Discard cinnamon stick.

2 Return potato to pan. Add 1½ tbsp maple syrup and all the butter. Mash. Serve drizzled with the remaining maple syrup.

per serving 166 calories, 2 g protein, 3 g fat (including 2 g saturated fat), 8 mg cholesterol, 33 g carbohydrates, 2 g fiber, 210 mg sodium

HINT **helpful HINT** HINTHINTHINT

Pure maple syrup has a smoother, more subtle flavor than imitation syrups, and is actually less sweet. You don't need the most expensive grade of syrup, which is often used for making candy. Medium amber is the best grade for table use.

baked sweet potato 'fries'

Baked fries are the way to go when you're cutting back on fat. These baked sweet potato sticks are so full of flavor, you'll never know the difference.

Serves 4   Preparation 7 minutes
Cooking 20 minutes

`QUICK RECIPE`

1 pound (500 g) orange sweet potatoes, peeled
    and cut into ½ inch (1.25 cm)-thick "fries"
1 tablespoon canola oil
¼ teaspoon salt
¼ teaspoon black pepper

1 Preheat oven to 425°F (220°C). Lightly coat a large baking tray with non-stick cooking spray.

2 Combine sweet potato, oil, salt and pepper in a large bowl. Toss to coat. Spread fries on the tray in a single layer.

3 Bake 10 minutes. Turn fries over. Continue baking until tender and lightly browned, or about 10 minutes longer.

per serving 102 calories, 1 g protein, 4 g fat (including 0 g saturated fat), 0 mg cholesterol, 17 g carbohydrates, 2 g fiber, 152 mg sodium

on the menu

Baked Sweet Potato "Fries" go especially well with veggie burgers or pork dishes like ham, sausages, chops or roasts.

193

HINT helpful HINT HINTHINTHINThintHINThelpfulHINTHIN

Twice-Baked Stuffed Sweet Potatoes can be made up to a day ahead. Bake and stuff the potatoes as directed. Place in a shallow dish, cover loosely and refrigerate. Remove from the refrigerator 30 minutes before baking, then follow the recipe as usual.

twice-baked stuffed sweet potatoes

Use a half-and-half combination of butter and oil to maintain a rich flavor while reducing the saturated fat that could hurt your heart.

Serves 4   Preparation 10 minutes   MAKE AHEAD
Cooking 1 hour 10 minutes, plus cooling

2 large orange sweet potatoes (1½ pounds/750 g total)
8 oz (250 mL) can crushed pineapple, drained
1 tablespoon canola oil
1 tablespoon butter
1 tablespoon brown sugar
1 teaspoon grated orange zest
½ teaspoon salt
2 tablespoons chopped pecans

1 Preheat oven to 350°F (180°C). Pierce each sweet potato twice with the tip of a knife. Place on a baking tray.

2 Bake until soft, or about 50 minutes. Set aside until cool enough to handle but still warm. Reduce heat to 325°F (160°C).

3 Cut potatoes in half lengthwise. Scoop out flesh and place in medium bowl, being careful not to tear skin. Reserve skins. Add pineapple, oil, butter, sugar, zest and salt to potato flesh. Whip with an electric mixer or whisk until slightly fluffy.

4 Place skin shells on baking tray. Fill with potato mixture, mounding it a little. Bake for 15 minutes. Sprinkle with pecans. Bake for a further 5 minutes.

per serving 236 calories, 2 g protein, 9 g fat (including 2 g saturated fat), 8 mg cholesterol, 38 g carbohydrates, 4 g fiber, 303 mg sodium

fresh ideas *Roasted tomatoes will keep for several days in the refrigerator. Eat them as is or use in pasta sauces and salads.*

roasted tomatoes with garlic & herbs

Slow-roasting fresh tomatoes in olive oil concentrates their lycopene, the cancer-fighting phytochemical, and makes it more readily available to the body.

Serves 4   Preparation 10 minutes   Cooking 3 hours

3 pounds (1.5 kg) plum tomatoes, halved lengthwise
2 tablespoons olive oil
5 cloves garlic, finely chopped
½ cup finely chopped basil
2 tablespoons finely chopped rosemary
1 teaspoon sugar
1 teaspoon salt

1 Preheat oven to 250°F (120°C). Line a jelly roll pan with foil.

2 Toss tomato halves with oil, garlic, basil, rosemary, sugar and salt in a large bowl. Place, cut side up, in prepared pan. Bake for about 3 hours, or until they have collapsed and their skins have wrinkled. Serve at room temperature or refrigerate and serve chilled.

per serving 148 calories, 4 g protein, 8 g fat (including 1 g saturated fat), 0 mg cholesterol, 19 g carbohydrates, 5.5 g fiber, 468 mg sodium

grilled vegetables with balsamic glaze

Boost your supply of vitamin C and B with this colorful Mediterranean-style combination of vegetables.

Serves 4   Preparation 10 minutes
Cooking 14 minutes

1 large red pepper, seeded and cut in
   1 inch (2.5 cm)-wide strips
1 medium zucchini, thinly sliced
1 medium red onion, thinly sliced
2 medium portobello mushrooms, stems removed
   and caps cut into 1 inch (2.5 cm)-wide strips
2 tablespoons extra virgin olive oil
1 teaspoon dried oregano, crumbled
1 tablespoon balsamic vinegar
¼ teaspoon salt
¼ teaspoon black pepper

1 Preheat broiler or barbecue. Lightly coat a grill rack with non-stick cooking spray.

2 Combine pepper, zucchini, onion and mushroom in a large bowl. Sprinkle with oil and oregano. Toss to coat. Place vegetables on the rack in a single layer.

3 Broil or barbecue about 2 inches (5 cm) from heat until vegetables are just crisp-tender and lightly flecked with brown, or 6 to 8 minutes. Turn over; cook until done, about 5 minutes.

4 Arrange vegetables on a platter. Mix the balsamic vinegar, salt and pepper in a small bowl. Brush over vegetables. Serve warm or at room temperature.

per serving 101 calories, 2 g protein, 7 g fat (including 1 g saturated fat), 0 mg cholesterol, 8 g carbohydrates, 3 g fiber, 152 mg sodium

HINT **helpful HINT** HINTHINTHINT

Cut vegetables for broiling or barbecuing into pieces that are of uniform size and no more than 1 inch (2.5 cm) thick. That way, they'll cook quickly and evenly. Soak the pieces in cold water for 30 minutes and then brush with oil to prevent them from drying out while they cook.

zucchini with parsley, garlic & lemon

There's a substantial helping of vitamin C in every serving of this simple side dish.

Serves 4   Preparation 5 minutes
Cooking 8 minutes

2 teaspoons olive oil
1¼ pounds (625 g) zucchini, halved lengthwise and cut
   thinly crosswise to make half-moon shapes
1 tablespoon minced garlic
¼ teaspoon salt
2 tablespoons chopped parsley
2 teaspoons freshly squeezed lemon juice

1 Heat oil in a large non-stick frying pan over medium-high heat. Add zucchini. Sauté 3 minutes. Add garlic. Sauté until zucchini is crisp-tender, or 3 to 5 minutes.

2 Remove pan from heat. Stir in salt, parsley and lemon juice. Serve warm or at room temperature.

per serving 4 calories, 2 g protein, 3 g fat (including 0 g saturated fat), 0 mg cholesterol, 5 g carbohydrates, 2 g fiber, 151 mg sodium

on the menu

Grilled vegetables go well with grilled bluefish, tuna or swordfish steaks. Grilling intensifies all the flavors. Serve with crusty bread and finish the meal with freshly baked blueberry cobbler topped with whipped cream.

asian vegetables with oyster sauce

Soy sauce, oyster sauce, lime juice, garlic, ginger and basil provide a taste of Thailand.

Serves 8   Preparation 20 minutes   QUICK RECIPE
Cooking 6 minutes

1 tablespoon low-sodium soy sauce
1 tablespoon oyster sauce
2 tablespoons freshly squeezed lime juice
1 tablespoon sugar
2 tablespoons canola oil
4 cloves garlic, minced
2 serrano or jalapeño peppers, seeded
    and thinly sliced diagonally
3 scallions, thinly sliced
1 medium red pepper, seeded and
    cut into small pieces
4 oz (125 g) snow peas
1 long Japanese eggplant, cut into small cubes
4 oz (125 g) mushrooms, stems removed and
    caps cut into wedges
1 tablespoon peeled and finely chopped fresh ginger
3 small heads baby bok choy, cored and thinly sliced
½ cup loosely packed basil leaves, cut into thin shreds

1 Combine soy sauce, oyster sauce, lime juice and sugar in a small bowl.

2 Heat oil in a large non-stick frying pan over medium-high heat. Add garlic and chili peppers. Stir-fry 30 seconds. Add the scallion, red pepper, snow peas, eggplant, mushroom and ginger. Stir-fry 2 minutes. Add bok choy. Stir-fry until wilted, about 1 minute. Add soy mixture. Stir-fry until all the vegetables are crisp-tender, or about 1 minute. Stir in basil and serve immediately.

per serving 78 calories, 3 g protein, 4 g fat (including 0 g saturated fat),
0 mg cholesterol, 9 g carbohydrates, 4 g fiber, 128 mg sodium

spring vegetable sauté with tarragon

Yellow zucchini that are very brightly colored contain more beta-carotene than paler ones.

Serves 4   Preparation 15 minutes   QUICK RECIPE
Cooking 4 minutes

1 tablespoon butter
1 tablespoon canola oil
1 bunch scallions, cut into 2 inch (5 cm) lengths
1 medium yellow zucchini, unpeeled, thinly sliced
¼ pound (125 g) snow peas, blanched
1 small bunch asparagus, trimmed, cut into 4 inch
    (10 cm) pieces, blanched
½ teaspoon salt
¼ teaspoon black pepper
1 teaspoon chopped tarragon
    or ½ teaspoon dried

1 Heat butter and oil in a large non-stick frying pan over medium-high heat. Add scallion and zucchini. Sauté for about 1 minute.

2 Add snow peas, asparagus, salt and pepper. Cover. Cook until vegetables are heated through, or about 2 minutes. Stir in tarragon. Serve immediately.

per serving 96 calories, 3 g protein, 7 g fat (including 2 g saturated fat),
8 mg cholesterol, 8 g carbohydrates, 3 g fiber, 310 mg sodium

roasted harvest vegetables

This winter vegetable combination is rich in fiber, potassium and beta-carotene.

Serves 4 Preparation 20 minutes Cooking 45 minutes

3 tablespoons olive oil
6 cloves garlic, thinly sliced
3 cups butternut squash chunks (1 inch/2.5 cm cubes)
10 oz (300 g) brussels sprouts, trimmed and halved lengthwise
½ pound (250 g) fresh shiitake mushrooms, stems discarded and caps thickly sliced
2 large red apples, unpeeled, cut into 1 inch (2.5 cm) chunks
¼ cup oil-packed sun-dried tomatoes, drained and thinly sliced
1 teaspoon dried rosemary
½ teaspoon salt
¼ cup grated Parmesan cheese

1 Preheat oven to 400°F (200°C). Combine the olive oil and garlic in a large roasting pan. Heat for 3 minutes in the oven. Add the pumpkin, brussels sprouts, mushroom, apple, sun-dried tomato, rosemary and salt. Toss to combine.

2 Roast for 35 minutes, or until vegetables are tender. Toss vegetables every 10 minutes. Sprinkle Parmesan over the top and roast for a further 5 minutes.

per serving 292 calories, 8 g protein, 14 g fat (including 3 g saturated fat), 4 mg cholesterol, 39 g carbohydrates, 9.3 g fiber, 464 mg sodium

bulgur with spring vegetables

Bulgur is a source of complex carbohydrates, protein, niacin, insoluble fiber and vitamin E, all of which work to keep your cardiovascular system healthy.

Serves 6 Preparation 45 minutes
Cooking 10 minutes

MAKE AHEAD
HEART HEALTHY

1¼ cups bulgur
3½ cups boiling water
2 tablespoons olive oil
3 tablespoons fresh lemon juice
1 teaspoon salt
½ teaspoon pepper
2 leeks, halved lengthwise, cut crosswise into 1 inch (2.5 cm) pieces, rinsed well
2 cloves garlic, crushed
12 asparagus spears, cut into 2 inch (5 cm) lengths
1 cup frozen peas
¼ cup chopped mint

1 Combine bulgur and boiling water in a large heatproof bowl. Let stand until bulgur is tender, or about 30 minutes; stir after 15 minutes. Drain bulgur in a large, fine-meshed sieve to remove any remaining liquid.

2 Whisk 1 tbsp oil, the lemon juice, salt and pepper in a large bowl. Add bulgur and fluff with a fork.

3 Heat remaining oil in a medium frying pan over low heat. Add leeks and garlic; cook until leeks are tender, or about 5 minutes. Transfer to the bowl containing bulgur.

4 In a steamer set over a pan of boiling water, steam the asparagus until tender, about 4 minutes. Add peas during the final 30 seconds. Add vegetables and mint to bulgur mixture; toss to combine. Serve at room temperature or chilled.

per serving 188 calories, 6 g protein, 5 g fat (including 0.5 g saturated fat), 0 mg cholesterol, 32 g carbohydrates, 8 g fiber, 330 mg sodium

DID YOU KNOW ...bulgur is made from parboiled wheat kernels that have been dried and cracked? It is good for stuffings and pilafs, but is traditionally used for tabbouleh and other salads.

VEGETABLE SIDE DISHES 201

white beans & swiss chard

Beans protect your heart with soluble fiber that helps lower cholesterol.

Serves 8   Preparation 10 minutes   MAKE AHEAD
Cooking 25 minutes

1 small bunch Swiss chard (about ½ pound/250 g)
2 tablespoons olive oil
1 small onion, finely chopped
1 medium carrot, peeled and finely chopped
1 teaspoon dried oregano
1 bay leaf
2 cloves garlic, crushed
1 cup low-sodium chichen stock
3 x 15 oz (540 mL) cans white kidney or lima beans, drained and rinsed
½ teaspoon salt
⅛ teaspoon black pepper
½ cup grated Parmesan cheese

1 Remove tough stems from Swiss chard and finely chop. Coarsely chop leaves.

2 Heat oil in a large non-stick frying pan over medium heat. Add onion, carrot, oregano and bay leaf. Sauté until onion and carrot are very soft, or about 8 minutes. Add garlic. Sauté for 30 seconds.

3 Add the Swiss chard and stock to the pan. Cook, stirring occasionally, until Swiss chard begins to wilt, or about 2 minutes. Stir in beans. Simmer, covered, 10 minutes. Uncover and cook until Swiss chard is tender, 5 minutes. Season with salt and pepper. Remove bay leaf. Sprinkle with Parmesan.

per serving 139 calories, 7 g protein, 5 g fat (including 1 g saturated fat), 4 mg cholesterol, 16 g carbohydrates, 5 g fiber, 482 mg sodium

fresh ideas

Instead of white kidney beans, you can use another type of white bean or, for a nutty flavor, try making this dish with chickpeas. Vary the herbs, too: Fresh thyme, parsley or chervil all work well.

mediterranean rice with green peas & sun-dried tomatoes

Combining rice and peas helps boost the muscle-building protein in any meal.

Serves 6   Preparation 15 minutes   MAKE AHEAD
Cooking 20 minutes   HEART HEALTHY

1⅔ cups low-sodium chicken stock
2 cups fresh or frozen peas
½ cup sun-dried tomatoes, thinly sliced
¼ teaspoon salt
1 cup long-grain white rice

1 Bring stock to a boil in a medium saucepan over high heat. Add peas, tomatoes and salt. Bring back to a boil. Add rice and stir. Cover and lower heat to a bare simmer. Cook just until liquid is absorbed and rice is tender, or about 15 minutes.

2 Remove saucepan from heat. Leave rice mixture to stand, covered, for 10 minutes. Uncover. Fluff up with a fork.

per serving 175 calories, 7 g protein, 0 g fat (including 0 g saturated fat), 0 mg cholesterol, 36 g carbohydrates, 3 g fiber, 437 mg sodium

vegetable fried rice

A balanced blend of vitamins and minerals is contained in this combination dish.

Serves 6   Preparation 20 minutes
Cooking 15 minutes

MAKE AHEAD
HEART HEALTHY

¼ cup low-sodium chicken
    or vegetable stock
2½ tablespoons low-sodium soy sauce
1½ teaspoons dark sesame oil
1½ tablespoons canola oil
2 medium carrots, peeled and cut into
    matchsticks
1 medium red pepper, seeded and
    coarsely chopped
4 scallions, thinly sliced (darker green
    tops reserved for garnish)
2 tablespoons finely chopped, peeled
    fresh ginger
1 cup quartered white, brown or shiitake
    mushrooms
2 cloves garlic, minced
2 cups sliced napa cabbage
¼ teaspoon salt
3 cups cooked long-grain
    white rice, chilled

1 Whisk stock, soy sauce and sesame oil in a small bowl.

2 Heat canola oil in a large, deep non-stick frying pan or wok over medium-high heat. Add carrot, pepper, white and pale green parts of scallions and the ginger. Cook just until crisp-tender, stirring once, about 5 minutes.

3 Add the mushroom and garlic. Cook, stirring occasionally, 5 minutes. Add cabbage and salt. Cook, stirring, just until the cabbage is slightly wilted, or about 3 minutes. Stir in rice and soy sauce mixture. Cook, stirring occasionally, until rice is heated through, or about 3 minutes. Slice darker green scallion tops. Sprinkle over rice before serving.

per serving 178 calories, 4 g protein, 5 g fat (including 1 g saturated fat),
0 mg cholesterol, 29 g carbohydrates, 2 g fiber, 542 mg sodium

on the menu

Vegetable Fried Rice becomes a substantial main dish if you add chopped cooked turkey, chicken, ham, pork or scrambled egg to the mix.

rice with kale & butternut squash

For a vegetable that's high in antioxidants and fiber, you can't beat butternut squash.

Serves 6   Preparation 15 minutes
Cooking 16 minutes

HEART HEALTHY

½ cup basmati rice
1 tablespoon curry powder
1 pound (500 g) kale, tough stems removed
    and kale leaves blanched
½ pound (250 g) butternut squash, seeded, peeled
    and cut in 1 inch (2.5 cm) pieces
¼ cup raisins
1 cup reduced-fat coconut milk
¾ cup water
1 teaspoon salt

1 Heat a large non-stick frying pan over medium-low heat. Add rice. Toast, stirring frequently, until lightly browned, about 3 minutes. Add curry powder. Cook, stirring, 1 minute.

2 Add kale, pumpkin, raisins, coconut milk, water and salt. Cover and simmer until the liquid is absorbed and the rice and pumpkin are tender, about 12 minutes. Remove from the heat. Leave to stand, covered, for 5 minutes.

per serving 143 calories, 4 g protein, 3 g fat (including 1 g saturated fat), 0 mg cholesterol, 29 g carbohydrates, 3 g fiber, 420 mg sodium

DID YOU KNOW

...rice rarely, if ever, causes food allergies and is a staple for half the world's population? Basmati rice is an aromatic rice native to India and Pakistan. It is suitable for pilafs, as the grains stay dry and separate during cooking.

tomato chutney

Tomatoes contain chlorogenic acid, which may help guard against certain cancers.

Makes 3 cups **Preparation** 20 minutes
Cooking 25 minutes, plus chilling

MAKE AHEAD
HEART HEALTHY

1¾ pounds (875 g) plum tomatoes, seeded and coarsely chopped
2 medium celery stalks, coarsely chopped
1 medium red onion, coarsely chopped
½ cup sultanas
⅓ cup packed brown sugar
⅓ cup cider vinegar
2 tablespoons peeled and finely chopped fresh ginger
2 tablespoons chopped, bottled pickled jalapeño peppers
¼ teaspoon ground allspice
¼ teaspoon salt
14 grape or small cherry tomatoes, each quartered

1 In a large non-aluminum saucepan, combine the plum tomato, celery, onion, sultanas, brown sugar, vinegar, ginger, chili, allspice and salt. Bring to a boil. Simmer, uncovered, stirring occasionally, until ingredients are tender and most of the liquid has evaporated, or 20 to 25 minutes.

2 Remove pan from heat. Stir in grape or cherry tomatoes. Let cool to room temperature. Transfer to a covered dish and refrigerate for at least 24 hours. This will keep for up to 1 week.

per serving 70 calories, 1 g protein, 0 g fat (including 0 g saturated fat), 0 mg cholesterol, 17 g carbohydrates, 2 g fiber, 79 mg sodium

on the menu

There are many types of chutney, but they mostly feature a single vegetable or fruit simmered in a spicy blend of seasonings. In this recipe, you can try substituting 2 cups of chopped unripe (hard) mango for the plum tomatoes. To make mango chutney, leave out the celery and grape tomatoes and follow the recipe as directed. Chutney goes well with grilled meats, grains, rice, curries and potato dishes. It is also makes an excellent appetizer served with cream cheese on crackers or wedges of toasted pita bread.

pumpkin pickles

Ginger, cinnamon and peppercorns add sweet and spicy flavors to the pickles, as well as healthy phytochemicals.

Makes 8 cups
Preparation 25 minutes
Cooking 20 minutes

MAKE AHEAD
HEART HEALTHY

1 lemon
5 cups sugar
3 cups cider vinegar
¼ cup finely chopped, peeled fresh ginger
2 cinnamon sticks
20 black peppercorns
1 tablespoon salt
1 sugar pumpkin (3–4 pounds/1.5–2 kg), seeded, peeled and cut into 1½ x ¾ x ¾ inch (4 x 2 x 2 cm) pieces

1 Combine zest, sugar, vinegar, ginger, cinnamon sticks, peppercorns and salt in a large non-aluminium saucepan. Simmer, stirring to dissolve sugar, for 5 minutes. Add the pumpkin. Simmer, stirring occasionally, until crisp-tender, about 15 minutes.

2 Transfer pumpkin pickles to sterilized canning jars, using a slotted spoon (you will need eight ½ pint/250 mL jars, or four 1 pint/500 mL jars). Pour in cooking liquid to within ¼ inch (5 mm) of the top. Seal. Refrigerate and use within 1 week.

per ½ cup 30 calories, 1 g protein, 0 g fat (including 0 g saturated fat), 0 mg cholesterol, 8 g carbohydrates, 1 g fiber, 208 mg sodium

sweet corn & pepper relish

Canned corn contains ferulic acid. This is an antioxidant that destroys naturally occurring toxins in the body.

Serves 6   **Preparation** 10 minutes
Cooking 5 minutes

QUICK RECIPE
MAKE AHEAD
HEART HEALTHY

1½ cups white vinegar
¼ cup sugar
¾ teaspoon dry mustard
¼ teaspoon salt
2 scallions, thinly sliced
½ small orange pepper, seeded and diced
½ small yellow pepper, seeded and diced
15 oz (450 mL) can corn kernels, drained

1 In a small non-aluminium saucepan, combine vinegar, sugar, mustard and salt. Simmer 5 minutes. Remove from heat.

2 Stir in scallions, pepper and corn. Cool. Refrigerate in a covered container for up to 1 week. Serve relish chilled or at room temperature.

per serving 70 calories, 1 g protein, 0 g fat (including 0 g saturated fat), 0 mg cholesterol, 16 g carbohydrates, 1 g fiber, 236 mg sodium

fresh ideas

To spice up this simple relish, add a tablespoon or two of finely chopped jalapeño or other chili peppers.

endive & watercress salad with almonds

Watercress and Belgian endive are super sources of beta-carotene.

Serves 6   Preparation 10 minutes   `QUICK RECIPE`

⅓ cup low-fat plain yogurt
1 tablespoon light mayonnaise
2 teaspoons honey
1 teaspoon Dijon mustard
¼ teaspoon curry powder
pinch of ground ginger
1 bunch watercress, tough stems removed
1 large Belgian endive, halved lengthwise and
    cut crosswise into ½ inch (1.25 cm)-thick slices
1 McIntosh apple, halved, cored and thinly sliced
2 tablespoons slivered almonds, toasted

For the dressing, whisk yogurt, mayonnaise, honey, mustard, curry powder and ginger in a small bowl. Combine watercress, Belgian endive and apple in a large bowl. Add the dressing, then toss to combine. Sprinkle with almonds.

per serving 54 calories, 2 g protein, 2 g fat (including 0 g saturated fat),
2 mg cholesterol, 8 g carbohydrates, 1 g fiber, 62 mg sodium

HINT helpful HINT HINTHINTHINT

To toast almonds, place the nuts in a small, dry frying pan. Cook over medium heat, shaking the pan often, until the almonds just begin to color. Remove from the pan and cool before using.

cucumber, radish & snow pea salad

Snow peas and radishes are great sources of folate and vitamin C, nutrients that work together to protect the health of your heart.

Serves 4   `QUICK RECIPE`
Preparation 10 minutes   `HEART HEALTHY`

6 oz (175 g) snow peas, trimmed
1 tablespoon rice vinegar
2 teaspoons sugar
2 teaspoons soy sauce
1 teaspoon dark sesame oil
pinch of salt
2 cucumbers, scored and thinly sliced
2 bunches radishes, thinly sliced
1 tablespoon sesame seeds, toasted *(optional)*

1 Cook snow peas in a saucepan of lightly salted boiling water until crisp-tender, or 2 to 3 minutes. Drain. Rinse under cold running water.

2 For the vinaigrette, whisk the vinegar, sugar, soy sauce, sesame oil and salt in a bowl until sugar and salt are dissolved.

3 Combine the snow peas, cucumber and radish in a large bowl. Add vinaigrette and toss to combine. Sprinkle with sesame seeds, if using.

per serving 64 calories, 3 g protein, 2 g fat (including 0 g saturated fat),
0 mg cholesterol, 10 g carbohydrates, 3 g fiber, 247 mg sodium

DID YOU KNOW

...radishes were first cultivated thousands of years ago in China? They were so highly prized in ancient Greece that gold replicas were made of them.

on the menu

This salad makes a cool first course before grilled chicken and corn on the cob. Serve wedges of chilled watermelon for a refreshing dessert.

asparagus, snow pea & tomato salad with ginger dressing

This salad is an excellent source of folate, beta-carotene and vitamin C—key nutrients for fighting cancer and heart disease.

Serves 6   Preparation 10 minutes
Cooking 7 minutes

QUICK RECIPE
MAKE AHEAD

1 tablespoon soy sauce
2 teaspoons rice vinegar
2 teaspoons freshly squeezed lemon juice
1 teaspoon dark sesame oil
3 tablespoons vegetable oil
2 scallions, finely chopped
1 tablespoon peeled, finely chopped fresh ginger
4 oz (125 g) snow peas
1 pound (500 g) thin asparagus, trimmed
1 head romaine lettuce, cored and separated into leaves
4 plum tomatoes, cut into wedges
¼ cup walnuts, toasted and coarsely chopped

1 For the dressing, whisk soy sauce, rice vinegar, lemon juice and sesame oil in a small bowl. Whisk in vegetable oil, then stir in scallions and ginger.

2 Cook the snow peas in a large saucepan of lightly salted boiling water until crisp-tender, or 2 to 3 minutes. Transfer to a colander with a slotted spoon. Rinse under cold running water.

3 Add asparagus to the same boiling water in the saucepan. Cook until crisp-tender, or 3 to 4 minutes. Drain in colander and rinse under cold water. Toss snow peas and asparagus in a large bowl with just enough dressing to lightly coat.

4 Arrange 3 or 4 romaine leaves on each serving plate. Top with snow peas, asparagus and tomato. Garnish with walnuts and serve remaining dressing separately.

per serving 146 calories, 5 g protein, 12 g fat (including 1 g saturated fat), 0 mg cholesterol, 9 g carbohydrates, 4 g fiber, 200 mg sodium

beef & pasta salad

Pasta is a good source of iron and contributes niacin and other B vitamins.

Serves 4   Preparation 15 minutes
Cooking 20 minutes

HEART HEALTHY

½ pound (250 g) small pasta shapes of your choice
1 pound (500 g) broccoli florets
10 oz (300 g) well-trimmed sirloin steak
1¼ cups low-fat plain yogurt
3 tablespoons light mayonnaise
1 tablespoon balsamic vinegar
¾ cup basil leaves
½ teaspoon salt
1 pound (500 g) plum tomatoes, quartered
1 medium red onion, halved and thinly sliced

1 Cook pasta in a large saucepan of lightly salted boiling water until al dente, following package instructions. Add the broccoli florets during the last 2 minutes of cooking; drain.

2 Preheat grill. Grill steak 4 inches (10 cm) from the heat for 4 minutes per side, or until done to taste. On a cutting board, slice thinly and diagonally across the grain.

3 For the dressing, combine yogurt, mayonnaise, vinegar, basil and salt in a food processor, and process until smooth. Pour dressing into a large serving bowl.

4 Add the steak and any juices that have accumulated on the cutting board; toss to coat. Add pasta, broccoli, tomato and onion to bowl and toss again. (Recipe can be made ahead and refrigerated. Bring back to room temperature before serving.)

per serving 471 calories, 29 g protein, 15 g fat (including 4.5 g saturated fat), 50 mg cholesterol, 58 g carbohydrates, 7 g fiber, 781 mg sodium

green vegetable salad with garlic & ginger

Crisp, fat-free and delicately flavored, these steamed vegetables are good hot or cold.

Serves 4 Preparation 20 minutes
Cooking 4 minutes

QUICK RECIPE
MAKE AHEAD
HEART HEALTHY

½ pound (250 g) broccoli
½ pound (250 g) baby bok choy
4 scallions
½ pound (250 g) sugar snap peas, trimmed
1 clove garlic, crushed
1 teaspoon finely grated ginger
1 tablespoon Thai fish sauce
1 teaspoon brown sugar

1 Fill a steamer pot or saucepan with water to just below the base of a steamer basket. Bring water to a boil.

2 Cut broccoli into small florets, trimming stalks to just under 1 inch (2 cm). Peel remaining stalk and cut diagonally into thin slices. Trim bok choy and slice stems. Trim scallions and slice thinly on the diagonal.

3 Combine broccoli, bok choy, scallion and sugar snap peas in a large bowl. Add garlic and ginger, and toss well. Transfer to steamer basket. Steam, covered, until vegetables are crisp-tender, or 3 to 4 minutes.

4 Place vegetables in a serving dish. Combine fish sauce and sugar in a small cup, stirring until sugar has dissolved. Drizzle over the vegetables. Serve hot or chill briefly in the refrigerator before serving.

per serving 50 calories, 4 g protein, 0 g fat (including 0 g saturated fat), 0 mg cholesterol, 6 g carbohydrates, 5 g fiber, 485 mg sodium

romaine lettuce with chunky tomato vinaigrette

Feta cheese is high in calcium and protein and a good source of vitamin B_{12}.

Serves 6 Preparation 12 minutes

QUICK RECIPE

2 large ripe tomatoes, halved, seeded and coarsely chopped
⅓ cup loosely packed fresh basil leaves
2 tablespoons tomato sauce
2 tablespoons olive oil
1 tablespoon balsamic vinegar
1 small clove garlic, crushed
½ teaspoon salt
1 large head romaine lettuce, torn into bite-sized pieces
¼ cup crumbled feta cheese

For the vinaigrette, place tomato, basil, tomato sauce, oil, vinegar, garlic and salt in a food processor. Pulse on and off until blended but still chunky. Toss the lettuce with vinaigrette in a large bowl. Sprinkle with feta. Serve immediately.

per serving 82 calories, 3 g protein, 5 g fat (including 2 g saturated fat), 6 mg cholesterol, 3 g carbohydrates, 2 g fiber, 237 mg sodium

fresh ideas

Chunky Tomato Vinaigrette also makes a tasty topping for grilled meats and chicken or pasta. It can be made several hours before it's needed and refrigerated. To dress up a simple pasta dish, grate some mozzarella and add with salami and black olives.

carrot-almond salad & raspberry vinaigrette

Almonds, like most nuts, are a rich source of vitamins, especially folate and vitamin E.

Serves 4 Preparation 15 minutes QUICK RECIPE
Cooking 8 minutes

2 tablespoons raspberry vinegar
1 tablespoon olive oil
1 tablespoon honey
¼ teaspoon salt
¼ teaspoon black pepper
1 pound (500 g) carrots, peeled and thinly sliced
    on the diagonal
¼ cup slivered or sliced almonds
1 scallion, thinly sliced

1 For the vinaigrette, whisk the vinegar, oil, honey, salt and pepper in a small bowl. Steam carrots over a medium pan of simmering water just until tender, or about 8 minutes. Rinse under cold running water and drain.

2 Toss the carrot, almonds, scallion and vinaigrette in a medium bowl. Serve immediately.

per serving 134 calories, 3 g protein, 6 g fat (including 1 g saturated fat), 0 mg cholesterol, 18 g carbohydrates, 4 g fiber, 204 mg sodium

DID YOU KNOW

...there are two varieties of almonds?
The edible variety is sweet while the inedible, or bitter, almond contains a form of cyanide.

three-vegetable salad with curry vinaigrette

Phytochemicals known as indoles, found in cauliflower and other cruciferous vegetables, may help prevent hormone-related cancers. Beans contain vitamin A, which aids vision.

Serves 4   Preparation 10 minutes
Cooking 7 minutes

QUICK RECIPE
MAKE AHEAD

2 teaspoons curry powder
¼ cup freshly squeezed lime juice
¼ teaspoon salt
3 tablespoons vegetable oil
½ pound (250 g) green beans, trimmed and cut in half crosswise
1 small head cauliflower, stalks removed for other use and head separated into small florets
1 cup corn kernels, fresh or frozen and thawed

1 Toast curry powder, stirring frequently, in a small, dry frying pan over low heat until fragrant, about 1 minute. For the vinaigrette, whisk lime juice, toasted curry powder and salt in a small bowl. Whisk in vegetable oil.

2 Cook beans in a large saucepan of lightly salted boiling water until crisp-tender, or about 3 minutes. Transfer with a slotted spoon to a colander. Rinse under cold running water.

3 Add cauliflower florets to the boiling water. Cook until crisp-tender, or about 4 minutes. Drain in colander. Rinse under cold running water.

4 Toss beans, cauliflower, corn and vinaigrette in a large bowl. Serve chilled or at room temperature.

per serving 197 calories, 6 g protein, 12 g fat (including 1 g saturated fat), 0 mg cholesterol, 22 g carbohydrates, 9 g fiber, 758 mg sodium

HINT **helpful HINT** HINTHINTHINT

Toasting curry powder in a dry frying pan gets rid of the raw taste and boosts the flavor. Other spices, such as cumin and chili powder, benefit from toasting, too. They can be added to foods that don't require further cooking.

grilled vegetable salad

Here's a vegetable combination that will help keep your heart healthy.

Serves 6   Preparation 25 minutes
Cooking 15 minutes

1 medium eggplant (¾ pound/350 g)
1 small bulb fennel (6 oz/200 g), trimmed
1 medium yellow zucchini
1 medium green zucchini
½ teaspoon salt
1 small red pepper, halved through
    stem end and seeded
3 plum tomatoes, halved through stem end
    and seeded
2 tablespoons olive oil
2 cloves garlic, crushed
1 teaspoon finely chopped fresh marjoram
    or ½ teaspoon dried
1½ tablespoons balsamic vinegar

1 Preheat a barbecue or electric grill to medium-high heat. Slice the eggplant, fennel and zucchini lengthwise into ½-inch (1 cm)-thick pieces. Sprinkle with half the salt and coat with cooking spray.

2 Barbecue pepper, skin side down, until the skin is blackened and blistered, or 3 to 4 minutes. Cook eggplant, fennel and zucchini on one side until grill marks are dark brown but vegetables are still very firm, or about 4 minutes. Turn over and barbecue until browned and just tender, or about 3 minutes for zucchini and 5 to 6 minutes longer for eggplant and fennel.

3 Coat cut sides of tomatoes with cooking spray. Barbecue, cut sides down, just until light grill marks appear, or 3 minutes.

4 Heat oil in a small frying pan over medium heat. Add garlic, marjoram and remaining salt. Sauté 1 minute.

5 Peel grilled pepper and cut into thin strips. Cut the rest of the vegetables into bite-sized chunks. Transfer to a medium bowl. Add olive oil mixture and vinegar. Toss to coat and serve at room temperature.

per serving 85 calories, 2 g protein, 5 g fat (including 1 g saturated fat), 0 mg cholesterol, 10 g carbohydrates, 4 g fiber, 211 mg sodium

wilted spinach salad

Multigrain bread is used to make croutons instead of the usual white bread.

Serves 4   Preparation 5 minutes
Cooking 5 minutes

½ pound (250 g) baby spinach leaves
2 tablespoons olive oil
1 red onion, thinly sliced
¼ cup tomato juice
1 tablespoon freshly squeezed lemon juice
1 teaspoon Dijon mustard
1 small clove garlic, crushed
¼ teaspoon salt
pinch of black pepper
2 slices rindless, short-cut bacon cooked and crumbled
2 slices multigrain bread, trimmed, toasted
    and cut into small cubes for croutons

1 Place spinach in large bowl. Heat the olive oil in a large non-stick frying pan over medium heat. Add onion. Sauté for 1 minute. Stir in tomato juice, lemon juice, mustard, garlic, salt and pepper. Bring to a boil, then remove from heat.

2 Pour hot dressing over spinach and toss to coat. Top with bacon and croutons. Serve warm.

per serving 140 calories, 5 g protein, 9 g fat (including 1 g saturated fat), 6 mg cholesterol, 12 g carbohydrates, 3 g fiber, 435 mg sodium

roasted eggplant & tomato salad

Brushing vegetables with a little oil and then roasting them is generally a healthier option than frying—particularly with eggplants, which soak up oil like a sponge.

Serves 4   Preparation 15 minutes   Cooking 20 minutes

1 pound (500 g) eggplant, cut crosswise into
    thin slices
1 pound (500 g) plum tomatoes, thinly sliced
2 tablespoons olive oil
¼ teaspoon salt
¼ teaspoon black pepper
1 clove garlic
1 tablespoon red wine vinegar
15 small basil leaves

1 Preheat oven to 500°F (240°C). Line a large baking dish with aluminum foil and coat lightly with non-stick cooking spray. Place eggplant and tomato slices in a single layer on the foil. Brush with half the oil. Sprinkle with salt and pepper.

2 Roast until eggplant is softened and golden, or 20 minutes. Let cool.

3 For the dressing, crush the garlic in a small bowl. Add the remaining oil and all the vinegar and whisk until blended. Overlap slices of tomato and eggplant on a serving plate and intersperse with basil leaves. Brush with dressing.

per serving 115 calories, 2 g protein, 7 g fat (including 1 g saturated fat),
0 mg cholesterol, 13 g carbohydrates, 4 g fiber, 160 mg sodium

sweet potato salad with raisins & orange dressing

Sweet potatoes are rich in vitamins A and C—and delicious, to boot!

Serves 4   Preparation 25 minutes   Cooking 20 minutes

1 pound (500 g) orange sweet potatoes, peeled,
    quartered lengthwise and cut crosswise into thin
    slices
3 tablespoons olive oil
1 tablespoon freshly squeezed lemon juice
1 tablespoon freshly squeezed orange juice
1 teaspoon honey
¼ teaspoon salt
¼ teaspoon black pepper
½ pound (250 g) arugula, torn into pieces
1 navel orange, peeled and segmented
1 small red onion, thinly sliced crosswise
3 tablespoons raisins

1 Preheat oven to 400°F (200°C). Line a large baking dish with aluminum foil and lightly coat with non-stick cooking spray. Toss the sweet potatoes in the baking dish with half the oil to coat, then spread in an even layer. Roast until tender and lightly browned, or about 20 minutes.

2 Whisk the remaining oil, lemon juice, orange juice, honey, salt and pepper in a small bowl. Taste dressing and add 1 tsp lemon juice, if desired.

3 Toss warm potatoes and dressing in a serving bowl. Add arugula, orange segments, onion and raisins. Toss to combine.

per serving 219 calories, 3 g protein, 11 g fat (including 1 g saturated fat),
0 mg cholesterol, 31 g carbohydrates, 4 g fiber, 163 mg sodium

fresh ideas

To make Sweet Potato Salad into a main course lunch dish, add slices of fresh mozzarella cheese, cubes of feta or another soft cheese of your choice before you drizzle on the dressing. Or, serve with slices of cooked chorizo sausage.

potato salad with sun-dried tomatoes & basil

Everyone's favorite outdoor party food, this salad is an excellent source of vitamin C from all three vegetables.

Serves 6   Preparation 10 minutes
Cooking 15 minutes

QUICK RECIPE
MAKE AHEAD
HEART HEALTHY

1½ pounds (750 g) small red potatoes, unpeeled and halved
2 tablespoons light mayonnaise
2 teaspoons Dijon mustard
¼ cup low-fat buttermilk
2 scallions, thinly sliced
¼ cup chopped sun-dried tomatoes (not oil-packed)
8 basil leaves, shredded or finely chopped
½ teaspoon salt
¼ teaspoon black pepper

1 Cook potato in a large pot of lightly salted boiling water until tender, or 10 to 15 minutes. Drain well.

2 For the dressing, combine mayonnaise and mustard in a small bowl. Stir in the buttermilk.

3 Combine potatoes, scallions, sun-dried tomatoes, basil, salt and pepper in a large bowl. Add dressing. Toss to coat.

per serving 103 calories, 4 g protein, 2 g fat (including 0 g saturated fat), 2 mg cholesterol, 17 g carbohydrates, 3 g fiber, 340 mg sodium

DID YOU KNOW

...the name coleslaw comes from the Dutch word *koolsla*, which means cabbage salad? Recipes for this salad have always been open to improvisation, from the vegetables used to the dressing—it can be mayonnaise, vinaigrette and anything in between.

carrot-broccoli slaw

Almonds are a source of thiamine, which is important for your metabolism. Here's a simple and delicious way to use them.

Serves 6
Preparation 10 minutes

QUICK RECIPE
MAKE AHEAD

3 tablespoons light mayonnaise
1 tablespoon white wine vinegar
1 large bunch broccoli
3 medium carrots, peeled and grated
¼ cup slivered almonds, toasted
3 tablespoons chopped parsley
pinch of black pepper

1 For the dressing, whisk the mayonnaise and vinegar in a small bowl.

2 Cut off broccoli florets and reserve for another use. Peel the stalks, then grate in a food processor or by hand.

3 Combine broccoli, carrot and dressing in a large bowl. Stir in almonds, parsley and pepper.

per serving 87 calories, 3 g protein, 6 g fat (including 1 g saturated fat), 3 mg cholesterol, 8 g carbohydrates, 3 g fiber, 114 mg sodium

corn, tomato & basil salad with red onion

A phytochemical in corn protects your eyes against age-related macular degeneration, which causes blindness.

Serves 6
Preparation 15 minutes

QUICK RECIPE

1 tablespoon olive oil
1 teaspoon balsamic vinegar
¼ teaspoon salt
2 cups corn kernels,
    fresh or frozen and thawed
2 large ripe tomatoes, seeded
    and coarsely chopped
½ cup loosely packed fresh basil leaves,
    finely chopped
¼ cup finely chopped red onion

Whisk oil, vinegar and salt in a large bowl. If you're using fresh corn, blanch the kernels for 30 seconds in a large saucepan of boiling water before adding them to the salad. Gently stir in the corn, tomato, basil and onion. Serve immediately.

per serving 77 calories, 2 g protein, 3 g fat (including 0 g saturated fat), 0 mg cholesterol, 13 g carbohydrates, 2 g fiber, 102 mg sodium

fresh ideas

A fresh vegetable salad can be made from a variety of vegetables and vinaigrettes. (Parboil tough vegetables beforehand.) Try carrots, celery, scallions and dill; turnips, peas, peppers and chives; or red onions, potatoes, radishes and parsley.

on the menu

Serve this simple, fresh salad with grilled fish or poultry and Baked Sweet Potato Fries (page 193). Finish the meal with a slice of Carrot-Pineapple Cake (page 245) and an espresso.

breads & muffins

sweet potato muffins with pecan streusel

Nuts can provide a good supply of protein in a vegetarian diet.

Makes 12 muffins   Preparation 20 minutes   MAKE AHEAD
Cooking 20 minutes

STREUSEL:
¼ cup packed brown sugar
¼ cup all-purpose flour
½ teaspoon cinnamon; pinch of salt
2 tablespoons butter, cut up
⅓ cup chopped pecans

MUFFINS:
1¾ cups all-purpose flour
1 teaspoon baking powder
1 teaspoon baking soda
1 teaspoon cinnamon
¾ teaspoon ground ginger
½ teaspoon salt
1 cup cooked, mashed orange sweet potato
⅓ cup packed brown sugar
¼ cup honey
¼ cup canola oil
1 tablespoon finely grated orange zest
2 large eggs, lightly beaten
½ cup low-fat buttermilk

1 For the streusel, combine sugar, flour, cinnamon and salt in a medium bowl. Cut in the butter until the mixture is crumbly. Using your fingertips, rub mixture briefly to blend the butter. Stir in pecans. Refrigerate the streusel mixture.

2 Preheat oven to 350°F (180°C). Coat a 12-hole muffin pan with non-stick cooking spray. Combine flour, baking powder, baking soda, cinnamon, ginger and salt in a small bowl.

3 Combine the sweet potato, sugar, honey, oil and zest in a medium bowl. Add eggs and buttermilk; beat until well blended. Add flour mixture, stirring until just moistened. Spoon into muffin cups, filling each two-thirds full. Sprinkle with streusel.

4 Bake until tops of muffins are springy to the touch, or about 20 minutes. Cool in the pan on a wire rack before turning out.

per muffin 253 calories, 4 g protein, 10 g fat (including 2 g saturated fat), 41 mg cholesterol, 38 g carbohydrates, 2 g fiber, 286 mg sodium

DID YOU KNOW

...muffin batter can be prepared, spooned into muffin pans and refrigerated overnight? All you need do in the morning is pop the pan into a preheated oven to have delicious fresh muffins to eat for breakfast.

carrot-raisin muffins

Sunflower seeds are rich in heart-protecting vitamin E as well as selenium, copper, fiber, iron, zinc, folate and vitamin B_6.

Makes 12 muffins   **Preparation** 10 minutes
Cooking 15 minutes

QUICK RECIPE
HEART HEALTHY

1 cup all-purpose flour
$\frac{1}{2}$ cup whole wheat flour
$\frac{1}{2}$ cup sugar
2 teaspoons baking powder
$\frac{1}{4}$ teaspoon salt
$\frac{1}{2}$ teaspoon cinnamon
$\frac{1}{4}$ teaspoon ground allspice
$\frac{1}{4}$ teaspoon ground nutmeg
$\frac{1}{2}$ cup unsweetened applesauce
$\frac{1}{4}$ cup canola oil
2 large eggs, lightly beaten
1 large carrot, peeled and finely grated
$\frac{1}{2}$ cup raisins
2 tablespoons unsalted, shelled
   sunflower seeds

1 Preheat oven to 400°F (200°C). Coat a 12-hole deep muffin pan with non-stick cooking spray or line with paper cases.

2 Mix all-purpose flour, whole wheat flour, sugar, baking powder, salt, cinnamon, allspice and nutmeg in a medium bowl.

3 Combine the applesauce, oil and eggs in a large bowl. Fold in the carrot and raisins. Add flour mixture, stirring just until evenly moistened. Spoon into muffin cups, filling each one two-thirds full. Sprinkle with sunflower seeds.

4 Bake until a skewer inserted in the center of a muffin comes out clean, or about 15 minutes. Cool muffins in the pan on a wire rack before turning out. Serve warm.

per muffin 177 calories, 3 g protein, 6 g fat (including 1 g saturated fat), 35 mg cholesterol, 28 g carbohydrates, 2 g fiber, 126 mg sodium

HINT **helpful HINT** HINTHINTHINT

The rule of thumb with muffins is not to overmix the batter. To make sure the finished result is light and well risen, stir the ingredients with a wooden spoon until just combined. Muffins are very versatile. Savory or sweet, they're perfect for breakfast and as a snack food at any time.

sweet potato scones

These scones are low in saturated fat because they're made with oil, not butter.

Makes 12 scones   Preparation 12 minutes   Cooking 15 minutes

QUICK RECIPE
MAKE AHEAD

1¾ cups all-purpose flour
¼ teaspoon salt
1 tablespoon baking powder
pinch of nutmeg
1 cup cooked, mashed orange sweet potato
¼ cup canola oil
¼ cup low-fat (1%) milk
1 large egg, lightly beaten
2 tablespoons brown sugar

1 Preheat oven to 425°F (220°C). Sift flour, salt, baking powder and nutmeg into a small bowl.

2 Stir together sweet potato, oil, milk, egg and sugar in a medium bowl. Stir in flour mixture just until evenly moistened.

3 Turn dough out onto a floured work surface. Pat out to a ¾ inch (2 cm)-thick round. Cut into rounds with a 2 ½ inch (6 cm) cookie cutter. Place rounds on a baking tray about 1 inch (2.5 cm) apart. Gather up remaining dough. Pat into a circle; cut out remaining scones.

4 Bake until golden, or 12 to 15 minutes. Serve warm.

per scone 143 calories, 3 g protein, 6 g fat (including 1 g saturated fat), 18 mg cholesterol, 21 g carbohydrates, 1 g fiber, 186 mg sodium

tomato scones

Bits of fresh tomato add antioxidant power to these easy drop biscuits, while yogurt adds calcium to every bite.

Makes 12 scones   Preparation 12 minutes   Cooking 12 minutes

QUICK RECIPE
MAKE AHEAD

1 medium tomato, seeded and finely chopped
2 cups all-purpose flour
1 tablespoon baking powder
½ teaspoon salt
1 cup low-fat plain yogurt
⅓ cup olive oil
2 tablespoons finely chopped scallion
1 tablespoon finely chopped sun-dried tomato

1 Preheat oven to 425°F (220°C). Lightly coat a baking tray with non-stick cooking spray. Drain the chopped fresh tomato on paper towels.

2 Combine flour, baking powder and salt in a medium bowl. Combine yogurt and oil in a small bowl; stir into flour mixture just until evenly moistened.

3 Stir fresh tomato, scallion and sun-dried tomato into flour mixture. Drop dough, ¼ cup at a time, onto the prepared baking tray, making 12 scones.

4 Bake until the tops are golden brown, about 12 minutes. Serve warm or at room temperature.

per scone 145 calories, 3 g protein, 7 g fat (including 1 g saturated fat), 1 mg cholesterol, 18 g carbohydrates, 1 g fiber, 111 mg sodium

HINT **helpful HINT** HINTHINTHINT

To make Sweet Potato Scones even healthier for your heart, substitute 2 egg whites for the whole egg. Use plain whole wheat flour in place of some or all of the white flour.

Using baking powder, canola oil and yogurt will help you produce soft, flaky scones. To make **the tops browner**, brush the scones with milk or oil before baking. To add more flavor, include 2 tablespoons of finely chopped ham, chives or **mild chili peppers** in the batter. Scones freeze well so it's worth making a double batch and storing some for later.

fresh ideas

Quick breads such as Cranberry-Walnut Pumpkin Bread make welcome gifts. They're called **quick breads** because they don't contain yeast, so no rising time is required. This means you can prepare a loaf for the oven in minutes.

cranberry-walnut pumpkin bread

Walnuts and walnut oil contain "good fats" that help keep your arteries clear and your heart healthy.

Makes 1 loaf (about 16 slices)   MAKE AHEAD
Preparation 15 minutes   **Cooking** 45 minutes

1¼ cups all-purpose flour
1 teaspoon ground ginger
1 teaspoon cinnamon
¾ teaspoon baking soda
¼ teaspoon salt
1 cup canned puréed pumpkin
⅔ cup packed dark brown sugar
¼ cup walnut oil or canola oil
2 large eggs, lightly beaten
1 teaspoon vanilla extract
½ cup walnuts, coarsely chopped
½ cup sweet dried cranberries

1 Preheat oven to 350°F (180°C). Lightly coat a 9 x 5 inch (23 x 13 cm) loaf pan with non-stick cooking spray.

2 Sift together flour, ginger, cinnamon, baking soda and salt in a medium bowl. Stir pumpkin, sugar, oil, eggs and vanilla extract until smooth in another medium bowl. Stir into flour mixture just until evenly moistened. Add the walnuts and cranberries. Spoon into prepared pan.

3 Bake until a toothpick inserted in the center comes out clean, or about 45 minutes. Turn out onto a wire rack to cool.

per slice 225 calories, 5 g protein, 10 g fat (including 0 g saturated fat), 40 mg cholesterol, 34 g carbohydrates, 2 g fiber, 161 mg sodium

HINT helpful HINT HINTHINTHINT

Scones are traditionally made with butter, sugar, eggs and cream. In Carrot-Ginger Scones, the eggs are omitted and buttermilk stands in for cream to cut back on the saturated fat content.

carrot-ginger scones

The classic scone gets a beta-carotene boost from grated carrot.

Makes 8 scones   **Preparation** 15 minutes   MAKE AHEAD
Cooking 20 minutes

1½ cups all-purpose flour
¼ cup plus 2 teaspoons sugar
1½ teaspoons baking powder
½ teaspoon salt
¼ teaspoon baking soda
2 tablespoons crystallised ginger
6 tablespoons chilled butter,
    cut into small pieces
1 large carrot, peeled
½ cup low-fat buttermilk

1 Preheat oven to 400°F (200°C). Lightly coat a large baking tray with non-stick cooking spray.

2 Combine the flour, ¼ cup sugar, baking powder, salt and baking soda in a food processor. Pulse to combine. Add ginger and pulse until finely ground. Add butter and pulse until the mixture resembles coarse polenta. Transfer to a medium bowl.

3 Grate carrot in food processor. Add to flour mixture. Fold buttermilk into flour mixture just until evenly moistened.

4 Scrape dough onto a floured work surface. Knead briefly, just until dough holds together. Pat out to a 1 inch (2.5 cm)-thick round. Sprinkle top with remaining 2 tsp sugar.

5 Cut dough into 8 equal wedges. Arrange 1 inch (2.5 cm) apart on the prepared baking tray. Bake until golden, or 18 to 20 minutes. Transfer to a wire rack to cool.

per scone 203 calories, 3 g protein, 9 g fat (including 5 g saturated fat), 24 mg cholesterol, 28 g carbohydrates, 1 g fiber, 278 mg sodium

carrot-flecked corn bread

Grated carrots transform an ordinary quick bread into a nutritious superfood.

Makes 9 squares   Preparation 10 minutes   HEART HEALTHY
Cooking 25 minutes

2 tablespoons canola oil
1²/₃ cups instant polenta
¹/₃ cup all-purpose flour
2 teaspoons baking powder
1 teaspoon baking soda
2 tablespoons sugar
1 teaspoon salt
1³/₄ cups low-fat buttermilk
1 large egg, lightly beaten
2 medium carrots, peeled and finely shredded

1 Preheat oven to 400°F (200°C). Swirl oil in a 8 x 8 x 2 inch (20 x 20 x 5 cm) baking pan. Preheat pan in oven for 5 minutes.

2 Combine the polenta, flour, baking powder, baking soda, sugar and salt in a large bowl. Stir in the buttermilk, egg and carrot. Carefully pour in oil from baking pan. Mix well. Pour batter into hot pan.

3 Bake until a toothpick inserted in the center comes out clean, about 25 minutes. Let cool in pan 10 minutes. Turn out onto a wire rack and cool slightly before cutting. Serve warm.

per square 202 calories, 6 g protein, 5 g fat (including 1 g saturated fat), 26 mg cholesterol, 34 g carbohydrates, 3 g fiber, 550 mg sodium

DID YOU KNOW

...buttermilk is produced by adding live cultures to low-fat milk? This thickens the milk and gives it a pleasantly creamy, tangy flavor. Buttermilk is a useful ingredient in baking, particularly in scones and muffins.

red pepper & chili pepper spoon bread

Whether it's fresh, frozen or canned, corn contributes powerful antioxidants that help fight age-related blindness.

Serves 6   Preparation 20 minutes   HEART HEALTHY
Cooking 55 minutes

1 cup instant polenta
1 cup low-fat (1%) milk
1 teaspoon salt
1 tablespoon butter
3¹/₂ oz (100 g) drained, pickled green chili peppers
1 medium red pepper, seeded and cut into small chunks
1 cup corn kernels, either fresh, canned and drained, or frozen and thawed
3 large eggs, separated

1 Preheat oven to 375°F (190°C). Coat a medium round casserole dish with canola oil.

2 In a small saucepan, bring 1¹/₂ cups water and the polenta to the boil. Lower heat. Simmer, stirring frequently, for 3 minutes. Transfer to a medium bowl. Place milk, salt, butter, chili peppers, red pepper and corn in the pan, then heat until butter melts. When cool, stir in lightly beaten egg yolks.

3 Beat egg whites in a medium bowl until stiff peaks form. Fold into polenta mixture. Pour into prepared casserole.

4 Bake until center is firm and top is browned, or 50 minutes. Serve right away.

per serving 183 calories, 7 g protein, 5 g fat (including 2 g saturated fat), 113 mg cholesterol, 27 g carbohydrates, 3 g fiber, 474 mg sodium

whole wheat pumpkin rolls with honey

The whole wheat flour and pumpkin purée add antioxidant vitamins and fiber to these rolls.

Makes 24 rolls Preparation 30 minutes
Rising about 2 hours 30 minutes
Cooking 12 minutes

MAKE AHEAD
HEART HEALTHY

1 envelope active dry yeast
½ cup lukewarm water
¼ cup honey
15 oz (540 mL) can puréed unsweetened pumpkin
2 tablespoons olive oil
4¼ cups all-purpose flour
1 cup whole wheat flour
2 teaspoons salt
1½ cups unsalted, shelled pumpkin seeds, lightly toasted

1 Sprinkle yeast over lukewarm water in a large bowl. Leave until foamy, about 5 minutes. Add honey and stir until it dissolves. Stir in pumpkin and oil. Stir in all-purpose flour, whole wheat flour and salt to form a dough.

2 Place dough on a lightly floured work surface. Knead until smooth and elastic, or about 10 minutes, adding more flour as needed to prevent sticking. Work in pumpkin seeds. Place dough in a lightly oiled bowl. Turn to coat. Cover loosely with plastic wrap. Leave to rise in a warm place until doubled in volume, or about 1 hour 30 minutes.

3 Line 2 baking trays with aluminium foil. Punch the dough down. Form dough into 24 equal-sized rolls. Place on prepared baking trays. Cover loosely with plastic wrap. Leave to rise in a warm place until doubled in volume, about 1 hour.

4 Preheat oven to 400°F (200°C). Uncover rolls. Bake until puffed and golden and rolls sound hollow when tapped on their bottoms, or about 12 minutes. Serve warm.

per roll 177 calories, 6 g protein, 6 g fat (including 1 g saturated fat), 0 mg cholesterol, 27 g carbohydrates, 2 g fiber, 197 mg sodium

fresh ideas

Save the seeds from your Halloween jack-o'-lantern. Let them dry for a day, clean off the fibers and spread the seeds on a baking sheet. Spray with non-fat cooking spray and sprinkle with salt and pepper or your favorite herbs. Bake in a 350°F (180°C) oven until toasted—about 20 minutes—and enjoy a great fall snack.

whole wheat winter loaf

The wheat germ and bran in whole wheat flour supply significant amounts of vitamin E and fiber that are lost in processing white flour.

Makes 2 loaves (about 12 slices each)
Preparation 25 minutes
Rising about 1 hour 50 minutes   Cooking 30 minutes

MAKE AHEAD
HEART HEALTHY

3½ cups whole wheat flour
3 cups all-purpose flour
2 tablespoons active dry yeast
⅔ cup low-fat (1%) milk
½ cup water
½ cup honey
2 teaspoons salt
2 large eggs, lightly beaten
1½ cups cooked, puréed pumpkin
2 tablespoons olive oil
2 bunches scallions, coarsely chopped
    (about 1½ cups)
2 tablespoons chopped rosemary
1 cup unsalted, shelled sunflower seeds

1 Combine the flours in a large bowl. Place 3 cups flour mixture in another large bowl with yeast.

2 Heat milk, water and honey in a medium saucepan until warm. Stir into flour-yeast mixture. Add salt and eggs. Beat with electric beaters on low speed for 30 seconds, scraping down side of bowl constantly. Beat on high speed 3 minutes.

3 Add pumpkin, oil, scallions, rosemary, sunflower seeds and remaining flour mixture, beating until well combined.

4 Place dough on a lightly floured work surface. Knead until smooth and elastic, or 6 to 8 minutes, adding more all-purpose flour as needed to prevent sticking. Shape dough into a ball. Place in a lightly oiled bowl, turn to coat and cover loosely with plastic wrap. Leave dough to rise in a warm place until doubled in volume, or about 1 hour.

5 Punch dough down. Turn out onto lightly oiled surface. Divide in half. Leave to rest for 10 minutes.

6 Lightly oil two 9 x 5 inch (23 x 13 cm) loaf pans. Pat each half of the dough into a loaf shape. Place in loaf pans and cover loosely with plastic wrap. Let rise in a warm place until almost doubled in volume, or about 50 minutes.

7 Preheat oven to 375°F (190°C). Bake until the loaves sound hollow when tapped, about 30 minutes. Turn onto a wire rack to cool.

per slice 150 calories, 5 g protein, 4 g fat (including 1 g saturated fat), 14 mg cholesterol, 26 g carbohydrates, 3 g fiber, 155 mg sodium

HINT helpful HINT HINTHINTHINT

Store all-purpose flour in a tightly covered container in a cool room for up to six months. Whole-grain flours can turn rancid more quickly. Store them in the fridge for up to six months or the freezer for up to a year. Bring chilled flour to room temperature before using in baked goods.

potato bread with poppy seeds

Poppy seeds give an attractive finish to the crust of this loaf. The potato provides plenty of potassium and vitamins C and B$_6$.

Makes 1 loaf (about 12 slices)
Preparation 25 minutes
Rising about 2 hours   Cooking 45 minutes

MAKE AHEAD
HEART HEALTHY

3 tablespoons sugar
¼ cup lukewarm water
1 envelope active dry yeast
1 cup cooked, mashed potato
1 cup low-fat (1%) milk
2 tablespoons butter
1½ teaspoons salt
4 cups all-purpose flour
1 large egg beaten with 1 tablespoon milk, for glaze
2 teaspoons poppy seeds

1 Stir 1 tbsp sugar into lukewarm water in a small bowl. Sprinkle the yeast over the top. Leave until foamy, or about 5 minutes. Stir to dissolve yeast.

2 Stir potato, milk, remaining sugar, butter and salt in a small saucepan. Heat to warm the mixture and melt butter. Using a rubber spatula, push mixture through a sieve into a large bowl to remove any lumps in the potato. Stir in yeast mixture and 3 cups of flour to form a dough.

3 Sprinkle remaining flour on work surface. Turn out dough and knead, working in flour, until smooth and elastic, or about 10 minutes. Add more flour as needed to prevent sticking. Place dough in a lightly oiled bowl, turn to coat and cover loosely with plastic wrap. Leave to rise in a warm place until doubled in volume, or about 1 hour 15 minutes.

4 Lightly oil a 9 x 5 inch (23 x 13 cm) loaf pan. Punch dough down. Knead briefly. Press into loaf pan and cover loosely with plastic wrap. Leave to rise in a warm place until doubled in volume, or about 45 minutes.

5 Heat oven to 350°F (180°C). Brush top of loaf with glaze. Sprinkle with poppy seeds. Using a serrated knife, cut a half-inch (1 cm)-deep slit lengthwise down the middle of the loaf.

6 Bake until browned and loaf has pulled away slightly from edges of pan, or 40 to 45 minutes. Turn out onto a wire rack. Cool for at least 1 hour before slicing.

per slice 164 calories, 5 g protein, 3 g fat (including 1 g saturated fat), 19 mg cholesterol, 30 g carbohydrates, 1 g fiber, 265 mg sodium

tomato-rye bread with rosemary & garlic

The red pigment in tomato juice gives this bread its sunny color.

Makes 1 loaf (about 12 slices)
Preparation 30 minutes
Rising about 2 hours   Cooking 50 minutes

MAKE AHEAD
HEART HEALTHY

½ cup tomato juice
1 tablespoon olive oil
1 teaspoon salt
½ teaspoon dried rosemary
2 cloves garlic, crushed
1 envelope active dry yeast
½ cup lukewarm water
⅔ cup rye flour
2 cups all-purpose flour
⅓ cup finely chopped sun-dried tomatoes
   (not oil-packed)

1 Bring tomato juice, ½ cup water, oil, salt, rosemary and garlic to a simmer in a small saucepan. Transfer to a medium bowl. Cool until lukewarm.

2 Sprinkle yeast over lukewarm water in a small bowl. Leave until foamy, or 5 minutes. Stir to dissolve.

3 Add yeast mixture to tomato juice mixture. Gradually stir in rye flour. Gradually knead in all-purpose flour until dough comes together and is workable (dough will still be sticky). Knead in sun-dried tomatoes. Turn dough out onto a floured work surface. Knead for 1 minute, then let rest for 10 minutes.

4 Knead dough again on lightly floured surface until smooth and elastic, or about 10 minutes, adding more all-purpose flour as needed if dough is very sticky (dough should be slightly sticky). Place dough in a lightly oiled bowl. Turn to coat. Cover loosely with plastic wrap. Leave to rise in a warm place until doubled in volume, or about 1 hour.

5 Punch dough down. Lightly coat a 9 x 5 inch (23 x 13 cm) loaf pan with olive oil. Place dough in pan, patting it into the corners. Cover loosely with plastic wrap. Leave to rise in a warm place until doubled in volume (risen above top of pan), or about 1 hour.

6 Preheat oven to 375°F (190°C). Bake until the loaf sounds hollow when tapped on the bottom, or 40 to 50 minutes. Turn out onto a wire rack. Cool completely before slicing.

per slice 95 calories, 3 g protein, 1 g fat (including 0 g saturated fat), 0 mg cholesterol, 18 g carbohydrates, 2 g fiber, 196 mg sodium

onion bread sticks

Freshly sautéed onions add a zesty taste to frozen bread dough.

Makes 12 bread sticks
Preparation 20 minutes
Rising about 1 hour   Cooking 35 minutes

1 pound (500 g) premade pizza dough, thawed if frozen
2 tablespoons olive oil
2 medium onions, very thinly sliced
½ teaspoon coarse salt, such as sea salt
   or kosher salt

1 Lightly oil 2 large baking trays. Pat dough out on a lightly floured surface to make a 12 x 6 inch (30 x 15 cm) rectangle. Cut evenly into 12 bread sticks, each 6 inches (15 cm) long. Gently twist each stick. Place on baking trays and cover loosely with plastic wrap. Leave to rise in a warm place until doubled in volume, or about 1 hour.

2 Heat oil in a large non-stick frying pan over medium heat. Add onion. Sauté until soft and golden, or about 12 minutes.

3 Preheat oven to 400°F (200°C). Place an oven rack in the lowest position and one in the highest position.

4 Just before baking, distribute sautéed onions over surface of each bread stick, taking care not to deflate dough. Sprinkle each stick with salt.

5 Bake on the low rack for 15 minutes. Then move to the top rack. Bake until the onion is crisp and golden, or 5 to 8 minutes. Transfer to a wire rack to cool.

per bread stick 110 calories, 3 g protein, 3 g fat (including 0 g saturated fat), 0 mg cholesterol, 19 g carbohydrates, 1 g fiber, 258 mg sodium

focaccia with tomatoes & parsley

Focaccia is a flat bread similar to a pizza, but softer and thicker.

Serves 8   Preparation 25 minutes
Rising 1 hour 55 minutes
Cooking 40 minutes

2 teaspoons sugar
2 cups lukewarm water
1 envelope active dry yeast
⅓ cup chopped parsley
3½ tablespoons olive oil
1½ teaspoons salt
½ teaspoon dried sage
5 cups all-purpose flour
2 cloves garlic, crushed
3 medium tomatoes, thinly sliced
1 large yellow pepper, seeded and cut in thin strips
2 tablespoons grated parmesan cheese

1 Stir sugar into lukewarm water in a large bowl. Sprinkle yeast over the top. Leave until foamy, or about 5 minutes. Stir to dissolve yeast.

2 Reserve 2 tbsp parsley for top of bread. Stir the remaining parsley, 3 tbsp oil, salt and sage into yeast mixture. Add 2 cups flour; mix vigorously. Stir in 3 cups flour to make a stiff dough.

3 Lightly flour a work surface. Knead dough until smooth and elastic, or about 10 minutes, adding more flour as needed to prevent sticking. Place dough in a lightly oiled bowl. Turn to coat. Cover loosely with plastic wrap. Leave to rise in a warm place until doubled in volume, or about 1 hour 15 minutes.

4 Lightly oil a 17 x 11 inch (43 x 28 cm) jelly roll pan. Punch dough down. Knead briefly. Pat into a rectangle and place in pan. Cover dough loosely with plastic wrap. Leave to rise in a warm place until doubled in volume, or about 40 minutes.

5 Preheat oven to 400°F (200°C). Place oven rack in lowest position. Make dimples in dough with fingertips. Brush with remaining oil. Sprinkle with garlic and arrange tomato slices over the top. Top with pepper and Sprinkle with parmesan.

6 Bake on lowest rack until browned at the edges, or 35 to 40 minutes. Transfer to a wire rack. Sprinkle with reserved parsley. Leave to cool for at least 20 minutes.

per serving 395 calories, 11 g protein, 7 g fat (including 1 g saturated fat), 1 mg cholesterol, 71 g carbohydrates, 3 g fiber, 468 mg sodium

*Focaccia is delicious when used for sandwiches. Try slices of **mozzarella** and tomato. Pita bread and **lavash** are also versatile flatbreads. Fill pita pockets with salad greens and slices of cooked meat, and use lavash to make wraps.*

cakes, cookies & desserts

fresh ideas

Instead of a thick layer of icing, you can take this cake from tea party to dinner party by topping it generously with freshly whipped cream and a sprinkling of fresh raspberries or sliced strawberries..

secret-ingredient chocolate cake

Cocoa, flour, sugar and eggs are ingredients you'd expect to find in a cake. The surprise addition here is healthy tomato juice.

Serves 16 Preparation 20 minutes
Cooking 30 minutes

MAKE AHEAD

¾ cup tomato juice
¼ cup water
⅔ cup unsweetened cocoa powder
2¼ cups all-purpose flour
1 teaspoon baking soda
½ teaspoon baking powder
¼ teaspoon salt
1½ cups sugar
½ cup canola oil
3 large eggs
1½ teaspoons vanilla extract
1 oz (30 g) unsweetened chocolate
2 tablespoons low-fat (1%) milk
1 tablespoon unsweetened cocoa powder
½ cup light cream cheese
2½ cups icing (confectioner's) sugar, sifted
½ cup seedless raspberry jam

1 Preheat oven to 350°F (180°C). Coat two 9-inch (23 cm) round cake pans with non-stick cooking spray.

2 Bring the tomato juice and water to a boil in a small saucepan. Whisk in cocoa powder until completely dissolved. Remove from heat.

3 Stir together flour, baking soda, baking powder and salt in a medium bowl.

4 Beat sugar, oil, eggs and 1 tsp vanilla extract in a large bowl to combine. Beat in cocoa mixture. Beat in flour mixture just until evenly moistened. Divide batter between pans.

5 Bake until a skewer inserted in the center of each cake comes out clean, about 25 to 30 minutes. Transfer pans to a wire rack. Leave cakes to cool for 10 minutes. Turn cakes out onto rack. Allow to cool completely before icing.

6 For the icing, place the chocolate and milk in a medium microwave-safe bowl and microwave on high power 1 minute. Stir until smooth. Whisk in cocoa powder until smooth. Whisk in cream cheese and ½ tsp vanilla extract. Stir in icing (confectioner's) sugar until combined.

7 Place one cake layer on a serving plate. Spread with jam and about a third of the icing mixture. Place second layer on top. Spread the rest of the icing over top and side of cake.

per serving 359 calories, 6 g protein, 14 g fat (including 4 g saturated fat), 56 mg cholesterol, 56 g carbohydrates, 2 g fiber, 268 mg sodium

HINT helpful HINT HINTHINTHINT

For a square cake, use two 8 x 2-inch (20 x 5 cm) square pans in place of the two 9-inch (23 cm) rounds. To make a single layer cake, substitute a 13 x 9 x 2-inch (33 x 23 x 5 cm) pan. Start checking that the cake is sufficiently well cooked about 10 minutes before the baking time recommended in the recipe given here.

For cakes with a lighter texture, separate the eggs before adding them. Add the yolks to the creamed sugar and oil (or butter) mixture. Beat the whites separately until stiff peaks form and gently fold into the batter.

To prevent cake layers from sticking to the wire racks while cooling, first spray the racks lightly with non-stick cooking spray.

whiskey-squash cake

This offers essential nutrients, including B vitamins, beta-carotene, vitamin C, iron and magnesium.

Serves 16   Preparation 15 minutes   Cooking 50 minutes

MAKE AHEAD

2 cups all-purpose flour
2 teaspoons baking powder
1 teaspoon baking soda
1 teaspoon salt
2 teaspoons cinnamon
1½ cups granulated sugar
1 cup canola oil
4 large eggs
1¾ cups cooked, mashed butternut squash
¼ cup whiskey
icing (confectioner's) sugar, for dusting *(optional)*

1 Preheat oven to 350°F (180°C). Coat a 10-cup fluted ring pan with non-stick cooking spray.

2 Stir flour, baking powder, baking soda, salt and cinnamon in a small bowl.

3 Beat sugar, oil, eggs and squash in a large bowl until well combined. Beat in flour mixture until evenly moistened. Beat in whiskey. Using a rubber spatula, scrape batter into pan.

4 Bake until a skewer inserted in the cake comes out clean, 45 to 50 minutes. Transfer pan to a wire rack. Leave cake to cool in pan for 15 minutes. Run a thin-bladed knife around the edge and center ring of the pan. Turn out cake onto rack and leave to cool completely. Dust with icing (confectioner's) sugar, if desired.

per serving 282 calories, 3 g protein, 15 g fat (including 1 g saturated fat), 63 mg cholesterol, 33 g carbohydrates, 1 g fiber, 289 mg sodium

carrot-pineapple cake

This is one of the sweetest ways to get your quota of vitamin A, with 80 percent of the daily requirement contained in each slice.

Serves 16   Preparation 20 minutes
Cooking 50 minutes

MAKE AHEAD

2½ cups all-purpose flour
2 teaspoons cinnamon
1 teaspoon baking powder
1½ teaspoons baking soda
½ teaspoon salt
1½ cups sugar
½ cup canola oil
4 large eggs
½ cup unsweetened applesauce
1 pound (500 g) carrots, peeled and grated (about 4 cups)
1 cup canned crushed pineapple in juice
½ cup seedless raisins
½ cup walnuts, chopped
1 cup light cream cheese, softened
4½ cups icing (confectioner's) sugar, sifted
1 teaspoon vanilla extract

1 Preheat oven to 350°F (180°C). Coat two 9-inch (23 cm) round cake pans with non-stick cooking spray.

2 Stir together flour, cinnamon, baking powder, baking soda and salt in a medium bowl.

3 Beat sugar, oil, eggs and applesauce in a large bowl until thoroughly combined. Beat in flour mixture just until evenly moistened. Stir in the carrot, pineapple and juice, raisins and walnuts. Divide batter between prepared pans.

4 Bake until a skewer inserted in the center of each cake comes out clean, 45 to 50 minutes. Transfer the pans to a wire rack. Leave to cool for 30 minutes. Turn cakes out onto racks. Leave to cool completely.

5 For the icing, beat cream cheese in a large bowl on low speed for 1 minute. Add icing (confectioner's) sugar and vanilla extract; beat just until smooth.

6 Place a cake layer on a serving plate. Spread with a third of the icing. Place second layer on top. Spread remaining icing over the top and side of cake.

per serving 479 calories, 8 g protein, 18 g fat (including 5 g saturated fat), 75 mg cholesterol, 75 g carbohydrates, 2 g fiber, 357 mg sodium

DID YOU KNOW

...that pineapple contains an enzyme called bromelian that is a natural meat and poultry tenderizer when it is added to marinades or stews? Bromelian is also an anti-inflammatory and may reduce the risk of blood clots.

pumpkin tartlets

These nutritious little tarts not only taste great; they look attractive, too.

Makes 8 tartlets   Preparation 35 minutes
Cooking 25 minutes

1 tablespoon canola oil
1 tablespoon butter
3 medium eggs
1 cup light evaporated milk
¼ cup brown sugar
¼ cup shredded coconut
grated zest and juice of 1 orange
½ teaspoon each ground cinnamon,
    ground ginger and grated nutmeg
15-oz (540 mL) can unsweetened puréed pumpkin
4 sheets phyllo pastry (20 x 11 inches/44 x 28.5 cm each)
24 blackberries
icing (confectioner's) sugar, for dusting

1 Preheat oven to 375°F (190°C). Warm the oil and butter in a small saucepan until the butter melts. Use a little of the mixture to grease 8 individual 3-inch (7 cm) tart pans.

2 Whisk the eggs, evaporated milk, brown sugar, coconut, orange zest and juice and the spices in a large bowl until well combined. Stir in the puréed pumpkin.

3 Cut phyllo pastry into even squares, 8 from each sheet (32 in total). Layer 4 squares into each of the 8 pans, brushing each layer with oil and butter mixture. To create a petal effect, layer squares at angles to one another. Spoon pumpkin mixture into the center of each tartlet.

4 Bake tartlets until filling is set, 20 to 25 minutes. Transfer the pans to a wire rack; cool tartlets briefly. Just before serving, top with blackberries and a light dusting of icing sugar.

per tartlet 170 calories, 5 g protein, 6 g fat (including 3 g saturated fat),
75 mg cholesterol, 26 g carbohydrates, 6 g fiber, 170 mg sodium

no-bake pumpkin pie with gingersnap crust

This is a quick-fix dessert that's packed with beta-carotene and fiber.

Serves 8   Preparation 10 minutes   MAKE AHEAD
Refrigerate 5 hours

2 cups fine gingersnap crumbs
¼ cup butter, melted
2 packages (3¼ oz/100 g each) instant vanilla
    pudding mix
1½ cups milk
15-oz (540 mL) can unsweetened puréed pumpkin
1¼ teaspoons cinnamon
¾ teaspoon ground ginger
¼ teaspoon ground nutmeg
pecan halves, for garnish *(optional)*

1 Stir gingersnap crumbs and the melted butter in a small saucepan until the crumbs are evenly coated. Lightly pat over bottom and up sides of a 9-inch (23 cm) pie pan.

2 Whisk pudding mixes and milk in a medium bowl until thick and blended. Stir in pumpkin purée, cinnamon, ginger and nutmeg. Spread evenly over gingersnap crust. Garnish top with pecan halves, if using. Cover and refrigerate for at least 5 hours or overnight.

per serving 335 calories, 5 g protein, 13 g fat (including 6 g saturated fat),
22 mg cholesterol, 51 g carbohydrates, 3 g fiber, 456 mg sodium

HINT **helpful HINT** HINTHINTHINT

Instead of a whisk, you can use a food processor or blender to combine the filling ingredients for this pie. Short on time? Make the pie even more quickly by using a store-bought, prepared crust.

sweet & spicy carrot pie with nut crust

Nuts add healthy fats and rich flavor to a crust in which most of the butter has been replaced by canola oil.

Serves 8   Preparation 20 minutes
Cooking 1 hour 10 minutes

MAKE AHEAD

½ cup walnuts, lightly toasted
½ cup hazelnuts, lightly toasted
1 cup graham cracker crumbs
¼ cup packed brown sugar
1¼ teaspoons cinnamon
1¼ teaspoons ground ginger
3 tablespoons canola oil or light olive oil
2 tablespoons butter, melted
1 pound (500 g) carrots, peeled and cut into chunks
1 cup granulated sugar
1 tablespoon all-purpose flour
½ teaspoon salt
¼ teaspoon ground nutmeg
pinch of cloves
4 large eggs, lightly beaten
¾ cup milk

1 For the crust, combine walnuts and hazelnuts in a food processor. Pulse until coarsely chopped. Add cracker crumbs, brown sugar, ¼ tsp cinnamon and ¼ tsp ground ginger. Pulse two or three times to combine. Add the oil and melted butter.

Pulse until crumbs are evenly moistened. Press crumb mixture over bottom and side of a 9-inch (23 cm) deep-dish pie plate.

2 Place carrots in a large pot of lightly salted boiling water to cover; cook until tender, about 20 minutes. Drain well. Purée in a food processor. Leave to cool slightly.

3 Preheat oven to 400°F (200°C). Stir sugar, flour, remaining ginger and cinnamon, salt, nutmeg and cloves in a small bowl. Add to carrot purée in food processor; process to combine. Add the eggs and milk; process until smooth and thoroughly blended. Pour mixture into crust.

4 Bake until a skewer inserted in the center of the pie comes out clean, about 45 minutes. Serve warm or cool to room temperature. Or, refrigerate for several hours.

per serving 415 calories, 8 g protein, 22 g fat (including 4 g saturated fat), 117 mg cholesterol, 51 g carbohydrates, 3 g fiber, 284 mg sodium

HINT helpful HINT HINTHINTHINT

Just as with cheesecakes, custard-type pies made with eggs and milk may develop a crack across the top during baking or cooling. This is often due to excessive moisture loss and has no effect on taste. To minimize cracks, try placing a shallow pan of hot water on the bottom shelf of the oven to keep the moisture levels up.

sweet potato pie with cranberry-pecan marmalade

A fresh cranberry and nut layer lightens the texture of this classic dessert and adds a special blend of antioxidants. Cranberries provide fiber along with some vitamin C.

Serves 8   Preparation 20 minutes
Cooking 1 hour   MAKE AHEAD

6 oz (175 g) whole cranberries, fresh or frozen
½ cup plus ⅔ cup sugar
½ cup water
¾ cup pecans, toasted and chopped
premade pie pastry for a single-crust pie
2 cups cooked, mashed orange sweet potatoes
12 oz (375 mL) can light evaporated milk
1 large egg, lightly beaten
2 large egg whites, lightly beaten
½ teaspoon vanilla extract
½ teaspoon cinnamon
¼ teaspoon ground nutmeg
¼ teaspoon ground allspice
pinch of salt

1 For the cranberry-pecan marmalade, place the cranberries, ½ cup sugar and the water in a small saucepan. Bring to a boil. Reduce heat; simmer until the cranberries pop and are softened, about 10 minutes. Remove from heat. Stir in pecans. Leave mixture to cool.

2 Preheat oven to 425°F (220°C). Roll out pastry to a 12-inch (30 cm) circle. Fit into a 10-inch (25 cm) pie plate. Crimp edges.

3 Thoroughly combine the mashed sweet potato, evaporated milk, ⅔ cup sugar, egg, egg whites, vanilla extract, cinnamon, nutmeg, allspice and salt in a large bowl.

4 Spread cooled marmalade over bottom of pie shell. Pour the potato mixture on top.

5 Bake for 10 minutes. Lower temperature to 350°F (180°C). Bake until the center is set, about 40 minutes. Transfer pie to a wire rack. Cool for 30 minutes. Refrigerate to cool completely.

per serving 455 calories, 8 g protein, 16 g fat (including 4 g saturated fat), 33 mg cholesterol, 72 g carbohydrates, 4 g fiber, 218 mg sodium

fresh ideas

If whole cranberries are unavailable, substitute 1½ cups (about 400 g) whole-berry cranberry sauce. Heat gently, just to soften. Stir in pecans and cool mixture before using.

on the menu

Sweet quick breads keep well if they are stored in a cool place in an airtight container. However, if they become a little dry, try lightly toasting slices and spreading them with butter or fruit preserve.

carrot-zucchini sweet quick bread

You'll get A, B and C vitamins from the vegetables, omega-3 fatty acids from the walnuts, plus fiber from the wheat bran in the whole wheat flour.

Makes 12 slices **Preparation** 15 minutes **MAKE AHEAD**
Cooking 1 hour

1½ cups all-purpose flour
½ cup whole wheat flour
1¼ teaspoons baking soda
1 teaspoon baking powder
1 teaspoon cinnamon
½ teaspoon salt
¼ teaspoon nutmeg
1¼ cups sugar
¾ cup canola oil
3 large eggs
1 teaspoon vanilla extract
2 cups grated carrots, blotted dry
2 cups grated zucchini, blotted dry
½ cup walnuts, chopped (optional)
½ cup icing (confectioner's) sugar
1½ tablespoons orange juice
1¼ teaspoons grated orange zest

1 Preheat oven to 350°F (180°C). Coat a 9 x 5-inch (23 x 13 cm) loaf pan with non-stick cooking spray and dust with flour.

2 Mix both flours, baking soda, baking powder, cinnamon, salt and nutmeg in a medium bowl.

3 Beat sugar, oil, eggs and vanilla extract in a large bowl until well blended. Stir in carrot and zucchini. Beat in flour mixture just until evenly moistened. Stir in walnuts, if using. Spread batter in prepared pan.

4 Bake until a skewer inserted in the center comes out clean, 55 to 60 minutes. Transfer pan to a wire rack. Leave cake to cool for 10 minutes. Loosen edges of loaf with a thin-bladed knife. Turn bread onto a rack. Cool completely before glazing.

5 Mix the icing (confectioner's) sugar, orange juice and zest in a small bowl. Add another 1 to 2 tsp orange juice to thin, if necessary. Pour half the glaze over the cooled bread, spreading it evenly. Leave to set for 5 minutes. Pour on remaining glaze.

per slice 325 calories, 4 g protein, 16 g fat (including 1 g saturated fat), 53 mg cholesterol, 43 g carbohydrates, 2 g fiber, 280 mg sodium

coconut-topped sweet potato pudding

Here's a dessert well worth adding to the repertoire: it's loaded with beta-carotene.

Serves 10 **Preparation** 15 minutes **MAKE AHEAD**
Cooking 2 hours **HEART HEALTHY**

2 medium orange sweet potatoes, peeled and grated
12 oz (375 mL) can light evaporated milk
2 tablespoons canola oil
½ cup packed brown sugar
2 tablespoons orange juice concentrate
½ teaspoon ground ginger
½ teaspoon ground cloves
½ teaspoon ground allspice
½ teaspoon salt
1 large egg, lightly beaten
4 large egg whites, lightly beaten
½ cup shredded coconut

1 Preheat oven to 350°F (180°C). Coat an 8-cup (2 L) baking dish with non-stick cooking spray.

2 Mix together sweet potato, evaporated milk, oil, brown sugar, orange juice concentrate, ginger, cloves, allspice, salt, egg and egg whites in a large bowl. Pour into the baking dish. Cover dish with aluminum foil.

3 Bake for 1 hour 30 minutes. Sprinkle with coconut. Bake, uncovered, until the center is set and coconut turns golden, about 30 minutes.

per serving 167 calories, 6 g protein, 5 g fat (including 3 g saturated fat), 72 mg cholesterol, 24 g carbohydrates, 1 g fiber, 220 mg sodium

homemade pumpkin spice ice-cream

For fiber and protective antioxidant vitamins along with a lovely fresh flavor and creamy texture, this ice cream is hard to beat.

Serves 6 (makes 3 cups)
Preparation 20 minutes

MAKE AHEAD
HEART HEALTHY

1¼ cups light evaporated milk
1 large egg
½ cup packed brown sugar
⅔ cup canned unsweetened puréed pumpkin
1 teaspoon vanilla extract
½ teaspoon ground ginger
½ teaspoon cinnamon
large pinch of ground nutmeg
pinch of salt

1 Bring evaporated milk to a boil in a medium saucepan.

2 Whisk egg and sugar in a large bowl. Gradually whisk in boiling milk. Stir in pumpkin, vanilla extract, ginger, cinnamon, nutmeg and salt. Refrigerate until well chilled.

3 Freeze in an ice cream maker, following manufacturer's instructions. Soften slightly before serving.

per ½ cup 141 calories, 5 g protein, 2 g fat (including 1 g saturated fat),
40 mg cholesterol, 26 g carbohydrates, 1 g fiber, 102 mg sodium

fresh ideas

Dress up your ice cream with chopped apricots, chopped toasted walnuts or a dash of maple syrup.

soft pumpkin cookies

These pumpkin cookies are packed with beta-carotene and fiber.

Makes 24 cookies
Preparation 15 minutes
Cooking 15 minutes

MAKE AHEAD
HEART HEALTHY

½ cup all-purpose flour
½ cup whole wheat flour
½ teaspoon cinnamon
¼ teaspoon salt
¼ teaspoon baking soda
¼ teaspoon ground allspice
¼ cup packed brown sugar
3 tablespoons honey
¼ cup canola oil
1 large egg white
1 cup canned unsweetened puréed pumpkin
½ cup dried sweetened cranberries
    (craisins) or seedless raisins
⅓ cup walnuts, chopped *(optional)*

1 Preheat oven to 350°F (180°C). Coat two large baking trays with non-stick cooking spray. Sift flours, cinnamon, salt, baking soda and allspice into a medium bowl. Beat the brown sugar, honey, oil and egg white in a large bowl to combine. Stir in puréed pumpkin. Stir in flour mixture until evenly moistened. Fold in dried cranberries and the walnuts, if using.

2 Drop heaped teaspoons of cookie dough onto the baking tray, spacing them about 1 inch (2.5 cm) apart. Bake until a skewer or toothpick inserted in the center of a cookie comes out clean, about 15 minutes. Leave the cookies on the tray for 1 minute. Use a metal spatula to transfer them to a wire rack to cool. Store in an airtight container for up to 1 week.

per cookie 63 calories, 1 g protein, 2 g fat (including 0 g saturated fat),
0 mg cholesterol, 11 g carbohydrates, 1 g fiber, 17 mg sodium

oatmeal cookies

Oats help protect your heart by lowering cholesterol levels.

Makes **48** cookies
Preparation **20** minutes
Cooking **10 to 12** minutes

MAKE AHEAD
HEART HEALTHY

1 cup all-purpose flour
2½ teaspoons baking powder
½ teaspoon salt
½ teaspoon cinnamon
¼ teaspoon ground cloves
1 cup old-fashioned rolled oats
1 large egg
½ cup canola oil
1 teaspoon vanilla extract
1 cup packed brown sugar
1 cup grated carrots
¾ cup seedless raisins

1 Preheat oven to 375°F (190°C). Coat 2 large baking trays with non-stick cooking spray. Stir the flour, baking powder, salt, cinnamon and cloves in a medium bowl. Stir in the oats.

2 Beat egg, oil and vanilla extract in a large bowl. Beat in sugar. Beat in flour mixture in batches until evenly moistened. Fold in carrot and raisins to make a stiff dough.

3 Drop heaping teaspoons of dough onto the baking trays, spacing them about 2 inches (5 cm) apart.

4 Bake until golden brown and slightly darker at the edges, 10 to 12 minutes. Leave cookies on baking trays for 2 minutes. Use a metal spatula to transfer them to a wire rack to cool. Store in an airtight container for up to 1 week.

per cookie 64 calories, 1 g protein, 3 g fat (including 0 g saturated fat), 4 mg cholesterol, 10 g carbohydrates, 1 g fiber, 49 mg sodium

HINT **helpful HINT** HINTHINTHINT

To freeze the dough for drop cookies, dispense dough as directed on baking trays. Place trays in the freezer until dough is frozen solid. Transfer dough drops to a container. To bake, put frozen drops on prepared baking trays. Thaw at room temperature. Bake as directed in the recipe.

A-Z guide to
to vegetables
guide to vege
vegetables A-

A-Z guide to vegetables

artichokes

The giant flower bud of a bushy thistle plant, the globe artichoke is high in fiber. The edible parts are the heart, with its buttery, nutty flavor, and the earthy-tasting fleshy part at the base of the meaty outer leaves.

packed into 1 large steamed artichoke

About **60 calories** • high in **fiber** • **iron**, **copper** and **magnesium** and other essential minerals • 20% of the daily **vitamin C** requirement • 15% of the daily B vitamin **folate** requirement

at the market

Season Springtime is peak season for artichokes, but you'll also see them at the supermarket at other times throughout the fall and winter.

What to look for Spring artichokes should be a healthy green. Artichokes harvested in cooler weather are darker and may have bronze-tipped petals. Choose meaty-leafed globes that are heavy for their size.

in the kitchen

Storing Store unwashed and with stems intact in a sealed plastic bag in the refrigerator for up to two weeks.

Preparation Wash well under cold running water. Trimming techniques are shown at left.

Basic cooking To steam, place washed and trimmed whole artichokes in a nonreactive steamer over boiling water. Cover and cook until an outer leaf easily pulls out, about 30 minutes. Drain upside down in a colander before serving. Or boil in a large pot of lightly salted boiling water with a few drops of lemon juice for 30 to 40 minutes.

Best uses in recipes Artichokes are usually served with a dip as a first course. Hot artichokes are usually served with melted butter or hollandaise sauce. The healthier option is to sprinkle them with lemon juice and salt, Also, serve cold with a simple vinaigrette or a low-fat mayonnaise.

at the table

Eat artichokes with your fingers. Pluck a leaf from the side and dip the free end into sauce. Bite down on that end and pull the leaf through your teeth, scraping off all the pulp. To get to the heart, remove the outer leaves, then pull out the pale center petals and scrape off the choke (the fuzzy layer that sits on top of the heart).

fresh ideas

Classic dip Pluck the leaves from just-cooked artichokes and arrange on a serving platter. Stir equal parts of olive oil and melted butter and a few drops of lemon juice in a small bowl. Serve as a dip for the leaves.

Tofu dip Combine mashed roasted garlic, freshly ground black pepper, soft silken tofu and lemon juice.

Pasta and pizza Cooked artichoke hearts work well in a pasta sauce and as a pizza topping with fresh tomato sauce, salami and Parmesan.

getting ready

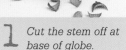

1 *Cut the stem off at base of globe.*

2 *Snip off sharp tips from petals with a pair of scissors.*

3 *Rub with lemon to stop discoloration.*

asparagus

A member of the lily family, asparagus is a springtime delicacy either lightly boiled or steamed. It is low in calories, high in fiber and contains vitamins C and E.

packed into one cup of asparagus

Less than **50 calories** • **thiamine** and other B vitamins necessary for energy metabolism • More than 25% of the daily requirement for **vitamin C** • a phytochemical called **glutathione**, which is one of the most potent antioxidants for fighting the cell destruction that leads to disease

at the market

Season Asparagus appears in Western markets as early as February with the first California crop. In the Midwest and East, the growing season lasts from May through July. Imported asparagus is sold in the fall and winter.

What to look for Asparagus should have firm round spears with tightly closed tips of deep green, purple or white. Purple spears are larger and less fibrous than green ones. It has a nutty flavor when cooked. White asparagus (grown shielded from sunlight) has a very delicate flavor, milder than either green or purple. Try to pick spears of uniform size to ensure even cooking.

in the kitchen

Storing Asparagus should be eaten as soon as possible after being picked. Stored at room temperature, it can, for example, lose half its vitamin C in two days. If you must keep it overnight, wrap the bottom ends in damp paper towels, cover it with plastic wrap, and put it in the refrigerator.

Preparation Wash carefully to get rid of any sand. Snap off and discard the tough ends *(right)*.

Basic cooking Asparagus can be cooked many different ways.
Steaming or boiling It takes about 3 to 5 minutes to cook asparagus either way. Do not overcook or spears will become soggy and limp. Remove from the pan when just crisp-tender; asparagus will continue to cook as it cools.
Microwaving Place spears, tips to the center, in a shallow microwaveable dish. Add ¼ cup water, cover tightly and cook at 100% power for 4 to 7 minutes.
Roasting Preheat the oven to 375°F (190°C). Lay the spears in a single layer in a shallow pan, sprinkle with olive oil and season with salt and pepper. Roast until spears are crisp-tender, about 20 minutes.
Barbecuing Brush spears with olive oil, sprinkle with salt and place cross-wise on the grill rack over a medium fire. Cook, turning often, until tender, 4 to 6 minutes. Sprinkle with pepper and lemon juice just before serving.

fresh ideas

To top it off Asparagus goes well with lemon or balsamic vinaigrette, mustard-mayonnaise, soy sauce and ginger, or grated Parmesan cheese.

Party nibbles Ham or prosciutto slices rolled around short spears of cold cooked asparagus – with or without a dab of mayonnaise.

Soup plus Leftover, cooked green asparagus can be puréed in a food processor and then gently heated with a little milk, chopped parsley and tarragon, and salt and pepper to taste to make asparagus soup.

trimming asparagus

1 Feel along the lower stalk for a natural breaking place – a divide between tough and more tender parts.

2 Snap off the end of the stalk. For a thick stem, peel the remaining part with a swivel-bladed peeler.

avocados

Healthy, unsaturated fats give this tropical fruit (it is not a vegetable) its creamy texture and nutty flavor. Called "midshipman's butter" by British seafaring crews over a century ago, avocados taste delicious simply mashed on toast. Avocados are used mostly in appetizers and salads.

packed into a quarter of an avocado

about **81 calories** • a significant amount of **vitamin E**, which slows the aging process and protects against cancer • **monounsaturated fats**, which help lower blood levels of LDL (bad) cholesterol • **lutein**, which protects against cancer and eye diseases • **folate** to help protect against heart disease • **glutathione**, an antioxidant that protects body cells from damage • **beta-sitosterol**, which helps block absorption of cholesterol in the intestine • **magnesium** to help with muscle function and energy metabolism • **potassium** to keep electrolytes in balance

at the market

Season Fresh avocados are available all year, because they don't start to ripen until they are cut from the tree. Farmers can wait months to harvest an avocado crop so that they always have fresh ones to go to market.

What to look for Variations in size, color and skin texture depend on the variety and where it is grown. No matter what type of avocado you buy, look for heavy fruit and avoid any that is bruised or has sunken spots in the skin. A ripe avocado will yield to gentle pressure from your hand.

in the kitchen

Storing If you buy an unripe avocado, it will ripen at room temperature over the course of a few days. To speed up the ripening process, place the avocado in a brown paper bag. Store at warm room temperature for a day or two or until the avocado yields to gentle pressure from your hand. You can ripen a cut avocado this way, too. The cut surface will eventually discolor but this can be delayed by coating the cut surface with lemon juice and then covering it with plastic wrap. Ripe avocados can be stored in the refrigerator for four or five days. Don't store unripe ones in the refrigerator because they will never ripen properly. If you find yourself with an excess of ripe avocados, peel and stone the fruit and purée it with a little lemon or lime juice to limit discoloration. You'll need about 2 teaspoons of juice for each avocado. Then pack the purée into a covered plastic container, label with the date and store in the freezer for up to four months.

fresh ideas

Use mashed avocado to bind a sandwich of sprouts and chopped vegetables, seasoned with salt and pepper and tucked neatly into a whole-wheat pita pocket.

For a creamy, tart salad dressing, mash an avocado with low-fat plain yogurt and add lime juice, salt and Tabasco to taste.

To make an avocado smoothie, purée the flesh of an avocado with milk, a touch of honey and a couple of ice cubes.

Avocado for dessert? Well, it *is* a fruit! Purée fresh avocado with some sugar or honey and lemon juice for an easy mousse. Top with toasted almonds.

The toothpick test
You can feel an avocado to see if it's ripe, but if you're still not sure, use a toothpick. Stick a pick into the stem end of the avocado, and if it moves in and out with ease, it's ripe and ready to eat.

Preparation To peel an avocado, first slice it into quarters *(right)* or halves lengthwise, cutting to the large center seed. You can twist the cut avocado to separate the halves. Remove the seed with a paring knife if it doesn't lift right out. If the avocado is ripe, use your fingers to peel back the skin *(right)*. Otherwise, use a paring knife. Always rub or sprinkle cut avocado with lime or lemon juice to prevent discoloration. This inevitable browning doesn't affect the flavor or nutritional value, but it does make the avocado look less appetizing. Cover mashed or puréed avocado with two layers of plastic wrap applied directly to the surface. The convenient belief that pressing the seed into mashed avocado will prevent browning is, unfortunately, not true.

Best uses in recipes Avocados are usually eaten raw. High heat causes them to turn bitter, so generally avocado should be added to hot dishes just at the end of cooking or after the heat has been turned off. Sliced or chopped avocado adds a richness to salads, wraps and sandwiches. Avocado is also a basis for many classic dishes such as avocado with crab or prawn salad, and avocado and grapefruit salad with a honey-mustard dressing.

Best recipe Mashed avocado is traditionally used as the basis of the Mexican dip **guacamole**, now enjoyed around the world as an easy-to-make, light, nutritious starter. To make guacamole, you will need 2 ripe avocados (preferably Hass), halved and pitted; 1 large tomato, peeled, cored, seeded and coarsely chopped; ½ cup finely chopped red onion; ⅓ cup chopped cilantro leaves; 3 tablespoons lime juice; ¾ teaspoon ground cumin; ¾ teaspoon salt and ¾ teaspoon Tabasco. Scoop the avocado flesh into a bowl and mash it with a fork until the texture is almost smooth. Add all the remaining ingredients and stir gently to combine. Cover with a double layer of plastic wrap; place in the refrigerator until ready to use. Guacamole is usually served with tortilla chips for scooping, but a healthier option is to serve it with sliced raw vegetables, such as carrot, celery and pepper.

varieties

Avocados were first grown in the United States in the mid-1800s in both California and Florida. These two states still have the world's largest avocado production. Between them the states raise twenty-odd varieties of avocado, which seem to depend on their specific growing conditions for their identities because the various species don't transplant well to other locations.

Almost 90% of U.S. avocados are grown in California. The state's most abundant variety is Hass, a medium-sized avocado that has a pebbly skin that turns from green to a purplish black as it ripens. More California varieties include Bacon, Fuerte and Zutano.

Florida raises larger and less expensive avocados than California that, ironically, contain about half the fat and two-thirds the calories. The texture of Florida avocados is, therefore, less creamy. Also, Florida avocados don't keep as well. Among the most popular Florida avocado varieties are Booth, Lula and Waldin.

cutting up an avocado

1 Using a sharp knife, cut out a quarter of the avocado.

2 Pull off the skin with your fingers; it is easily removed if the avocado is sufficiently ripe.

3 Slice the flesh with a paring knife. Sprinkle with lemon juice to stop the fruit from quickly discoloring.

fresh ideas

Cooked beans can be jazzed up with various seasonings and other ingredients. Before adding them, toss cooked beans in a hot frying pan to rid them of moisture. This way, the beans will better absorb the additional flavors.

To make garlic oil, mix 2 tbsp olive oil per 500 g beans with 2 cloves finely chopped garlic. Heat until just beginning to sizzle. Add beans and cook, tossing, until heated through. Season with salt and pepper.

To make lemon butter, toss 500 g cooked beans with 1½ tbsp melted butter in a hot frying pan. Sprinkle lightly to taste with fresh lemon juice, salt and pepper.

To add toasted almonds, lightly brown slivered almonds in peanut oil or butter. Mix with the cooked beans and season to taste.

Thinly slice prosciutto or ham and heat in a little olive oil or butter in a large frying pan. Add cooked beans and toss to mix.

Add Parmesan cheese after tossing beans in melted butter. Season with freshly ground black pepper.

beans

Depending on where you're from, the most familiar fresh bean is called a green bean, snap bean or string bean. This category also includes wax beans, Chinese yard-long beans and France's famous *haricots verts*.

packed into one cup of beans

about **35 calories** • **insoluble fiber**, which serves as a digestive aid and may help lower cholesterol • more than 30% of the daily requirement for **vitamin C** • phytochemicals called **saponins**, believed to stimulate the immune system • **folate**, important in pregnancy and for normal growth

at the market

Season Fresh green beans are a year-round staple in the supermarket produce section, but just-picked beans from a summer farm stand usually offer the very best flavor and texture. That's because fresh beans, like corn, will lose their crunchy sweetness during prolonged storage; the sooner they make it from field to table, the better.

What to look for Regardless of which variety you are shopping for, choose beans that snap rather than bend when folded over. The pods should be straight with a "peach fuzz" feel and no blemishes or brown spots. Limp beans will be tough and bland. Try to select slender beans of a uniform size to ensure even cooking.

in the kitchen

Storing Keep beans in the vegetable drawer of the refrigerator, loosely wrapped in plastic; and use as soon as possible.

Preparation To prepare fresh beans, snap or trim off the stem end; the fine point at the tip is edible so there's no reason to remove it. Beans can be left whole or cut to any length needed; they look good cut on the diagonal.

Basic cooking Steam or simmer beans for 3 to 10 minutes, depending on their thickness, until they're cooked but still retain a bit of crunch – take a test bite to determine this. Beans also cook well and retain their color in the microwave. Or, try blanching beans for 1 or 2 minutes in a large pan of lightly salted boiling water and then finishing them when needed by sautéing them in butter or olive oil just before serving. However you cook them, drain beans immediately. If you're planning to finish them later or use them chilled for a salad recipe, plunge the crisp-tender cooked beans into iced water to stop the cooking process and to retain their bright color; drain and pat dry before refrigerating or adding to other ingredients.

varieties

The beans that we eat fresh are not different species from the dried beans that are cooked for hours to make chili con carne and Boston baked beans. Fresh beans are edible pods that are picked at a different time in the plant's growth cycle. Green beans and wax beans, for example, are the immature pods of kidney beans. Here is a guide to some of the edible pods and beans.

borlotti or pinto beans are grown not for the pods but for the mature beans inside the pods. The beans are also sold in dried form.

chinese long beans These mild-tasting green beans are very long. They are related to black-eyed peas, but taste like other green beans when cooked. Often cut up for use in stir-fries, they are a staple of Chinese cooking. Although the beans can grow to as long as 30 inches (85 cm), they are at their best when they are half that size.

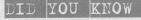

green beans range in length from about 4 to 8 inches (10 to 20 cm). Green beans are picked young when their carbohydrate content is present in the form of sugar. Hence, they are the sweetest of all the types.

italian green beans Recognizable for their broad flat shape and deep green color. These beans, also called "romano beans," are a specialty of Italian cuisine.

purple wax beans These exotic-looking beans with their deeply colored pods are the smaller cousins of yellow wax beans. They lose their hue during cooking, turning green and tasting like other wax beans.

yellow wax beans Color and nutrition separate wax beans from green beans, which they resemble in both size and flavor. Green beans, however, have eight times as much beta-carotene as the paler yellow beans.

Best uses in recipes Fresh green beans, sautéed in butter and seasoned with salt and pepper, make a refreshing accompaniment to almost any main dish. Any fresh bean, cut to a manageable length, is a good addition to a stir-fry or a hot pasta dish, adding texture and bulk. Cold cooked green beans add color and texture to potato and pasta salads.

-----

shell beans — lima, fava and soybeans (or edamame) — fall nutritionally between fresh green beans and dried beans that have developed high-protein and carbohydrate and low-vitamin counts. Used much like dried beans (except they don't need to be soaked), shell beans have protein, potassium, iron and vitamin C in different degrees. Lima beans, which indeed do come from Lima, Peru, are the most popular shell bean in North America. They provide high amounts of iron and potassium. Fava beans, or broad beans, are similar to lima beans, just a little larger and richer in folate and vitamin C. Both are used cold in salads and hot as a side dish alone or in soups or stews. Soybeans are a staple of Asian food markets. Fresh soybeans are unique among beans in having high amounts of complete protein. They also contain unsaturated fat. Soybeans have a mild flavor. Keep refrigerated and shell them right before you cook them.

beets

Ruby-red beets taste sweet because they contain more natural sugar than any other vegetable that we eat. They are, however, still low in calories, very low in fat and packed with important vitamins and minerals.

fresh ideas

Young beets up to 1¼ inches (3 cm) in diameter have tender, edible skin that doesn't require peeling. Baby beets also have the sweetest greens. The leaves and roots can be cooked separately and then served together. Steam the roots for about 15 minutes. Meanwhile, sauté the greens in olive oil and butter. Drain the beets. Cut them in half and sprinkle with salt and pepper. Place sautéed greens on a plate and top with the warm beets.

Sprinkle hot beets with lemon juice, salt and pepper and dot with little pieces of butter.

Serve hot or cold beets with a yogurt-horseradish sauce.

Team cooked beets, sliced and chilled, with orange segments, thin slices of red onion and a handful of toasted walnuts. Add vinaigrette.

DID YOU KNOW

...that betalains, the bright red pigments in beets, can be extracted for use as a natural food coloring and dye?

packed into a half-cup of cooked beets

about **37 calories** • **magnesium**, **potassium** and **vitamin C**, plus a significant amount of **folate**, which is important for growth and protein metabolism and reduces the risk of birth defects such as spina bifida

at the market

Season Beets are available all year long, but are at their best during the summer and early fall months, when baby beets are also available.

What to look for Choose beets with their tops on; those that have been clipped have most likely been in storage. The leafy tops should look fresh and the roots should be firm, smooth and unbruised. Pick uniform-sized beets up to 3 inches (7 cm) in diameter. If you shop at a specialty food market, you may also see golden beets. They can be cooked and used the same way as the red variety, but their roots and greens are milder in flavor.

in the kitchen

Storing First cut off the leafy tops, leaving an inch or two (about 3 cm) of the stem attached to the bulbous root. Leave the long, stringy root intact. Store the greens and beets in separate plastic bags in the vegetable drawer of your refrigerator. The greens should be used within a couple of days. The roots will keep for up to a couple of weeks.

Preparation Gently scrub beets under cold running water and dry on paper towels. Leave 1¼ inches or so (3 cm) of stem attached to the unpeeled root to prevent color (and nutrients) from bleeding out during cooking.

Basic cooking To preserve their color and nutrients, beets should not be peeled or cut before cooking. To retain the color and flavor, baking, microwaving and steaming are the best methods of cooking. To bake, wrap in aluminum foil, place in a baking tin, and cook in a preheated 350°F (180°C) oven for 1 hour 30 minutes to 2 hours. Leave to cool just until they can be handled for peeling. Serve hot or cool and refrigerate for salads.

Best uses in recipes Cooked beets are eaten hot as a side dish and cold in salads. They are used in a borscht, a soup which can be served hot or cold. They are also pickled. Raw grated beets add crunch to a salad.

broccoli

Super-high in fiber and vitamins and jam-packed with phytochemicals that help fight off disease, broccoli is one of the healthiest stars of the vegetable world.

packed into one cup of broccoli

Less than **25 calories** • more than a day's requirement for **vitamin C** • almost half a day's requirement for **vitamin A** • **folate** to fight birth defects • **calcium** to fight bone disease • **indoles** to fight cancer

at the market

Season Broccoli is at its best and most abundant in mid-fall through the winter.

What to look for Select dark green heads and leaves and bright green stems. The stalks holding the florets should be slender and crisp and the florets themselves tightly closed and uniformly green. Yellowed, flowering buds are a sign of old age and a toughness that longer cooking can't cure.

in the kitchen

Storing Keep in a plastic bag in the vegetable drawer of the refrigerator for three or four days.

Preparation Wash well. Peel tough skin from stalks with a swivel-bladed peeler or sharp paring knife, if desired. If cooking long spears with florets attached, slice spears lengthwise as far up as the florets. The leaves are full of vitamins and good flavor and can be cooked. Add to soups or stir-fries.

Basic cooking Short cooking time brings out the best flavor and color and helps prevent broccoli's valuable vitamins from leaching into the cooking water. It also prevents the breakdown of chemicals in broccoli that release strong-smelling sulfur compounds that smell like rotten eggs. Blanch, steam, sauté or stir-fry florets and chopped-up stems and leaves with a little added liquid for just 3 to 5 minutes.

Best uses in recipes Raw broccoli often features on vegetable platters for dips or in salads. Broccoli florets can be sautéed with olive oil and garlic, added at the beginning of a vegetable stir-fry, or steamed and topped with cheese sauce, white sauce or a squeeze of fresh lemon juice. Broccoli stems and leaves can be cooked in chicken stock as the base for a cream of broccoli soup: Purée the cooked broccoli, add milk or cream and season to taste with salt, pepper and a little oregano.

fresh ideas

Broccoli stalks, which many people discard, are tender and tasty parts of the plant that can be put to good use in cooking. Cut stalks into thin rounds and add to stir-fries. Blanch, steam or stir-fry broccoli stems. Or, grate them coarsely and serve raw in salads or slaws.

Purée cooked broccoli with a little chicken stock, some milk or cream, a pinch of dried marjoram and a seasoning of cayenne pepper and salt to make a quick, creamy soup.

cutting up broccoli

1 *Cut off stem and side shoots but don't discard. They're tender and delicious when cooked.*

2 *Remove individual florets for use in a stir-fry or include them in a raw vegetable platter for dips.*

broccoli rabe (rapini)

Not even a distant cousin of broccoli, rapini is a member of the turnip family. But its pleasantly peppery, bitter flavor is similar to that of broccoli and thereby comes its name.

packed into one cup of rapini

Less than **20 calories** • nearly a day's requirement for **vitamin C** • **indoles** to help fight cancer • **sulforaphane**, a phytochemical that helps fight cancer • 2.7 mg of **beta-carotene**

at the market

Season Rapini, also known as broccoli rape, broccoli raab or broccoli rabe, is a cool-weather plant that is at its best and most abundant from fall to midwinter. It is popular in southern Italy, where it grows wild, as well as under cultivation. It is used in Italian and Chinese cooking.

What to look for Rapini resembles broccoli but has thinner stems, smaller florets and more and bigger leaves. The stalks should be crisp and the florets themselves tightly closed. Stalks, florets and leaves should all be uniformly green and fresh-looking. Avoid limp stalks or discolored leaves.

in the kitchen

Storing Keep rapini, unwashed, in a plastic bag in the vegetable drawer of the refrigerator for three or four days at most.

Preparation Wash rapini well. Peel or remove tough lower stalks with a sharp paring knife. Stalks, florets and leaves are all edible.

Basic cooking Many cooks like to blanch rapini in a large pan of lightly salted boiling water for 2 to 3 minutes before using it in a recipe. This slakes its bitterness. Put the cooked vegetable into ice-cold water to stop the cooking process. Drain well and chop into manageable pieces. You can sauté the pieces in olive oil with a little garlic until tender, about 3 minutes. Season with salt, pepper and lemon juice as a side dish for meat or poultry. Or, braise in a little chicken or vegetable stock.

Best uses in recipes Rapini has been described as having stalks that taste like asparagus, florets that taste like broccoli and leaves that taste like mustard greens. It offers a nice sharp note to dishes like pasta sauces, omelettes, frittatas and polenta.

fresh ideas

Use cooked rapini with a little sautéed onion and bacon and a sprinkle of thyme (fresh or dried) to stuff mushroom caps for a hot hors d'oeuvre. Bake for 5 minutes before serving.

rapini gives a lift to white beans cooked with tomatoes. Add the cut-up vegetable for the final 15 minutes of cooking.

Sauté blanched, cut-up rapini with sultanas and pine nuts.

Cook pasta in the water that you have used to blanch rapini; this will intensify the flavor. Sauté finely chopped rapini in olive oil with garlic and other seasonings of your choice. Serve over the pasta.

DID YOU KNOW

...that rapini is a best-selling vegetable in the food markets of Hong Kong?

brussels sprouts

Thanks to generations of overcooking, brussels sprouts may be the most maligned vegetable in the world. Savvy cooks know, however, that these mini cabbages have a delicious, earthy flavor if treated well in the kitchen.

packed into a half-cup of brussels sprouts

30 calories • 80% the recommended daily requirement of **vitamin C** • the B vitamin **folate** • **fiber** • phytochemicals called **indoles** and **isothiocyanates**, which help protect against cancer

at the market

Season Brussels sprouts are autumn vegetables, usually not seen in markets until September or October.

What to look for Look for bright green, tightly packed leaves. Avoid any whose leaves have begun to yellow and unfurl or whose stem ends are dry and browned. A strong off-flavor and aroma develops with brussels sprouts that have been stored too long. If serving sprouts whole, choose ones roughly of uniform size so that they will cook evenly. Smaller sprouts generally have a milder, sweeter taste than larger ones.

in the kitchen

Storing Store unwashed in a paper bag in the refrigerator for two days.

Preparation Before cooking, proceed as shown *(right)*. Sprouts that are more than 1 inch (2.5 cm) thick are best halved or quartered to make them easier to cook and eat.

Basic cooking Boil, uncovered, in lightly salted water for 5 to 10 minutes, depending on thickness; they should be just tender enough to be pierced by a skewer. Avoid overcooking, which will render the sprouts mushy, pale and strongly flavored. Brussels sprouts can also be steamed or microwaved.

Best uses in recipes Thinly sliced sprouts can be used in stir-fries and sautés, more easily absorbing savoury sauces and dressings than whole ones. Brussels sprouts can be threaded on skewers, brushed with a little olive oil and barbecued until lightly charred and just tender.

fresh ideas

Pair brussels sprouts with one or several of the following: butter and lemon, caraway seeds, apple slices, crushed juniper berries, balsamic vinegar, dill, toasted walnuts, ham, cheddar cheese.

Loose leaves from brussels sprouts make a nutritious garnish for soups, stews, salads or any dish that could use a little color. Peel off the outer leaves and steam them over boiling water for about 3 minutes, or until they are crisp-tender.

to prepare brussels sprouts

1   *Trim stems and discard discolored or wilted outer leaves.*

2   *To bring heat to the center when cooking sprouts whole, score an X on the bottom of each one.*

cabbages

Now that more is known about the health benefits of this once-humble vegetable, cabbage has become a nutritional superstar. There are hundreds of different types.

-----

packed into one cup of raw cabbage

Less than **25 calories** • 3.5 g **fiber** • **sulforaphane**, **isothiocyanates** and **dithiolethiones**, all phytochemicals that have known disease-fighting capabilities • one-third or more of the daily requirement for **vitamin C** • phytochemicals called **indoles**, which help protect against breast, prostate and colon cancers • **anthocyanins** in red cabbage that fight inflammation

-----

at the market

Season Available all year, with peak season in mid-winter. Savoy cabbage is available throughout fall, winter and early spring.

What to look for When choosing red or green cabbage, select firm heads that are quite heavy for their size. Looser-leafed, elongated varieties such as Chinese or napa cabbage will also be heavy for their size. Choose heads with fresh-looking cores and no wilted leaves or yellowing. A 2-pound (1 kg) head serves four to six people for a side dish and makes about 10 cups of shredded cabbage.

in the kitchen

Storing All varieties of cabbage should be stored, unwashed, in a paper bag, in the vegetable drawer of the refrigerator. Green or red cabbages with tight heads will keep for up to two weeks; loose-leaf napa cabbage will keep for up to one week.

Preparation Remove and discard any damaged or wilted outer leaves and trim away any brown spots. Remove and discard tough outer leaves from the larger heads of cabbage. Rinse cabbage in cold water just before cooking. Use a knife, grater or food processor to shred heads of green or red cabbage. First, cut the head into quarters with a large, heavy knife. Then remove the core. You can then shred the cabbage by slicing it vertically, or using a hand-held grater or a food procesor with the grating disk attached.

Basic cooking Whatever the type of cabbage, always cook it very briefly and drain it well. Cabbage has a bad name simply because it has a history of being overcooked. The simplest technique for cooking all types of cabbage is to first slice or chop it and then steam it over boiling water until it is barely tender, about 5 minutes. Drain well. Just before serving,

fresh ideas

Use cabbage leaves as steamer wrappers. Sprinkle thick fish fillets with fresh herbs such as tarragon or dill, and wrap in cabbage leaves. Steam over stock to which more of the same herbs have been added. The whole parcel can be eaten.

Steam cabbage or bok choy leaves and wrap them around matchsticks of carrot and peppers. Serve the packets with a spicy dipping sauce.

Stir-fry sliced cabbage and onions and add to coarsely mashed potato. Use as a stuffing for chicken or turkey for roasting.

DID YOU KNOW

...that sauerkraut is simply pickled cabbage?

sauté in a little butter or olive oil to heat through, and season with salt and pepper.

Best uses in recipes Grated raw cabbage is used to make salads and slaws. Crisp cabbage leaves can be cut up and substituted in any recipe that calls for lettuce, including sandwiches. Whole raw cabbage leaves, especially savoy cabbage leaves, can be used in place of tortillas for a tasty, low-calorie wrap for sandwich fillings. Cooked cabbage is served as a side dish with meat, poultry and sausages. It is also used as a filling for small pastry cases, such as the Russian piroshki, and for dumplings. Cabbage is a useful ingredient in a wide variety of soups, stews, salads and stir-fries.

Best recipe One of the most popular and easy-to-make recipes for cabbage is **coleslaw**, a mixture of shredded cabbage, carrots and an almost sweet creamy dressing, traditionally made from mayonnaise, but increasingly made from sour cream and/or yogurt. In a medium bowl, whip 3 tablespoons low-fat, plain yogurt, 2 tablespoons sour cream, 1 teaspoon prepared mustard, ½ teaspoon sugar, ½ teaspoon cider vinegar, ¼ teaspoon celery seeds and a pinch each of salt and black pepper. For the salad, add 2 cups coarsely shredded cabbage and 2 coarsely grated carrots. Mix well, then refrigerate for 3 hours, tossing occasionally. Serves 4.

cutting up bok choy

1 Use a sharp knife to separate the leaves from the white base.

2 Chop the leaves evenly into 2-inch (5 cm) pieces.

3 Slice base into slivers along ribs, perpendicular to the base.

varieties

bok choy is a variety of Chinese cabbage; it is used extensively in Asian cooking. It does not form a head and looks more like a leafy green vegetable than a cabbage. It is richer in beta-carotene and calcium than green cabbage.

green cabbage is an all-purpose vegetable. It is the most common cabbage. The head is tight and has pale- to medium-green very crisp leaves.

napa cabbage is also called Chinese cabbage. It has long white ribs and tender, pale green leaves. Its relatively mild taste works well raw in salads as it does not dominate. It is also good cooked in soups and stir-fries.

red cabbage, with its distinctive purplish red leaves, can be teamed with sweet ingredients in soups such as borscht and sides such as sweet and sour cabbage with apples. It is much used in Central European cuisines.

savoy cabbage has tender, crinkled, pale green leaves. It has a milder flavor than that of green cabbage, with which it can be interchanged in recipes. It is used extensively in European cuisines.

carrots

If one vegetable gets top prize for nutritional value and versatility, it's the carrot. Recipes for them feature in cookbooks from just about every country in the world.

packed into a half-cup of cooked carrots

35 calories • almost twice the daily requirement for **vitamin A**, in the disease-fighting form of beta-carotene • a good supply of **vitamin B6** to maintain brain function • **fiber** to keep the digestive tract healthy

at the market

Season Available all year, but most abundant during winter and early spring.

What to look for Whether you buy them long and tapered or short and stubby, in bunches or in plastic bags, choose smooth, firm, evenly colored and evenly shaped carrots. Avoid carrots that are soft, withered, oversized or green around the shoulders. For carrots sold in bunches, look for ones with bright green, fresh-looking feathery tops. Small, slender carrots are usually the sweetest.

in the kitchen

Storing Discard the leafy green tops before storing carrots because they steal nutrients from the roots. Keep carrots, loosely wrapped, in the vegetable drawer of the refrigerator. Tiny, early carrots keep only a day or two, while large carrots keep for at least a week. Small, bagged carrots are usually good for a couple of weeks.

Preparation Many of a carrot's nutrients are concentrated just below the skin's surface. For this reason, scrub tender young carrots rather than peel them. Large not-so-young carrots may require peeling.

Basic cooking Carrots can be boiled, steamed, roasted, grilled and added to soups and stews. Raw carrot sticks and raw baby carrots are a nutritious snack. Grated carrots add color and nutrients to salads and sweets. Sliced carrots can be steamed, stir-fried or roasted to serve with or without other vegetables as a side dish. Turn freshly cooked carrots in butter, dill, salt and pepper to coat. To glaze carrots, combine brown sugar, salt, ginger and a little cornflour in a small saucepan. Add orange juice. Cook, stirring, until the mixture thickens. Stir in butter and spoon over hot roasted carrots. To braise, place carrots in a saucepan with butter, orange juice and zest, sugar, salt and pepper. Bring to the boil, cover, lower heat and cook for 5 minutes. Uncover, raise heat, and stir until liquid has evaporated and carrots are tender.

fresh ideas

Use carrot juice instead of water in homemade bread or pizza dough to add extra nutrients.

Sauce barbecued chicken with a carrot-based gravy: sauté sliced carrots with olive oil and garlic until very soft and then purée with carrot juice and lemon juice to taste.

Substitute carrot juice for stock in soups, stews and sauces.

Use grated carrot as a substitute for coconut in biscuits and cakes to cut calories and boost nutrition.

making matchsticks

1 Section peeled carrots into 2-inch (5 cm) lengths; then cut into broad slices.

2 Put several broad slices in a pile and cut off matchstick slices in bunches.

cauliflower

Creamy white, purple or a brilliant chartreuse – these
are the colors of today's cauliflower. A close relative
of broccoli, cauliflower has the nutritional attributes of
its cousin, but a much milder flavor.

packed into one cup of cauliflower

29 calories • **folate** to protect your heart • **fiber** to maintain good
digestion • **indoles** and **isothiocyanates** which are cancer-fighting
phytochemicals • 100% of the daily requirement for **vitamin C**

at the market

Season Available all year, with peak season in the fall.

What to look for Choose a head with fresh, crisp, creamy-white curd.
The size of the head has no bearing on quality. Avoid cauliflower that is
turning brown or with curd that appears to have been trimmed. These are
indicators of old age. Old cauliflower has an unpleasant odour when cooked
and has a strong taste. Try to buy cauliflower with some or all of its leaves
intact; they protect the curd from damage and help retain its freshness.

in the kitchen

Storing Cauliflower generally does not keep well, especially if it has been
trimmed of its leaves. If you can't use a head of cauliflower the day you buy
it, place it, unwashed, in a perforated or open plastic bag and refrigerate for
no more than a day or two. The same goes for leftover cooked cauliflower.
Rather than reheat it as a side dish or serve it cold as a salad vegetable, it's
best to purée leftovers with a little stock and use it for soup the next day.

Preparation Wash cauliflower just before cooking or eating raw. Use a
sharp knife to separate the florets into bite-sized pieces, retaining a bit of
stem. To keep florets crisp and white until serving, place in a bowl of iced
water, stir in a squeeze of lemon juice and refrigerate. Drain and pat dry
just before serving.

Basic cooking Cook cauliflower carefully, checking it often because it
goes from undercooked to overcooked in a flash. Florets are cooked as soon
as the stem end is tender. Cauliflower will discolor if cooked in aluminum or
iron pans.

Best uses in recipes Serve raw cauliflower with dips. Cooked, it can be
served with a sauce, made into soup or added to combinations of vegetables
for use in curries.

fresh ideas

Try mashed cauliflower for a
lower-carb version of mashed
potatoes. The similar taste makes
mashed cauliflower very popular
with those who are watching their
carb intake.

Top cauliflower with sauces, add
seasonings and dressings. Try some
of the following with either cooked
or raw cauliflower.

Cheese sauce

Vinaigrette dressing

Mustard-mayonnaise sauce

Curry sauce

Yogurt with fresh or dried herbs

DID YOU KNOW

...that purple cauliflower is a
cross between broccoli and
cauliflower? It has more beta-
carotene than white and turns
white when cooked. The acid
green, chartreuse cauliflower
retains its color on cooking.
It has a relatively mild flavor.

celery

Although celery will never win a star for its nutritional properties, it's an excellent snacking vegetable with a low calorie count that comes from its water content.

packed into 2 medium stalks celery

10 calories • **polyacetylene**, a medicinal substance that helps reduce inflammation • **potassium** to maintain blood pressure • **vitamin C** for healthy gums and teeth

at the market

Season Available all year.

What to look for Choose firm stalks that are pale to medium green, with crisp, fresh-looking leaves. The greener the stalk, the more intense the celery flavor. Celery can be sweet or bitter and it's hard to tell just by looking at it which it is. Scratch the bottom of a bunch with your fingernail. If it smells bitter, it will taste bitter.

in the kitchen

Storing Wrap in layers of damp paper towel and store in the crisper section of the refrigerator for up to two weeks. Keep away from the coldest parts of the refrigerator – the back and side walls – because it freezes easily and then becomes limp and unusable.

Preparation After trimming celery, cut into either end of the stalk with a small, sharp knife and pull down and out to remove stringy fibers.

Basic cooking To cook as a side dish, slice stalks and sauté in peanut oil. Alternatively, cut stalks into 2-inch (5 cm) lengths and simmer in stock. Eat as is, or sprinkle with grated cheese and place under the grill until lightly browned.

Best uses in recipes Every part of the celery plant is usable. Add the strongly flavored leaves to soups and stews for seasoning. Cut up the outer ribs and sauté, braise or stir-fry with other vegetables. Tender inner stalks can be included on raw vegetable platters or to snack on. Along with onions, chopped celery is an essential seasoning in many traditional soups, stews, casseroles and other mixed dishes, such as the stuffing for poultry.

fresh ideas

For finger food, fill 2-inch (5 cm) lengths of celery stalk with:

Cream cheese with chopped onions and chives or chopped peppers

Curried egg salad

Chicken salad combined with dill mayonnaise

A blend of cottage and blue cheeses

Peanut butter

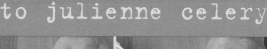

to julienne celery

1 Trim off top and bottom of stalks.

2 Cut into 2-inch (5 cm) pieces; line up cut pieces as guides.

3 Sliver each piece into matchsticks.

corn

When those first plump corn cobs appear at the market, it's time to fire up the barbecue or boil a saucepan of water and set up a table outdoors for supper.

packed into an ear of corn

about **75 calories** • plenty of **fiber** • a mix of **B vitamins** that aid in energy metabolism • **magnesium** to help maintain nerves and muscles • **phosphorus** to help generate energy • **ferulic acid**, an antioxidant that destroys naturally occurring toxins in the body known as free radicals, reducing the risk of heart disease and cancer

at the market

Season Corn is at its sweetest and most abundant during the summer months. However, supersweet varieties from Florida and California have extended the season considerably.

What to look for Always buy corn with intact, bright green husks, as the sugar in the kernels transforms into starch as soon as the husk is removed. Pull back the husk to inspect the kernels; there should be evenly formed straight rows of plump, smooth, shiny kernels. Check the silky end to make sure there's no decay or worm holes.

Corn has a high sugar content – up to 6% of its weight – and is picked at an immature stage to be eaten on the cob. Field corn is picked at a more mature, starchier stage and is used as livestock feed and, after refining, in a number of products from whisky to plastics.

in the kitchen

Storing The sooner you use it, the sweeter it will be. If you must store corn, place ears in a plastic bag and keep it in the vegetable drawer of your refrigerator for a day or two.

Preparation Remove the husk and silk from corn just before cooking. For grilling or roasting, you may want to keep the husks attached (*right*) to protect the kernels during cooking.

Basic cooking Corn-on-the-cob can be steamed, boiled, grilled, roasted in the oven or cooked in the microwave. Keep cooking times brief. You can grill corn on the barbecue rack or nestled in the coals. Either way, pull back the husks and brush the kernels with vegetable oil or melted butter. Refit the husks back over the corn and put the cobs in iced water until you are ready to cook them. Grill over medium-hot coals for 10 to 20 minutes, turning often.

fresh ideas

Corn kernels aren't just for eating off the cob. Try using them in or with some of the following.

Pancake or waffle batter

Cornbread or corn muffin batter

Tomato salsa, along with finely chopped coriander

Carrots, pepper, stock and leftover chicken to make a soup.

for the grill

1 *Shuck corn from tip to stem; husk must not be removed all the way.*

2 *Remove the corn silk by hand.*

3 *Pull husks back up over kernels. Soak corn in iced water.*

cucumber

Cucumbers are cool to the tongue and refreshing to the mouth. They go well with hot foods such as curries, and also add crunch and a little fiber to salads and salsas.

packed into one cup of sliced cucumber

About **14 calories** • plenty of **water** to help maintain normal body temperature • **vitamin C** to help your body absorb iron from other foods

at the market

Season Available all year, but best in summer months. Pickling cucumbers, like Kirbys and gherkins, are also at their peak in warm weather. Kirbys are crisp and delicious without being pickled. Hydroponic cucumbers are hothouse grown in water and available all year, wrapped in plastic

What to look for Select firm cucumbers that are heavy for their size, with no soft spots or shriveled skin.

in the kitchen

Storing Cucumbers that are plastic wrapped will keep for up to a week in the vegetable drawer of the refrigerator. Cut cucumbers must be tightly wrapped and checked daily for signs of decay – soft spots develop quickly.

Preparation Some people prefer to remove the seeds from cucumbers before eating. Peel the cucumber, if you wish, then cut lengthwise in half. Use the tip of a spoon to scoop out the center row of seeds from each half. Discard seeds. Chop, slice or fill the cucumber as directed in a recipe.

Basic cooking Cucumbers aren't just for eating raw in salads. Sliced or chopped, they can be steamed, sautéed or stir-fried in a little oil, sprinkled with salt and chopped fresh dill and served warm as a side dish.

Best uses in recipes Cucumbers are most commonly eaten in salads and mixed vegetable platters, as snacks, and as part of chilled, uncooked soups such as gazpacho. They are also the basis for many types of pickles. To make a speedy sweet-and-sour cucumber salad without pickling, simply marinate thinly sliced cucumber and onion in vinegar, sugar, salt and pepper for several hours in the refrigerator. Serve chilled with meat or fish.

fresh ideas

Add slices of chilled cucumber to almost any sandwich.

Stir grated or diced cucumber with plain yogurt, chopped mint, ground cumin and pepper to make the Indian condiment raita that is a cooling accompaniment to curries.

Slice a cucumber lengthwise, scoop out seeds, poach in water to cover for 5 minutes and fill with hot, seasoned rice.

Sauté cucumber slices in butter or oil and sprinkle with dill.

Purée peeled cucumber in a food processor with yogurt, a peeled garlic clove, fresh dill, lemon juice, salt and pepper for a chilled soup.

DID YOU KNOW

...that scoring the skin of a cucumber gives slices a green and white edge that looks attractive in salads? Trim the ends, stand the cucumber on one of them, and, pressing gently, run the tines of a fork down its length. Repeat the process around the circumference of the cucumber.

legumes

Black, white, pink, green and many colors in between, dried beans play an important role in foods around the world. In this age of fusion cooking, beans jump from cuisine to cuisine, mixed and matched into a variety of intriguing dishes.

packed into 1 cup of black beans

About **225 calories** • more than 30% the daily requirement for **protein** • more than half the daily requirement of **folate** to fight birth defects • **fiber** to maintain a healthy digestive system • **iron** to help prevent anemia • **magnesium** to keep bones healthy • **phosphorus** to maintain strong teeth • **zinc** to fight off infection

at the market

Season Legumes are available dried, canned or frozen year round.

What to look for Name-brand products are usually better quality than generic or store-brand products, but the nutritional value is the same. Generically labeled packages and cans may or may not contain more broken or squashed beans. When buying dried beans in bags or bulk, look for clean, smooth, evenly shaped beans with little or no debris.

Where to buy the best A good health food store or natural foods market may be best for buying dried beans in bulk. Health food stores are also the best source for dried and canned organic beans and lentils. All supermarkets carry packaged dried beans and canned beans; some carry organic brands.

in the kitchen

Storing Dried and canned beans keep indefinitely. Store dried beans in a sealed package or covered container to keep out dust, debris and insects. Once cooked, store, covered, for up to 5 days in the refrigerator.

Preparation Dried legumes should be well rinsed before using and picked over to remove any foreign particles such as pebbles or clumps of dirt that may have slipped through. With the exception of lentils, all dried beans should be soaked before cooking. Place in a large bowl with plenty of cold water to cover. Leave to stand at room temperature for at least eight hours or overnight. Or, combine the beans with water to cover in a large saucepan. Heat to boiling; let boil for 2 minutes. Remove from heat, cover, and let stand for 1 hour. Whichever pre-soaking method you use, discard the soaking water before cooking and add fresh water.

fresh ideas

Combine mashed white beans with tuna, chopped onion and dill to make a sandwich spread or dip.

Mash chickpeas with parsley, garlic, lemon juice, salt and pepper to make a low-calorie, low-fat hummus. Serve with small triangles of pita bread.

Mix several types of beans (black, red, pinto, for example) in a vegetarian chili dish.

Toss warm lentils in a vinaigrette dressing and combine with chopped onion, cherry tomatoes, arugula and coarsely chopped romaine lettuce to make a warm side salad.

DID YOU KNOW

...that in India, where there is a large vegetarian population, dhals, made from mung beans and other legumes, are a vital source of fiber and protein?

adzuki These small reddish-brown beans with a white stripe have a sweet flavor and are particularly popular in Japanese cooking.

black (turtle) beans A staple in Latin American dishes, these earthy beans are lower in folate than red kidney beans but are still high in nutritional value.

black-eyed peas Medium-sized, creamy white beans with a black spot, they are used in Cajun and Caribbean cuisines.

cannellini Large white Italian kidney beans, available canned and dried, cannellinis are used in salads and soups.

chickpeas (garbanzo beans) Medium-sized, tan and acorn-shaped, these beans are often featured in Mediterranean and Middle Eastern dishes.

cranberry beans Medium-sized and oval, these are pink and beige in color and nutty in flavor – a good addition to soups and stews.

fava beans Large and brown when dried, fava beans, also known as broad beans, are staples in Middle Eastern and Mediterranean cooking.

flageolets These pale green kidney beans are traditionally served with lamb, but can also be used with other meats, and in soups, stews and salads.

great northern Kidney-shaped and mild, these large white beans are used in classic French cassoulets, stews and dips.

kidney beans Large pink or red kidney-shaped beans, this variety is often served with rice and is a favorite for chili con carne, stews and soups.

lentils Very small brown, green, orange, or yellow legumes, lentils are featured in Middle Eastern and Central European cuisines in soups, stews, salads and side dishes.

lima beans Starchy and filling, limas come in two sizes: a large variety and the smaller butter beans or baby limas. They are popular in casseroles and soups.

mung beans (moong dhal or green gram) Greenish-brown, yellow or black, these small beans cook quickly and have a sweet, fresh flavor. Use in Asian recipes.

navy (haricot) beans These small, white rounded beans have a mild flavor. Use in traditional recipes for baked beans. They are interchangeable with other white beans.

pigeon peas These small, creamy white beans with orange mottling are used in Caribbean, African and Indian cooking. They contain high levels of protein.

pinto beans Medium-sized, mottled pinkish-tan, kidney-shaped beans, pinto beans are used in Latin American cooking and are one of the most nutritious types.

soybeans Medium-sized, round, and green when fresh, soybeans are black or yellow when dried. Highly nutritious, they are processed into tofu, soy drinks and flour.

split peas Made from fresh green peas, these legumes split when dried. They are a favourite ingredient in soups and a good thickening agent in stews and curries.

Basic cooking All legumes can be cooked using a ratio of 1 part beans to 3 parts water. Combine beans and water in a saucepan. Do not add salt; it hardens the skins and lengthens cooking time. Boil over medium-high heat for 10 minutes. Reduce heat to low, cover, and simmer until tender, about 2 hours for most beans. (For black beans and lima beans, check after 1 hour.)

eggplant

Like tomatoes and avocados, eggplant is a fruit that is treated like a vegetable. Eggplant is a key ingredient in Middle Eastern and Asian recipes.

packed into one cup of eggplant

About **25 calories** • more than 2 g **fiber** to help prevent constipation and formation of hemorrhoids • **B vitamins** for energy production

at the market

Season Available all year, but at their best in the summer months.

What to look for From purplish-black to light violet and white, eggplants can be long and narrow or short and plump. Select fruit that is heavy for its size, with firm, glossy, unblemished skin and a healthy-looking crown. The tastiest are firm with thin skins. Larger ones are more likely to be seedy, tough and bitter.

in the kitchen

Storing Use eggplant within a couple of days of purchase. If you must store it, keep it in a cool place but preferably not in the refrigerator because it's likely to soften and become bitter very quickly.

Preparation It's not necessary to peel an eggplant before cooking, unless the skin is especially thick or you simply prefer your vegetables peeled.

Basic cooking Eggplants soak up oil during cooking, which is one of the drawbacks from a health point of view. Some have a bitter taste, but this is easily eliminated with salt before cooking *(right)*. Wipe off the salt and dry the slices before cooking. The salting not only removes bitter juices, it reduces the amount of moisture, making it less oil-absorbent. When eggplant is used as the basis of a dip, such as Middle Eastern baba ghanoush, however, it is often baked whole or boiled until the flesh is soft enough to mash, avoiding the oil issue altogether.

To barbecue eggplant for a side dish, cut crosswise into ½-inch (1 cm) slices and brush with oil and cook, oiled side facing the heat source, until browned on both sides. Brush with oil and turn slices twice during cooking. Sprinkle with salt, pepper and chopped fresh parsley or basil before serving.

fresh ideas

Coat slices of small eggplants in bread crumbs. Bake in a hot oven until tender. Top with chopped basil or oregano leaves and serve as an hors d'oeuvre.

Grilling gives eggplant a meaty, rich flavor. Halve a large eggplant lengthwise; prick skin. Place cut-side down on a barbecue or under a grill and cook until skin blisters and blackens. Place in a paper bag for a few minutes to loosen skin. Peel, then mash flesh. Drizzle with oil and season with salt and pepper.

salting eggplant

1 *First slice the eggplant into uniform pieces with a sharp knife.*

2 *Lay slices on paper towels and sprinkle with salt. Let stand 30 minutes to release moisture.*

fresh ideas

Sprinkle chopped fresh fennel leaves on cooked prawns or clams.

Use fennel stalks as "boats," similar to celery sticks, for carrying fillings such as cream cheese or tuna salad.

Add fennel stalks along with other "soup greens" to flavor chicken and fish stocks.

Add chopped fennel stalks to the other seasoning vegetables (onion, garlic and carrot) when making a fresh tomato sauce.

preparing fennel

1 *Cut feathery fronds from fennel.*

2 *Peel bulb with a vegetable peeler.*

3 *Cut bulb vertically; let slices fall away.*

fennel

From seed to stem, the entire fennel plant is edible and used in many different ways to impart a mild, anise flavor to foods. Fennel's unusual licorice taste goes especially well with tomato and fish dishes.

packed into one cup cooked fennel

about **130 calories** • **vitamin C** to help keep skin healthy • 20% of the daily requirement for **fiber** to maintain intestinal health • a good source of **folate** and **potassium**

at the market

Season Fennel is widely available in fall and winter months.

What to look for Choose stalks with fresh-looking feathery fronds and smooth whitish-green bulbs and stems with no cracks.

in the kitchen

Storing Separate fennel stems from the bulb before storing. Wrap stalks and bulb separately in plastic bags and put in the vegetable drawer of the refrigerator for up to four days. Use the stalks first, because they don't keep as well. Fennel loses its flavor with longer storage; it dries out and starts to turn brown.

Preparation To prepare fennel for cooking or eating raw, trim the base and remove any tough outer ribs. Trim off stalks with feathery leaves. Halve, core and slice the bulb. Raw fennel will turn brown soon after slicing so, to prevent discoloring, drop sliced fennel into a bowl of water with a little lemon juice and refrigerate until ready to cook or serve.

Basic cooking Fennel can be steamed, boiled, braised, stir-fried or eaten raw. To braise, combine 2 sliced fennel bulbs and ½ cup chicken stock or white wine in a large frying pan. Bring to the boil over medium heat. Reduce heat, cover, and simmer until fennel is tender when pierced with a fork, about 20 minutes. Sprinkle with salt and pepper. Makes 4 servings. The stalks and feathery leaves can be used as a seasoning or garnish for soups, salads and seafood.

Best uses in recipes Fennel has an affinity for fish. In French cuisine, for example, fish is often baked on a bed of sliced fennel. Try barbecuing fish over fennel stalks or add leaves to the poaching stock for a large salmon.

garlic

In addition to its culinary virtues, garlic has a long history of healing and curing. It has anti-bacterial and anti-fungal qualities that help keep the immune system in good shape.

packed into one clove of garlic

about **5 calories** • the phytochemical **allicin** which may help to lower cholesterol and reduce the risk of cancer • **calcium** and potassium

at the market

Season Available all year.

What to look for Select firm garlic with dry, tight-fitting skin. A head of garlic should feel heavy and firm in your hand and the cloves appear plump and well formed. Garlic can be a creamy white or tinged a pinkish purple.

in the kitchen

Storing Depending on how fresh it is when purchased, garlic will keep in a cool, dark, dry place for up to three months. Vented and lidded garlic jars made of a porous material, such as terracotta, make ideal storage containers. Do not refrigerate.

Preparation To peel a garlic clove, lay it under the flat side of a large knife and then hit the side of the knife with your fist, sufficiently hard to split the clove so that the skin is easily removed.

Basic cooking Garlic is a basic seasoning in dishes worldwide. Rub a wooden serving bowl with a cut garlic clove to season a salad. For roasts and braises, the longer garlic cooks, the more mellow its flavor. When sautéing or stir-frying garlic, however, take care not to burn it or it will taste bitter.

Roast garlic cloves to a soft paste to make a low-fat spread for bread and grilled meats. Add sliced roasted garlic to soups, stews and pasta sauces.

To roast a whole bulb of garlic, preheat oven to 375°F (190°C). Cut across the top of the bulb with a sharp knife to expose all the cloves. Brush the tops of the cloves with olive oil and season with salt. Wrap the bulb in aluminum foil and bake until very soft, 30 minutes to 1 hour. When cool enough to handle, push the softened garlic cloves from their skins.

To roast individual cloves, separate them from a bulb and toss, unpeeled, with 1 tablespoon olive oil in a small baking dish. Roast in the oven until tender when pierced with a knife, about 15 minutes. Serve with roast meats, stir through mashed potatoes or use to season stir-fried vegetables.

fresh ideas

For the maximum health benefits, chop or crush garlic and let it stand for 10 minutes before using. This allows allicin, associated with anti-cancer and cholesterol-lowering effects, to be activated.

Cook garlic slowly in olive oil over a low heat, then discard. Use the oil to impart a mild flavor to foods.

Tuck slivers of raw garlic into lamb, beef and veal for roasting.

Make garlic bread with olive oil (no saturated fats), not butter.

roasted garlic

1   *Cut ½ inch (5 mm) off the top.*

2   *Roast as directed (see text). Push out the roasted cloves.*

3   *Mash garlic with a fork until smooth.*

Leafy green vegetables meant for cooking rather than salad making (although there is some overlap) are a large and diverse group.

packed into one cup of cooked mixed greens

About **33 calories** • **beta-carotene** that is converted into vitamin A in the body • half the daily requirement for **vitamin C** • antioxidant **vitamin E** to protect the heart • phytonutrients known as **organosulfur compounds** that detoxify potential carcinogens • **carotenoids** to reduce the risk of age-related eye disease and certain kinds of cancer

at the market

Season A variety of cooking greens is always available.

What to look for Regardless of the variety, pick brightly colored, crisp leaves. Avoid bruised or excessively dirty leaves as well as limp or yellowing specimens – both are sure signs of age. Woody stems and coarse veins in the leaves practically guarantee that the vegetable will be tough and bitter.

Where to buy the best At a local farmers' market, greens will be newly picked. In a supermarket, greens that are displayed in a refrigerated section of the produce department are likely to stay fresh, since cool temperatures discourage decay and bacteria.

in the kitchen

Storing Do not wash greens before storing them – too much moisture encourages the leaves to rot. Use perforated plastic storage bags or boxes, which allow air to circulate around the leaves and maintain just enough moisture to preserve their crispness.

Preparation Soak in cold water and then rinse thoroughly immediately before cooking to release any dirt trapped in stems or crinkly leaves. Trim any bruised outer leaves and cut off tough stems. Stems can be used in stock or soups. Swiss chard stems taste good sautéed briefly in olive oil and garlic, although they do not retain their bright appearance.

Basic cooking Greens are frequently the victim of overcooking, which leaves them soggy, bland and an unappetizing shade of gray. Brief, gentle cooking or quick cooking over a high heat, however, brings out their subtle flavors without ruining the delicate texture of the leaves. Cavolo nero is the exception *(overleaf)*. There is one general rule that applies to all greens, which is that they cook down to about one third of their original volume.

fresh ideas

Purée steamed greens with garlic and plain yogurt. Top with sliced spring onions and serve cold as a summer soup.

For a quick pasta sauce, purée steamed spinach with parsley and lemon juice.

Make a salad dressing in a food processor or blender with steamed Swiss chard and a handful of parsley and basil. Add olive oil, lemon juice, crushed garlic, salt and pepper.

Some simple seasonings for cooked greens.

Balsamic vinegar

Fresh lemon juice

Sesame oil and soy sauce

Finely chopped fresh dill

Toasted sesame seeds

Greens can be simply tossed in butter over a high heat until just wilted and then sprinkled with a little grated nutmeg, which takes the edge off any coarseness in the flavor. Finely chopped greens are a good addition to egg dishes such as soufflés, omelettes and quiches and to stuffings for roasts. The classic dish Eggs Florentine comprises two soft poached eggs on a bed of cooked spinach, topped with mornay (cheese) sauce and grated cheese such as cheddar or Parmesan. This is an ideal dish for Sunday brunch.

Best recipe To make **ribollita**, the traditional hearty Tuscan soup, soak 10 oz (300 g) white kidney beans in water for at least 8 hours, or overnight. Drain and then boil in 8 cups of water until cooked. Drain, reserving the cooking liquid. Slice an onion and sauté in olive oil in a large, deep frying pan. Meanwhile, coarsely chop a head of cavolo nero, a quarter of a savoy cabbage, 1 bunch of Swiss chard, 1 leek, and two each of potatoes, carrots, zucchini, celery stalks and peeled plum tomatoes. Add the vegetables to the pan and allow to soften slowly over medium heat, about 10 minutes. Add the reserved cooking liquid with half the cooked beans. Purée the remaining beans in a food processor and add to the pan. Season with salt and pepper to taste. Simmer, partially covered, for 2 hours. Add 8 slices stale Italian bread, stir well and let the mixture boil for 10 minutes. Turn off the heat and let soup stand for a day to allow flavors to develop and soup to thicken. Reheat just before serving. Spoon into large bowls; drizzle with olive oil.

cavolo nero – literally means black cabbage. It is also known as black-leaf kale. This leafy, dark green vegetable can be prepared in many of the same ways as spinach and cabbage. Cavolo nero features widely in Italian cuisine, especially in recipes from Tuscany. It has a good, strong flavor. While leafy greens are often ruined through overcooking, cavolo nero is unique in that it benefits from long, slow cooking. One of the most famous recipes showcasing this type of greens is the classic soup, ribolitta. After it is made, it is traditionally left to sit for a day before serving to allow it to thicken and the flavors to develop. Cavolo nero also tastes delicious fried in good-quality olive oil with garlic and finely chopped chili peppers.

cavolo nero

cutting up greens

1 To quickly chop up greens, roll a bundle of leaves together into a cigar shape.

2 Slice across the cigar to reduce the greens to shreds for fast cooking or to add to soups.

DID YOU KNOW

...that a pinch of baking soda added during cooking makes greens even greener? However, it also breaks down the plant tissues, making the texture mushy and destroying many of the vitamins. Flavor and nutrients should be the major issues, not looks. If you cook greens briefly, they'll be a lovely fresh green anyway.

greens continued on the next page ▶

beet greens Like fresh spinach leaves, beet greens are tender and cook quickly. They have a mild flavor. Cook greens in a covered frying pan using just the water that clings to the rinsed leaves. Add butter or olive oil. Other ingredients to add to give the greens more flavor include crushed garlic, ground cumin or a good dash of Tabasco.

kale comes in several varieties with leaves that are very crinkly, serrated or feathery and tones of blue-green, reddish purple, gray-green or light green. All but the season's first tender kale leaves tend to be quite tough – they need braising for 12 to 15 minutes. Kale has a full flavor and is especially good chopped and added to hearty winter soups near the end of cooking.

mustard greens These light green, crinkly leaves pack a hot punch, especially if simmered for no more than 15 minutes. Longer cooking mellows the flavor. They are an excellent complement to Asian pork dishes that have a rich sauce. Grated ginger, soy sauce and toasted sesame seeds are all good matches for mustard greens. Pickled mustard greens are also available.

swiss chard is sometimes confused with spinach, with which it is interchangeable. However, Swiss chard has an earthier taste. The leaves can be blanched, sautéed, steamed or stir-fried. The wide stem, or rib, which comes in vivid red, yellow or a bright white, can be chopped and sautéed in oil or butter. The stems take a little longer to cook than the leaves.

spinach The best-known of all the cooking greens, spinach comes with dark green, crisp crinkly leaves. English spinach, which has a shorter season, has paler green flat leaves. Trimmed spinach leaves can be cooked in a pan with just the water left clinging to the leaves from rinsing. Cover and steam for 1 or 2 minutes. Do not overcook.

Packing a punch

The flavor of peppery mustard greens may be too strong for some palates. If you find them too pungent or bitter, quickly blanch the leaves in salted water to reduce their sharpness. Mustard greens are also known as curled mustard, mustard spinach, Indian mustard or leaf mustard.

DID YOU KNOW

...that Popeye didn't get his strength from spinach because it is not, in fact, a great source of iron? While it is true that it does contain good quantities of iron, it also contains oxalic acid, which limits how much iron the body can absorb.

kohlrabi

Sometimes called cabbage turnip, kohlrabi has a bulblike stem that tastes like a mild sweet turnip with traces of its cruciferous cousins, cabbage and brussels sprouts, and a bit of radish. It has edible greens that are rich in iron.

packed into a half-cup of cooked kohlrabi

About **29 calories** • half the daily requirement for **vitamin C** • vitamin A precursor **beta-carotene** to protect eyes and aid in normal cell division and growth • **antioxidant bioflavonoids** to prevent cell damage by free radicals • plenty of **fiber** • 200 mg **potassium** to maintain fluid balance and proper metabolism and muscle function

at the market

Season Fresh kohlrabi is available from mid-spring to mid-fall.

What to look for Choose fresh-looking deep-colored green leaves with no yellowing and firm bulbs with smooth skin and no soft spots. Bulbs should be heavy for their size. Bulbs less than 3 inches (7 cm) in diameter are the most tender; larger ones tend to be tough and woody. Kohlrabi bulb and stem color can run from white to pale green and from red to purple, depending on variety. The flesh is always white and the flavor is essentially the same.

in the kitchen

Storing You can keep fresh kohlrabi in a ventilated plastic bag in the vegetable drawer of the refrigerator for up to 2 weeks.

Preparation Kohlrabi leaves are even more nutritious than the bulb, which is an argument for cutting them up and cooking them with the bulb. Discard the leaf stalks. The bulb can be easily peeled with a small, sharp knife, but some cooks think the flavor is better if the vegetable is cooked with its peel still in place. Once cut, kohlrabi flesh is quick to discolor, so you may want to put slices or cut-up pieces in a bowl of water with a little lemon juice until ready to cook.

Basic cooking Kohlrabi is usually peeled, sliced or chopped, and steamed until tender, then buttered and seasoned with salt and pepper. It is also delicious braised in a beef or chicken stock, seasoned with onions and herbs. Many cooks steam or microwave kohlrabi pieces and then mash them with butter and seasonings. Sliced kohlrabi is often used in Asian stir-fries as a substitute for the more expensive water chestnuts – it has the same crispness with a bit more flavor.

fresh ideas

Add small amounts of grated raw kohlrabi to salads to give a sweet, pungent accent.

To pickle kohlrabi, soak slices of kohlrabi and onion for several hours in a litre of iced water to which 4 tablespoons pickling salt have been added. Drain the vegetables and place in a medium bowl. In a saucepan, boil 2 cups vinegar, ¾ cup sugar, 1 tablespoon mustard seed, 1½ teaspoons celery seed, and ¼ teaspoon turmeric for several minutes, stirring to make sure sugar is dissolved. Pour mixture over the vegetables and leave to cool. Cover and refrigerate for 3 days.

If the leaves attached to the bulb are fresh and green, wash them and remove the ribs. Blanch the leaves until just wilted. Drain thoroughly and chop. Sauté in butter or olive oil and season with salt and pepper.

DID YOU KNOW

...that more than 40,000 tons of kohlrabi are harvested every year in Germany?

leeks

With a milder, sweeter flavor than onions and a crunchy bite when cooked, leeks are a great vegetable for savory, nutritious side dishes, and to add to soups and stews.

packed into one cup cooked leeks

About **61 calories** • 20% of the daily **vitamin C** requirement to fight infection • 34% of the daily requirement for **folate** to regulate growth • the phytochemical **diallyl sulfide** that is thought to lower the risk of stomach cancer • **kaempferol**, a substance that may block cancer-causing compounds • **quercetin**, another phytochemical that helps fight cancer and heart disease • **fiber** for protection against high cholesterol

at the market

Season Available all year, leeks are most abundant from fall to early spring.

What to look for Fresh leeks look like giant spring onions with straight root ends. Check both ends – the tops should be a healthy-looking dark green and the root end, white for several inches with unblemished skin that gives a little when you press it. The root end shouldn't be bigger than 1½ inches (4 cm) in diameter with a bush of small roots still attached.

in the kitchen

Storing Loosely wrap unwashed, untrimmed leeks in plastic and store in the vegetable drawer of the refrigerator for up to a week.

Preparation Leeks need careful cleaning (they are grown in furrows that are filled in with dirt as they grow to keep the bottoms white). Trim off tough outer leaves and the roots at the base. Slit a leek lengthwise from the base to the top and fan out the leaves under water, checking every layer for grit.

Basic cooking Whole leeks are often braised in stock or wine (you'll need 2 to 3 cups of liquid for 8 medium leeks) for 20 minutes or more. Be careful not to overcook them or they will lose their crispness and turn slimy. Cut-up leeks cook more quickly: steam or microwave them for 5 to 8 minutes. Sliced leeks add texture and flavor to soups and stews. Vichyssoise is the classic cold leek-and-potato soup: In a medium saucepan, sauté 2 sliced leeks and 1 chopped onion in butter until tender, about 5 minutes. Add 2 peeled and sliced potatoes and 2½ cups chicken stock. Simmer until potatoes are tender, 10 to 20 minutes. Let cool and then purée in batches in a food processor. Stir in a little light sour cream and salt and pepper to taste. Chill before serving.

lettuces

There is an astonishing diversity of lettuce types and salad greens, with more appearing all the time. Tossed green salads are always more interesting, more flavorful and more nutritious when you combine the shapes, textures, hues and tastes of several varieties. Three lettuces should be the minimum.

packed into one cup of romaine lettuce

9 calories • 22% of the daily requirement for **vitamin C** • the B vitamin **folic acid**, for protein metabolism • **carotenoids**, which help prevent age-related blindness due to macular degeneration

at the market

Season Many varieties are available in food markets throughout the year. Farmers' markets have especially fresh lettuce in summer.

What to look for Regardless of the variety, lettuce should always look clean and fresh, with no wilted leaves or rust-colored spots. Avoid large heads of lettuce with tough outer leaves and ribs.

in the kitchen

Storing Wash lettuce before storing and dry well. Discard any wilted or discolored outer leaves. Wrap loosely in paper towels, then overwrap in plastic. Store in the the vegetable section of the refrigerator. Tender leaf lettuces will keep for a day or two; sturdier ones, such as romaine and iceberg, will keep well for up to four days.

Preparation Tear small, tender lettuce leaves by hand. To shred large lettuce leaves, stack several of them on a cutting board. Roll the leaves up tightly from one long end. Slice the roll crosswise. Shredded lettuce makes an attractive, edible bed for grilled seafood and marinated cooked meats.

Serving Never toss a green salad with dressing until it's time to eat or you'll end up with a soggy heap. To be well prepared ahead of time and to save on clean-up, mix salad dressing in the bottom of the salad bowl, top with salad greens, then refrigerate up to two hours ahead of time. Toss the greens and dressing together just before serving. Be careful not to drown greens in dressing – a little goes a long way.

fresh ideas

Coarsely shred a mix of sturdy, spicy lettuces, such as watercress or arugula, to use as a bed for grilled lamb chops or slices of steak.

Use individual leaves of Belgian endive to hold a savory dip such as herbed goat cheese as an appetizer.

Wrap sandwich fillings such as egg or tuna salad, in lettuce leaves instead of bread to cut down on calories and carbohydrates.

Grill fish in a generous covering of lettuce to keep it moist. Spicier lettuces will add some flavor, too.

DID YOU KNOW

...that lettuce was originally regarded as a weed? Today, it is cultivated in many varieties all around the world.

a glossary of salad greens

 **arugula** has several rounded and spiked leaves jutting from stems. The peppery flavor becomes stronger with age. Arugula can be eaten raw or added at the last minute to stir-fries.

 **belgian endive** is a tightly closed head of smooth leaves with a slightly bitter taste. The whitish creamy leaves are the result of its not being exposed to sunlight during growing.

 **butterhead** is a category of lettuces that form small heads with soft leaves (like Boston or Bibb). The heart is tender and the leaves have a mild flavor.

 **curly endive,** or chicory, has leaves tapering to sharp points. Outer leaves are lacy and green-rimmed; inner leaves are pale yellow. The flavor is slightly bitter.

 **iceberg** is a tight-head lettuce that looks like a type of cabbage. It has pale green leaves and a mild flavor.

 lollo rosso is dark copper red fading to bright green. The leaves are crisp and finely crinkled, with jagged edges resembling lace. They have a refreshing taste.

 **mache,** lamb's lettuce or field salad, is high in beta-carotene, with tender, round leaves and a mild flavor. Sold with its roots still attached, it is highly perishable and should be used right away.

 **mignonette** is a loose-head lettuce with small, soft leaves that have a mild flavor. It is available in green and red varieties which look attractive mixed in a salad.

 **oak leaf** is a loose lettuce with thin, tender reddish-brown or green scalloped leaves. It has a distinctive mild, nutty flavor.

 **radicchio** comprises a tight head of crisp leaves which are a vibrant red or reddish-purple with white veins. The very bitter flavor works well in a salad of mixed leaves.

 romaine is a loose-head lettuce with sturdy, rich green outer leaves, paler green inner leaves, and crisp ribs. It has a mild tangy flavor.

Dressing The classic vinaigrette blends one part vinegar to three parts olive oil. Beating them together with a fork or a whisk will emulsify them. Experiment with seasonings such as garlic, herbs, mustard or lemon juice.

watercress Although watercress is a popular salad vegetable, it's not actually a lettuce, but rather a member of the high-nutrition cruciferous vegetable family. It has small dark green leaves and a pungent, peppery, mustard-like flavor. The best-quality watercress is available in spring and has small leaves and thin stems. It is also available at other times of the year. Do not buy watercress with flowering stems. Use in soups and as a garnish.

watercress

mushrooms

Thousands of varieties of fungi, including edible mushrooms, cover the planet. Many wild mushrooms are toxic, even deadly, so unless you're an expert, it's best to pick your exotic mushrooms at a supermarket or farmers' market.

packed into one cup of common mushrooms

Less than **20 calories** • a variety of **B vitamins** for energy • **copper** to support thyroid activity • **potassium** to regulate blood pressure

at the market

Season All but the most exotic mushrooms are available all year.

What to look for Choose mushrooms with smooth, dry skin and stems and no bruises. Buy only as many as you will use within a day or two. One pound (500 g) yields about 5 cups sliced, which cooks down to 1 or 2 cups.

in the kitchen

Storing Keep mushrooms in a paper bag, or layered between sheets of paper towel, in the refrigerator for up to two days.

Preparation Just before using, clean mushrooms with a damp paper towel or a soft vegetable brush to remove dirt. Trim stems as desired.

fresh ideas

When you want to add flavor to button mushrooms, trying using a few reconstituted dried mushrooms. These have a rich, intense flavor, while the buttons give the dish the texture you expect of mushrooms.

To flavor soups and stews, use the liquid from the reconstituted dried mushrooms, strained through cheesecloth. Add to sauces, too.

Brush portobello mushrooms or field mushrooms with oil, salt and pepper and barbecue or grill them as you would hamburgers. Serve sprinkled with chopped thyme.

varieties

button mushrooms are white or off-white with round caps and a very subtle flavor and fine texture. Larger, open, field mushrooms have a stronger flavor.

cremini or brown mushrooms are a milky brown color with round caps similar to button mushrooms. They have a meatier, richer flavor and more texture.

enokis are unique among edible mushrooms in having a crunchy texture and are best eaten raw. Creamy-colored enokis have long, thin stems with a tiny button cap.

oysters have no stalk and are creamy white to gray with a very delicate texture. They actually do have an oysterlike flavor, and it intensifies with cooking.

portobellos are older, larger flatter creminis and come in a variety of sizes from average to extra-large. They have a rich, earthy flavor.

shiitakes are quite strongly flavored, with a meaty texture. The tough stems are usually discarded. They are often used in Asian cooking.

okra

Also known as lady's fingers or gumbo, okra has long been a staple in Creole and Cajun cooking and a popular Middle Eastern dish. It is sold fresh, frozen, dried and in cans.

fresh ideas

Barbecue okra. Thread 4 or 5 pods onto two parallel skewers, to create a vegetable "ladder." Brush the pods with olive oil and sprinkle with salt. Barbecue on both sides until lightly charred. Sprinkle with vinegar or lemon juice. Serve hot.

Serve raw okra on a vegetable platter with a dip.

Okra and stewed tomatoes make a great combination. Okra keeps the tomato from becoming too watery, and the acid in the tomato keeps okra from becoming too gelatinous.

Add slices of raw okra to a salad for an extra crunch.

packed into one cup of okra

About **65 calories** • One third the daily requirement for **vitamin C** • over half the daily requirement for **folate**, which prevents birth defects and promotes normal growth • fibrous **pectin**, which reduces cholesterol in the blood and protects against stomach ulcers and other intestinal disorders • **lutein** and **carotenoids**, phytochemicals that help prevent blindness due to macular degeneration and cataracts

at the market

Season Fresh okra's prime season is summer, but it can sometimes be found in fall as well.

What to look for Choose bright green pods no more than 3 inches (7 cm) long, avoiding any oversized okra, which will be fibrous and tough. Pods should be firm with no browning or discoloration at the tips.

in the kitchen

Storing Okra is quite perishable; if you must store it, spread the unwashed pods in a single layer in a perforated plastic bag and refrigerate for a day or two. If kept longer, the okra will lose its texture and color.

Preparation Wash okra just before using it. Some cooks prefer to gently scrub the pods with a soft brush or towel to remove the fine fuzz on the surface, while others contend that this is not necessary, because the fuzz is imperceptible after cooking. In any case, do cut off and discard the stem end. Avoid cutting into the okra's interior flesh – except when chopping the okra for stews or sautés – or its slippery juice will be released.

Basic cooking Okra can be steamed, stewed, cooked in the microwave, or fried. One of the most popular ways to cook okra as a side dish is to fry it: For a pound (500 g) trimmed whole okra, you'll need some flour and cornmeal in a bowl for coating, 2 eggs lightly beaten in a bowl, plus vegetable oil for deep-frying. Once the oil is hot (about 375°F/190°C), toss the okra in the flour, dip it in the eggs, and then roll it in cornmeal. Fry in batches, without overcrowding, until well browned – about 3 minutes. Drain on paper towels. Sprinkle with salt and serve.

DID YOU KNOW

...that okra releases sticky, gelatinous juices as it cooks, that thicken whatever liquid it is in? That's why it is such an important ingredient in gumbos and other Creole dishes that don't use a roux of flour and fat for thickening.

onions

There are very few kitchens where onions are not a staple food. White, brown and red onions, which are left in the ground to mature and have a tough outer skin for longer storage, are used almost daily. Fresh scallions or shallots should be purchased as needed.

packed into a half-cup of chopped onion

30 **calories** • **vitamin C** to fight infection • a phytochemical known as **diallyl sulfide** that is thought to lower the risk of stomach cancer • **quercetin**, another phytochemical that fights cancer and heart disease

at the market

Season Onions are available all year round. While at their peak in spring, spring onions (long and thin with a bulb at the end) and green onions (long and uniformly thin) are also available all year.

What to look for Choose firm, evenly shaped onions and spring onions with smooth, brittle, papery skin. Avoid onions that have soft spots or wet, discolored skin. Spring onions should be a bright white, with deep green leaves and fresh-looking roots. Spring onions and green onions are juicy and mild enough to eat raw.

in the kitchen

Storing Store onions in a mesh bag in a cool, dry open space away from bright light. Don't store them with potatoes; the potatoes give off moisture and a gas that causes onions to spoil more quickly. They should keep up to a month. Milder, sweeter onions such as Vidalia onions and eschalots often don't keep as long as sharper-tasting onions. Spring onions are not meant to be stored for long periods. Wrap them in plastic, refrigerate and use within a few days of purchase.

Preparation Onions contain a substance called a lachrymator, which is released into the air when the vegetable is peeled or cut. When these vapours combine with moisture from your eyes, sulfuric acid is formed, resulting in a painful burning sensation and tears. To prevent or minimize this, try peeling the onion while holding it under cold running water. Some people suggest chewing on a piece of bread while you chop, to stop tears forming. If you use a sharp knife and make quick work of chopping *(p.288)*, tears won't be too much of a problem. Onions are best chopped by hand. If you use a food processor, pulse gently off and on to avoid mashing the onion.

fresh ideas

Cook sliced red or sweet white onions in olive oil over low heat until they are very tender and golden brown. Serve them with meat, fish or poultry, or as a hamburger relish.

Stuff large sweet onions that have been cored with a seasoned rice mixture. Bake in the same way as you would stuffed peppers.

Add sautéed onions and chopped fresh dill to bread doughs.

Stuff cored apples with sautéed red onions and bake until tender. Serve with sausages and scrambled eggs for brunch or a light lunch.

DID YOU KNOW

...that in Ancient Egypt, onions were seen as a symbol of the universe, and were represented in carvings in pyramids built between in 2500 and 2200 BC?

cutting up an onion

1 Halve onion lengthwise. Make several horizontal cuts, stopping about ¼" (10 mm) from the root.

2 Make vertical cuts from top to bottom, keeping root intact.

3 Hold onion by the root end, slice crosswise, letting onion fall apart into small, even pieces.

varieties

brown onions have a brown skin and creamy flesh, and are more strongly flavored than white onions. Brown onions store well.

red onions are mild enough to eat raw in salads and sandwiches, but they are often added to cooked dishes as well. They have a red to purplish-red flesh, and are sometimes called Spanish onions or salad onions. Red onions are hotter than the real, white or yellow-skinned Spanish onion, which has an even milder flavor.

scallions or green onions are immature onions with a semi-developed or unformed bulb. They can be thinly sliced and served raw in salads or as a garnish to hot foods. They are also good cooked and are often added to stir-fries and other Asian dishes. Scallions are also known as green onions or spring onions.

shallots grow in bunches, similar to garlic. They have light brown skin and white or purplish flesh. Eschalots have a delicate but distinctive and delicious flavor that defines many French sauces and braised dishes. The shallot should not to be confused with scallions, which some cooks mistakenly refer to as shallots.

sweet onions such as Vidalia, Walla Walla or Maui Sweet, have white or tan skin and are generally larger and sometimes flatter than regular yellow onions. They are eaten raw in salads and sandwiches and are also good on the barbecue.

white onions have white skin and flesh, and are milder than brown onions. They are suitable for salads as well as cooking.

yellow onions are a pale form of brown onions with yellowish-brown skin and creamy white flesh. They are the most popular cooking onion. Their flavor ranges from pungent to almost sweet, but they can hold up to the long cooking sometimes required for soups and stews.

Basic cooking Onions can be steamed, microwaved, battered and deep-fried, roasted or grilled on their own to be served with meat, poultry or fish as a side dish. But onions are most often used – raw or sautéed – to season soups, stews, sauces, cooked vegetables, casseroles, stir-fries and stocks. Caramelizing is a popular way to cook onions to accompany meat. To serve four, thinly slice 3 yellow onions. In a heavy pan over medium heat, heat a tablespoon of olive oil. Add onions and cook, covered, for 10 minutes, stirring often. Remove cover; cook for 10 more minutes, stirring occasionally. A pinch of sugar speeds the caramelizing process, producing browned, soft, aromatic onions to complement any dish.

parsnips

Related to carrots but lacking the orange color (and beta-carotene), parsnips look like pale versions of their cousins. They have a sweet, herby and slightly nutty flavor – and are high in fiber and nutrients.

packed into one cup cooked parsnips

Less than **126 calories** • about a quarter of the daily **vitamin C** requirement for heart health • **folate** for making red blood cells • **magnesium** for bone growth and metabolism

at the market

Season Parsnips are in greatest supply from fall through early spring, but many markets carry them year-round. They are grown mainly in northern California, Michigan, southern Ontario, British Columbia and Manitoba. Growers place parsnips in cold storage for two weeks or so before shipping them to market, to allow their starch to convert to sugar, making them much sweeter. That is why many farmers and home gardeners in colder climates allow parsnips to winter over in the ground, enjoying a natural cold storage.

What to look for Choose firm, medium-sized roots that are uniformly shaped and free from bruises or soft spots. Parsnips more than 8 inches (20 cm) long may have a woody core. Young parsnips are high in natural sugars, so they caramelize well when baked.

in the kitchen

Storing Keep parsnips – without their greens – in a perforated plastic bag in the vegetable drawer of the refrigerator for up to four weeks.

Preparation For most uses, trim the tops and bottoms of parsnips and peel with a vegetable peeler *(right)*. If you are intending to purée parsnips, you can cook them first, and peel them easily afterwards by hand.

Basic cooking Parsnips are best when they are cooked until just tender. Steaming is a good method to use, as is microwaving. You can also braise parsnips in stock and season them with herbs or bake them as you would sweet potatoes with fruit juice, brown sugar and spices such as cinnamon and ginger. Purée cooked parsnips in a blender or food processor and serve with butter and salt and pepper. Or, combine puréed parsnips with puréed pumpkin or sweet potatoes. Parsnip enriches the nutritional value and the flavor of soups and stews; be careful not to put them in to cook too early or they will become mushy.

fresh ideas

Grate tender young raw parsnips into salads to add flavor, texture and vitamin C.

Puréed parsnip can be used as the basis for delicious pancakes. Add 1 medium grated carrot, 2 sliced spring onions, 1 egg, 1 tablespoon flour and a pinch of salt. Cook pancakes in batches in a non-stick frying pan with a little peanut oil. Serve warm topped with apple sauce or a dollop of sour cream.

cutting up parsnips

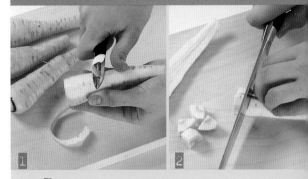

1 Trim top and bottom from parsnips. Then use a vegetable peeler to trim away a thin layer of peel.

2 To dice, cut parsnip in two along the length and remove any woody core. Then cut across each piece.

fresh ideas

Toss a handful of blanched peas into fresh salads.

Pluck a handful of fresh green peas from their pods and eat them for a nutritious snack.

Add raw shelled peas to stews, soups and vegetable sautés during the last minutes of cooking.

Add peas to plain grains such as rice, couscous and pasta.

Garnish a platter of sliced roasted meat with a handful of blanched shelled peas.

For a smoky taste to complement their sweetness, sauté sugar snap peas with a little chopped bacon.

Cut blanched snow peas into small pieces and add them to egg salad or tuna salad to provide texture.

DID YOU KNOW

...that a three-quarter-cup serving of fresh green peas has more protein than an egg?

...that snow peas, so closely associated with Chinese stir-fries, were actually developed in Holland in the 1500s?

peas

Thanks to the popularity of snow peas and subsequently sugar snap peas – both peas with edible pods that require little preparation – more people are enjoying the benefits of fresh peas today than ever before.

packed into a half-cup of cooked peas

About **65 calories** • **B vitamins** for energy production • **vitamin C** for resistance to infection • **folate** to promote normal growth • **iron** to carry oxygen through your body • plenty of **fiber** to maintain digestive health

at the market

Season Fresh sweet peas are available late spring and early summer. The season for fresh sugar snap peas and snow peas extends throughout the summer. Crops from California, Florida and Central America extend the season into the winter months.

What to look for The freshest pea pods at the market will look shiny and firm; if rubbed together they squeak a little. Avoid any pale green or yellow pods, an indicator that their sugars have begun to turn to starch. If possible, taste one to test. The sweetest green shell peas are best small to medium sized. They should fit snugly inside their pods without looking swollen or crowded. Large, heavy, shell pea pods usually signal that the peas will be tough and starchy. On the other hand, light, thin pods indicate bland peas.

in the kitchen

Storing Like corn, time is of the essence when it comes to serving fresh peas, so storage is not recommended. If you must, store peas briefly in plastic wrap in the coldest part of the refrigerator.

Preparation To shell green peas, snap off the top of the pod and pull the string down the side, opening the pod in the process. The peas will pop right out. Sugar snap pods are edible, but you may encounter some varieties that need stringing. To string sugar snaps, bend the stem tip toward the flat side of the pod to snap it, then gently pull downward, removing the string with the stem. Snow peas need only the stem tip trimmed.

Basic cooking Nothing could be simpler than cooking fresh peas. Boil water, add a good pinch of salt and stir in the peas. Sugar snap peas and snow peas will be crisp-tender in 1 to 2 minutes; shell peas, depending on their size and freshness, will cook in 2 to 4 minutes. A pinch of sugar in the cooking water boosts the flavor of peas that are not perfectly sweet.

peppers, bell

Like a string of colored lights, red, yellow, orange, purple and green peppers brighten the produce section of almost every supermarket these days.

packed into a half-cup of raw red pepper

Less than **14 calories** • the antioxidant **beta-carotene** to fight chronic disease • **folate** for normal growth • more than the daily requirement for **vitamin A** • more than twice the daily requirement for **vitamin C**

at the market

Season Available all year, but most plentiful in summer.

What to look for Choose well-shaped globes with firm, glossy skin and no cuts, blisters or bruises. Reject any with moldy stems, which might be a sign of rot on the inside. Peppers should feel heavy for their size and look crisp, not limp or spongy.

in the kitchen

Storing Store, unwrapped, in the vegetable drawer of the refrigerator. Green peppers keep for about a week. Yellow, orange and red ones keep for up to five days.

Preparation Cut pepper in half through the stem end and remove the stem, seed pods and white ribs. Cut the pepper into flat panels for slicing and chopping. To peel a pepper, you must first char it over a barbecue or under the broiler, turning it often for even blackening. Steam the charred peppers in a paper bag for 15 minutes. Scrape off the skin, cut out the stem and core and discard the seeds.

Basic cooking Barbecue whole peppers for 20 minutes or slow-roast them in a 375°F (190°C) oven for 30 minutes. Use purple peppers in salads; they turn an unpleasant color when cooked. Whole peppers, tops cut through to make a lid, can be stuffed with meat or grain mixtures. First microwave the shells for 2 minutes, then stuff and heat the whole dish.

Best uses in recipes Raw or cooked, red, yellow and orange peppers are sweeter than green ones. Raw peppers, chopped or sliced, are good additions to all kinds of salsas as well as salads – pasta, potato, rice or mixed salad greens. Chopped and sautéed in oil, peppers enhance pilafs, pasta sauces, soups, stews and stir-fries.

peeling peppers

1 Roast peppers on a barbecue grill lined with foil. Cook until the skins are charred and blistered.

2 Place in a paper bag and seal tightly. Allow to steam for 10 minutes.

3 Peel away skin, then remove stem and seeds.

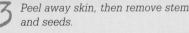

4 Cut pepper into bite-sized chunks.

peppers, chili

Mild to fiery, chili peppers spice up the cuisines of many countries, in particular those of Mexico and Thailand.

packed into a quarter cup of chili peppers

less than **20 calories** • more than 150% of the daily requirement for **vitamin C** • **beta-carotene** to help fight chronic disease • **folate** for normal growth • **vitamin B$_6$** for normal brain function and formation of red blood cells • the antioxidant **capsaicin** to fight cancer and ulcers

fresh ideas

Add finely chopped chili to corn bread or corn muffins.

Make a hot chili and sweet pepper salsa by finely chopping red, green and orange peppers and jalapeño and chipotle chili peppers. Add finely chopped red onion and cilantro and vinegar. Serve with meat or poultry.

A sprinkling of chopped chili peppers adds a kick to tomato sauce, meat loaf or a cheese sauce.

DID YOU KNOW

...that red chili peppers contain more than 10 times the amount of beta-carotene found in green? Pimentos are often confused with chili peppers; they're a variety of pepper. Pimentón, a spice much used in Spanish cooking and similar to paprika, is made from dried, ground pimentos.

at the market

Season Most supermarkets carry fresh chili peppers all year, though some have a wider variety than others. Asian markets are usually the best source.

What to look for Fresh chili peppers should have fresh-looking green stems and be well shaped, firm and glossy, with no wrinkles. Dried hot chili peppers should be glossy and unbroken.

in the kitchen

Storing Wrap unwashed chili peppers in paper towels. Don't use plastic bags because moisture causes chili peppers to decompose. Keep fresh chili peppers in the vegetable drawer of the refrigerator for up to three weeks. Dried chili peppers can be stored in an airtight container at room temperature; they will last as long as four months. In the refrigerator, they'll last even longer.

Preparation Take care when handling chili peppers. The membranes and seeds harbor capsaicin, the substance that makes chili peppers hot. It can badly irritate the skin and cause considerable discomfort if it gets in your eyes. You might want to wear rubber gloves while you prepare them. Wash chili peppers, cut them open and remove the membranes and seeds if you prefer a milder flavor in your dish. After chopping chili peppers, wash the cutting board and the utensils, as well as your gloves. If you grind dried chili peppers to use in powder form, be careful not to inhale the fumes or expose your eyes to them. To minimize discomfort, try soaking chili peppers in hot water for 30 minutes, then puréeing them with a little of the soaking liquid. Then proceed with your recipe.

Basic cooking Just a sprinkling of chopped chili adds zing to all kinds of dishes from hamburgers to salad dressings. Roast and peel large mild chili peppers just as you do peppers *(page 268)*, then stuff them with cheese or meat and deep-fry. Remove the ribs and seeds when you peel them.

varieties

Most chili peppers have a predictable heat level, depending on what kind they are. A chili pepper's pungency, however, is determined not only by its variety, but also by its growing conditions. Some of the milder varieties are eaten as low-calorie snacks. Others have a searing heat. Chili peppers are a good source of beta-carotene and vitamin C. They may help relieve nasal congestion.

anaheim peppers range from mild to medium hot. These long, slender red or green chili peppers are among the most popular in North America. The Mexican dish *chiles rellenos* often uses these flavorful peppers.

bird's eye or Thai chili peppers have a deep fiery heat. Flavor varies from mild to sweet. Colors range from red to cream, yellow or orange. Use in Thai salads and noodle dishes.

cayenne peppers have long, thin red pods that can grow as long as 10 inches (20 cm). They are fiery hot with a tangy flavor. Use in salsas, sauces and soups. Used for ground cayenne pepper, a staple seasoning in North American cooking.

habanero or scotch bonnet peppers have a fiercely hot and fruity flavor. They can be 30 times hotter than jalapeños. Use to flavor oils, vinegars and salsas.

jalapeño peppers are thick-fleshed and very hot. They are sold fresh as well as canned, sliced and pickled. Usually, they are found in their mature green stage, not the fully ripe red stage. Chipotles are smoked jalapeños.

pasilla peppers are a dark greenish-red. Moderately hot, they are usually used in dried form.

poblano/ancho peppers (poblano refers to the fresh chili, ancho to the dried one) are mild to medium hot. One of Mexico's most popular chili peppers, it is often roasted to intensify the flavor. Poblanos can be stuffed with other ingredients, or blended and added to soups.

serrano peppers range from bright green to red (the sweeter of the two). They have thick flesh and a biting heat. Another favorite in Tex-Mex cooking, they often feature in hot salsas. They can also be pickled and roasted.

Putting out the fire

Although they all go under the name of capsaicin, several different substances give a chili its characteristic "heat" and have varying effects when they reach your mouth. Some give the back of your throat a quick burn; others seem to explode on your tongue and linger on the roof of your mouth. If you bite into an unbearably hot chili pepper, the best way to extinguish the fire is by eating or drinking a food that's high in fat, such as 3.25% (whole) milk, ice cream, avocado, peanut butter or buttered bread. Water just won't do it!

seeding chili peppers

Wear plastic gloves to protect you from the heat. Remove seeds and ribs with a melon baller or a sharp knife.

potatoes

It's hard to believe the ever popular and highly nutritious potato was once thought to be poisonous. Today, many varieties of red, white, yellow and blue potatoes regularly compete for space on grocery store shelves.

packed into 1 medium baked potato

Less than **200 calories** • plenty of **potassium** to maintain normal blood pressure • more than one third the daily requirement for **vitamin C** • flavonoids and other protective **phytochemicals**, especially in its skin • insoluble **fiber** for better digestion

at the market

Season Since most mature potatoes store well, they are available all year. New potatoes are only harvested from spring through fall.

What to look for Choose potatoes that are firm, dry, and well formed, with no bruises, cuts, cracks or sprouted eyes. Avoid potatoes with green spots, which indicates the presence of a toxin that develops when potatoes are exposed to light.

in the kitchen

Storing Keep potatoes loosely wrapped in paper, netting or ventilated plastic bags in a cool, dry place with good air circulation. Under the best conditions, potatoes will keep for several months. New potatoes (*see below*) are the exception; they should be eaten within a week of purchase.

Preparation Scrub potatoes well before cooking. Cut off and discard any sprouted areas.

Basic cooking depends on the variety. **All-purpose (chef's)** potatoes — round, with smooth, pale skin and waxy flesh — are best when steamed, boiled, or roasted. **Bliss** potatoes, red-skinned and no larger than 1½ inches (4 cm) in diameter, are excellent for roasting and steaming. Early summer is their peak-season. **Blue (purple)** potatoes with their deep bluish-purple skin and flesh are used to make potato salads, home fries and sautés. Summer is peak-season for blue potatoes. **Idaho (russet)** are long potatoes with russet brown skin. They are best for baking and frying and also excellent for mashing. **New potatoes** are young potatoes, no more than 1½ inches (4 cm) in diameter, with thin, tan or red skin. They are usually boiled, steamed, or cut up and roasted. It's not necessary to peel new potatoes. Unlike more mature potatoes, new potatoes don't store well and should be kept in the refrigerator for use within a week of purchase. **Yukon golds** are tan-skinned potatoes with

fresh ideas

Add potatoes to soups and, once cooked, remove some of them, mash and return to the pan to thicken the soup without adding extra flour.

Make a colorful potato salad with unpeeled red, white, bluish-purple and yellow-skinned potatoes.

Substitute mashed potato for some of the oil in a salad dressing. Then add chopped garlic and lemon juice or vinegar and whisk until smooth. The potato will give the dressing a creamy texture.

Bind meat loaf or hamburgers with cubes of cooked potato instead of using bread crumbs.

Top a baked potato with low-fat cream cheese and chopped fresh herbs such as parsley, chives or dill. Season with salt and pepper.

golden yellow flesh and a buttery flavor. They can be baked, boiled and mashed as a side dish, or sliced and incorporated into salads or casserole-style dishes. They can also be fried.

Best recipe To make **Potatoes with Hazelnut Sauce** as a side salad, boil 2 pounds (1 kg) small potatoes until tender; drain. In a small bowl, whisk together 4 egg yolks, 1 teaspoon Dijon mustard, 2 teaspoons wine vinegar, a pinch of sugar and salt and a generous grinding of black pepper. Place the bowl over a pan of simmering water and whisk until the egg mixture begins to thicken. Cut ¼ pound (125 g) unsalted butter into cubes. Whisk into the mixture, a cube at a time, then whisk in 3½ oz (100 mL) hazelnut oil. Adjust seasoning, if necessary. Spoon sauce over potatoes and scatter with 2 oz (60 g) lightly roasted hazelnuts.

varieties

The range of potatoes on offer can be bewildering. Basically, potatoes are either waxy or floury and it is these qualities that determine their suitability for certain cooking methods. Skin and flesh colors are numerous, as the following guide reveals.

désirée The pink hue of the skin varies depending on the soil and climate in which this potato is grown. Désirées have golden flesh, and can be boiled, mashed, baked, roasted or mircowaved. They are good for salads and sliced potato dishes, but are not ideal for deep-frying.

goldrush This distinctive tuber is long in shape, with slightly rough dark brown skin and white flesh. Goldrush potatoes are well-suited to baking, boiling and in some cases, french frying. It was developed in North Dakota.

nipigon This Canadian-developed variant has white, smooth skin with the hint of flakiness, and shallow eyes with a hint of purple. They are good for boiling and baking, but unsuitable for fries.

pontiac This attractive variety has a red skin with deep eyes. The flesh is white and waxy. It is good for most cooking methods, in particular boiling and baking and for using in salads and for making chips.

russet (idaho) This long, cylindrical tuber has brown, slightly rough skin with many shallow eyes and white flesh. It is an excellent choice for boiling, mashing, roasting of french-frying.

sebago A starchy variety with a cream skin and white flesh, sebago is a good all-rounder. It is particularly useful for making chips or mash, and it also bakes well.

yukon gold This is a light yellow-fleshed, oval potato variant with pale skin and shallow, pink eyes. It is a waxy tuber that is good for boiling, baking and french-frying.

fresh ideas

If you like a little spiciness but can't take the heat of chili peppers, try garnishing dips, salads, stir-fries and other dishes with slivered or grated radishes.

Simmer daikon slices in stock and then glaze with orange juice, just as you do carrots.

For an easy side salad, combine any of the following pairings with a well-seasoned vinaigrette dressing: cucumber slices and radishes; peas (shelled or snow peas) and radishes. orange segments and radishes.

matchstick radishes

1   *With a paring knife, cut radishes into coins about 1/8 inch (3 mm) thick.*

2   *Stack 3 or 4 coins and cut crossways into 1/8-inch (3 mm) sticks.*

radishes

A bunch of round red radishes or tapered white radishes can go a long way towards enlivening a salad or a plate of appetizers. Radishes add a pleasant crunch as well as a hint of heat without the burn.

packed into a half-cup of radishes

about **6 calories** • 14% of the daily requirement for **vitamin C** • cancer-fighting phytochemicals known as **flavonoids**

at the market

Season   Radishes are available throughout the year but are most abundant in early spring.

Varieties   Although **red radishes** are the best known, in most vegetable markets, you can now find long, tapered **white radishes**, which are milder than red ones, and **daikons**, which are large white carrot-shaped radishes, native to Asia, that have a sharper flavor than red radishes. **Black radishes**, popular in Polish and Russian cooking, are shaped like turnips but have dull black or brown skins and pungent white flesh. **Horseradish** is a cousin that is long and tapered with a brown skin. It is usually sold prepared as a sauce, but can be bought fresh and grated.

What to look for   Choose firm red radishes with taut, brightly colored skin and fresh-looking leaves. White radishes, daikons and horseradish should be firm, unblemished and smooth. Black radishes should be heavy for their size and free of cracks.

in the kitchen

Storing   Remove and discard any leaves before storing. Wrap red and white radishes, daikons and horseradish in plastic wrap and store in the refrigerator for a week. Store black radishes in perforated plastic bags in the refrigerator for up to a month.

Preparation   Scrub radishes and trim ends. Peel daikons, horseradish and thick-skinned black radishes. If radishes have started to wither, it is possible to revive them by soaking them in iced water for an hour before serving.

Basic cooking   Though red radishes are most often eaten raw in salads, they can also be steamed or sautéed until tender and served as a side dish. The flavor of all radishes mellows with cooking. Steam whole, trimmed red or white radishes for about 10 minutes. Sauté sliced radishes for 4 minutes. The simplest seasoning is a sprinkling of salt and a bit of butter.

fresh ideas

Sticks of zucchini, resembling fat French fries, can be briefly roasted, then used for dipping into savory sauces and spicy dips.

Blanch zucchini. Slice lengthwise, stuff with crumbled feta cheese and top with bread crumbs. Place under the grill until cheese starts to melt and crumbs begin to brown.

Add small cubes of cooked summer squash to pasta sauces.

Make ribbons to garnish salads by running a cheese grater lengthwise down the sides of a raw zucchini.

Overgrown, tough squash can be used as serving containers. Scrape out and discard the flesh and seeds. Brush "container" with lemon juice. Fill with crudités or salads.

Add cooked squash to an omelette with tomato, herbs and onion for a Mediterranean-style brunch.

summer squash

Summer squash are wonderfully versatile and quick to cook. When you buy fresh ones, you'll know that they will be good any number of ways: sautéed, roasted, stir-fried or even mixed into a muffin batter.

packed into one cup of zucchini

25 calories • more than half the daily requirement for **vitamin C** • several **B vitamins** used in energy production • **magnesium** to help regulate nerves and muscles

at the market

Season Despite their name, summer squash and zucchini can be found at other times of the year. But summer is when you usually find the freshest, tastiest examples of these easy-to-grow vegetables. Another bonus of the summer harvest is the availability of squash blossoms – a true delicacy.

What to look for Zucchini and summer squash are best when young and small. Choose zucchini that are no longer than about 7 inches (15 cm) in length. These and some of the squash can grow to enormous sizes, but they will be seedy, watery and tough. Choose squash and zucchini with bright, shiny skins and a firm texture. Don't be put off by a few surface scratches; because the skins are so tender and thin, they are practically unavoidable.

in the kitchen

Storing Store zucchini and other summer squash in a perforated plastic bag in the refrigerator for up to 4 days.

Preparation Give zucchini and squash a good rinse and trim their ends. Small and medium-sized squash have edible skin. With oversized summer squash, it's best to peel the tough skin and scoop out the seeds. Discard any dry, pulpy parts. Squash can be precut for later use, covered with a damp towel, and refrigerated for several hours. To use squash in baking breads and muffins, grate the raw vegetable and blot with paper towels to remove as much of the excess liquid as possible.

Basic cooking Summer squash can be steamed, sautéed, stir-fried or barbecued. An easy way to prepare summer squash is to cut green and yellow varieties into thin slices, and sauté in a little olive oil until they just begin to soften and brown. Add chopped garlic, fresh herbs, salt and pepper, and cook for another minute or two. Drizzle with lemon juice and serve. To barbecue, cut small squash in half lengthwise and lightly oil the cut surface. Place cut-side down on the grill just until lightly charred and tender.

Best recipe To make **Potato and Zucchini Cakes**, grate 1 large potato and rinse well, squeezing out excess moisture. Grate 1 large zucchini. Combine with 1 large egg white, 1 tablespoon plain flour, black pepper to taste, 1 tablespoon sesame seeds and 2 cloves garlic, crushed. Shape into 8 cakes. Grease a large frying pan and fry cakes on both sides over a medium heat until lightly browned. Keep warm. Meanwhile, poach 24 peeled uncooked prawns lightly in fish stock until pink. Drain and set aside. Place 2 cakes on each serving plate and arrange 3 prawns on each. Sprinkle with finely chopped chives.

squash varieties

bitter melon This pale green, wrinkled, cucumber-like vegetable is eaten while still unripe. It has bright red seeds that must be removed before eating, and a bitter taste which improves when cooked. Bitter melon features in southeast Asian dishes such as cooked salads and stir-fries and is made into a tart pickle that is popular in Indian cuisine.

pattypan squash, also called button squash, come in several varieties: green, white, bright yellow and orange. Pattypans have a pretty scalloped border. The French name "pâtisson" comes from the Provençal word for a cake made in a scalloped mold. Picked young, these squash are firm and sweet.

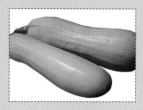

yellow zucchini, also called straightneck squash, is a medium-sized variety with thin yellow skin that can be left on and a straight neck. The flesh is mild and can be used to replace zucchini in many recipes. This squash is a close relative of the curved, bumpy-skinned yellow crookneck squash, which has a taste closer to that of winter squash than to other summer varieties.

zucchini blossoms can be stuffed and cooked to serve as an attractive appetizer. Male flowers – those without the tiny squash attached – are the best to cook. Fill the blossoms with goat cheese and fresh herbs, then pinch them shut and sauté briefly in hot oil. Drain on paper towels. Squash and okra also have edible flowers. Okra flowers are ivory or yellow with a funnel shape. Pumpkin flowers are similar to zucchini.

zucchini blossoms

sweet potatoes

These orange tubers belong to a select group of power vegetables loaded with important nutrients. beta-carotene, the carotenoid that gives the color to sweet potatoes, is a powerful antioxidant linked to lowered risk of certain cancers and heart disease.

packed into a half-cup of sweet potatoes

170 calories • almost half of the daily requirement for **vitamin C** • more than five times the daily requirement for **vitamin A** • more than 10% of the daily requirement for **fiber**

at the market

Season Sweet potatoes are available all year but are most abundant and at their best from early autumn through the winter months.

Varieties Sweet potatoes can be white, purple or orange/red/gold. The white skinned sweet potatoes have white flesh, and the purple sweet potato has a creamy-white flesh.

What to look for Choose firm sweet potatoes with smooth, dry skin and no cracks or blemishes. Check the tips of the potatoes, which is where decay usually begins.

in the kitchen

Storing Keep sweet potatoes in a cool, preferably 55°F (12°C), dark place for up to a month. At normal room temperature, they will last up to a week. Don't put raw sweet potatoes in the refrigerator; they tend to harden and develop an off taste. You can freeze cooked sweet potatoes for longer storage.

Preparation Scrub unpeeled potatoes well before baking. Potatoes to be cut up for cooking can be peeled with a swivel-blade peeler. Alternatively, peel whole potatoes after cooking.

Basic cooking To bake whole sweet potatoes, preheat oven to 425°F (220°C). Pierce each potato in several places with a fork or knife tip. Arrange potatoes in a foil-lined baking pan. Bake until very tender, about 1 hour.

Best uses in recipes Baked sweet potatoes are served split and mashed with butter as a side dish. Their sweetness can be enhanced by cooking sweet potatoes with pear, apple or orange juice. For a different taste, season sweet potatoes with lime juice and cilantro, or mash with roasted garlic, salt and pepper. Mash boiled sweet potatoes to use as a side dish.

fresh ideas

Mash sweet potatoes with maple syrup and serve as a pudding for dessert.

Make a salad with chunks of cooked sweet potato. Dress with lime juice, olive oil, curry powder and salt and sprinkle with finely chopped spring onions.

Mash cooked sweet potatoes with grated Parmesan cheese. Use in place of half the cheese in your favorite lasagna recipe.

Make sweet potato chips by thinly slicing sweet potatoes and drizzling them with olive oil. Bake in a 400°F (200°C) oven until tender and crisp.

DID YOU KNOW

...that sweet potatoes are called yams in some countries, although the two vegetables are unrelated? Yams grow on vines while sweet potatoes grow under the ground.

tomatoes

Although Italy and other Mediterranean countries are probably best known for dishes that feature tomatoes, they are, in fact, native to Central America.

packed into 1 medium tomato

about **25 calories** • more than one third the daily requirement for **vitamin C** • sight-protective **lutein** and **zeaxanthin** that help stave off vision loss • **beta-carotene** that is converted to vitamin A in the body • a phytochemical called **lycopene** that fights prostate cancer • anti-cancer chemicals **caffeic**, **ferulic** and **chlorogenic acids**

at the market

Season There are tomatoes in the market throughout the year, but summer is the best time to buy and enjoy fresh tomatoes from local growers – or your own backyard.

What to look for Choose firm, ripe, evenly shaped, deeply colored tomatoes with no tears or bruises in the skin. Ripe tomatoes have a very distinctive earthy fragrance.

Where to buy the best Farmers' markets and shops that specialize in organically grown produce are most likely to have the sweetest, juiciest fruits (tomatoes are technically a fruit, not a vegetable).

in the kitchen

Storing Always store tomatoes at room temperature. Store any slightly underripe tomatoes in a brown paper bag to ripen them and improve their flavor. Refrigeration destroys a tomato's taste and texture.

Preparation Use a sharp, serrated knife to slice tomatoes. To remove seeds, cut the tomato in half and gently squeeze out seeds and liquid. To peel tomatoes, follow instructions and photographs *(p. 301)*.

Basic cooking Tomatoes can be halved and barbecued, or roasted in a hot oven until they start to shrivel, 10 to 15 minutes. Do not overcook them or they will collapse. Large varieties can be stuffed.

Best use in recipes Most tomatoes are used to make sauce. They are also used in soups, stews, casseroles and sautés and eaten raw in salads. Cherry and pear tomatoes are served on vegetable appetizer platters and eaten just as they are as snacks.

fresh ideas

Cook fresh tomatoes with sugar, cinnamon and orange zest to make a savory jam.

Combine tomato juice with an equal amount of carrot juice and chill. Garnished with chopped fresh tomato and a dollop of yogurt, the mixture serves as a refreshing summer soup.

To give a nutritional boost to savory soups, replace half of the water with tomato juice.

Make a quick sauce for pasta salad by combining tomato paste, tomato juice, olive oil, balsamic vinegar and chopped fresh basil.

DID YOU KNOW

...that lycopene-rich food may protect against prostate cancer? In a six-year study of 48,000 men who consumed 10 or more servings per week of tomato products, participants experienced a 45% reduction in prostate cancer.

varieties

beefsteaks are very large, deeply ridged, dark red tomatoes that are wonderful for salads and sandwiches.

cherry tomatoes are small red or yellow tomatoes that are often sweeter and lower in acid than regular slicing tomatoes.

grape tomatoes are also called pear tomatoes. They are small, red or yellow, grape-shaped, and, like cherry tomatoes, can be eaten just as they are.

green tomatoes are merely tomatoes that were picked from the vine prior to ripening. If they are wrapped in paper and left at room temperature, they'll slowly ripen and turn red, though don't expect them to be sweet. Firm and tart, green tomatoes are commonly used for pickling or frying.

plum tomatoes are a red, egg-shaped, fleshy variety that is especially good for sauces, soups, and other cooked dishes. Plum tomatoes can also be eaten raw in salads and can be used to make dried tomatoes. They are a very good pantry ingredient in cans.

tomatillos are small, round, green tomatoes that are encased in a brown, papery husk. Very tart, they are usually cooked before eating. Tomatillos are most often used in Mexican and southwest American-style sauces.

yellow slicing tomatoes are medium to large in size, round in shape, and a deep, bright yellow. Yellow tomatoes can be eaten raw in salads or sliced for sandwiches as a substitute for red slicing tomatoes.

peeling a tomato

1 Cut a shallow X in the base of each tomato.

2 Blanch in boiling water for about 1 minute. Skin will shrivel. Place in cold water.

3 Remove skin with a paring knife or with your fingers.

heirloom tomatoes

With global mass marketing of food, many ancient varieties of fruits and vegetables can no longer be found. What's available instead are hybrid varieties preferred by farmers, marketers and many consumers for their uniform good looks and hardiness to travel. Unfortunately, many of today's hybrids aren't as rich in flavor as the originals. But thanks to devotees who, years ago, began saving non-hybrid seeds, heirloom tomatoes with unusual coloration and interesting shapes can still be found in specialty food markets, farmers' markets and the home gardens of anyone who buys seeds descended from the originals. Several varieties of heirlooms are considered among the best-tasting and most interesting in appearance. These include Black Plum, Carbon, Sweet Olive, Sungold and Green Zebra.

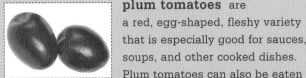

black plum

turnips & other root vegetables

A member of the cabbage family, turnips are prized for their roots as well as their greens. A staple vegetable since early Roman times, turnips were brought to North America by both French and British settlers.

fresh ideas

Steam sliced turnips, carrots and potatoes and mash them together. The combination is smoky and delicious.

Sauté cubes of turnip in olive oil with garlic and shredded turnip greens as a side dish.

Add shredded turnips and dill to the shredded potatoes you are using to make potato pancakes, for a fresh new taste.

Make a slaw of shredded turnips and shredded apples; dress with a combination of apple cider, apple cider vinegar, and Dijon mustard.

packed into three-quarters of a cup of turnips

about **28 calories** • more than a third of the daily recommendation for **vitamin C** to control blood cholesterol • **indoles** to fight cancer • **lysine** to prevent cold sores • **soluble and insoluble fiber** to lower cholesterol and prevent constipation

at the market

Season Turnips are mainly winter vegetables, but because they store well, you can find them year-round.

What to look for Choose smooth, heavy, firm turnips, preferably on the small side – closer to a golf ball than a baseball – with a minimum of fibrous root hairs at the bottom. Large turnips can develop a strong flavor that's too assertive for most tastes. If greens are attached, they should be crisp and a vibrant green.

in the kitchen

Storing Keep turnip roots in a plastic bag in the vegetable drawer of the refrigerator for up to a week. Detach and store turnip greens separately and use within a few days.

Preparation Trim a slice from the top and bottom of each turnip and peel as thinly as possible with a swivel vegetable peeler to save nutrients.

Basic cooking Before cooking, place cut-up turnip in cold water with lemon or vinegar added to prevent the flesh from darkening. For the same reason, do not cook turnips in aluminum or iron pans. To preserve the mild, peppery flavor, do not cook turnips beyond the crisp-tender stage because overcooking intensifies the flavor.

Turnip chunks can be roasted with meat or poultry or in a shallow roasting pan by themselves (30 to 45 minutes at 375°F/190°C). Turnips can be

DID YOU KNOW

...in the late fourth century BC, when King Nicomedes of Bithynia (now part of northern Turkey) was traveling far from the sea and craved anchovies, his cook served him thin slices of turnip sprinkled with poppy seeds and salt?

other root vegetables

celeriac or celery root is a knobby root that tastes like celery and has a crisp texture. It is low in calories and rich in phosphorus, potassium and vitamin C. Grate it fresh for salads or braise it in stock as a side dish. Or, dice it and add to soups. Scrub the root well and peel before cutting up for cooking or raw vegetable platters. Roast celeriac in its skin and peel afterwards. Celeriac goes well with pork.

jerusalem artichoke

or sunchoke is a native American tuber. This gnarled root is packed with vitamin C, iron, fiber and calcium, and has a nutty taste and a crisp texture. Grated or sliced fresh, jerusalem artichoke adds a smoky flavor and lots of crunch to salads and slaws. Dunk cut-up or peeled jerusalem artichokes in cold water with lemon or lime juice to keep the flesh from turning brown. Do not use iron or aluminum cookware. Bake the vegetable for 30 to 60 minutes or boil for 10 to 20 minutes. Mash or purée the artichokes with parsley and other fresh herbs and a little butter or oil. For a side dish to accompany roasts, chops or chicken, braise with potatoes, carrots and celery

in beef or chicken stock. Use slices in place of water chestnuts in stir-fries for both their flavor and crunchy texture. Despite the name this vegetable is no relation of the spiky-leaved globe artichoke.

jicama A Mexican tuber, the jicama has white flesh and a thin brown skin. It has a bland flavor and a juicy crispness more like an apple than a turnip. Fresh jicama slices – sprinkled with lime or lemon juice to keep them from browning – are a good addition to salads or to raw vegetable platters and add crunch to stir-fries. Jicama is rich in vitamin C and potassium, iron and calcium. Pick roots that feel heavy and peel the papery skin with a knife. Store in water in the refrigerator for up to a week.

lotus root This buff-colored fibrous, starchy root is the rhizome of the water lily. Slices of lotus root have a delicate lacy appearance because the rhizome is riddled with air tunnels. Slightly sweet-tasting, it is used raw in salads and cooked in stir-fries and soups. Whole roots can be refrigerated for up to a week. Lotus root can also be purchased canned, frozen and candied.

salsify or oyster plant With tan skin and white flesh, salsify looks like a parsnip and is treated like parsnips in cooking. Its flavor is more like an oyster, however. A serving (about ⅔ cup) has 80 calories, vitamin C and potassium. Salsify is available in fall and winter.

---

boiled, steamed, microwaved or braised, whole or in pieces. Cooking turnips whole takes longer – up to 30 minutes. Sliced or matchstick turnips can be successfully stir-fried or sautéed. Turnip chunks add a sweet, peppery note to soups and stews. Mashing boiled, steamed or microwaved turnips with butter, salt and pepper is a classic way to serve the vegetable. But mashed turnip also goes well with other mashed vegetables, such as potatoes, spiced with some onion or roasted cloves of garlic and fresh herbs such as chives or parsley.

Puréed turnips on their own are deliciously sweet, but their bulk and texture tends to be a little on the thin side. Adding one medium potato for every three turnips makes a creamier, richer purée.

DID YOU KNOW

...that turnips are one of the only vegetables that you can plant near potatoes, because potatoes tend to need lots of space to spread and grow and are poor garden companions?

winter squash

Each type of winter squash is a powerhouse of good nutrition, the kind that fights heart disease, cancer, depression and vision loss due to macular degeneration.

packed into 1 cup of butternut squash cubes

82 calories • half the daily requirement for **vitamin C** • more than 100% the daily requirement for vitamin A in the form of the cancer-fighting antioxidant **beta-carotene** • **B vitamins** for energy production • **fiber** to help maintain digestive health • eye-protective **lutein** • heart-helping **magnesium** and **potassium**

at the market

Season Although some varieties are available all year round, winter squash are at their peak from late autumn through the winter months.

What to look for When choosing any variety of squash, look for dry, hard, tough-looking skin with no soft spots or bruises. Pick smaller squash for their sweeter flavor and more tender flesh. Make sure they still have their stalks to be sure that insects have not burrowed into them. A 2-pound (1 kg) butternut squash yields about 3 cups of mashed or puréed cooked squash.

in the kitchen

Storing At home, store pumpkin in a paper bag in the refrigerator for up to a week. For the best flavor, use the same day. Whole squash can be stored at room temperature for up to three months.

Preparation To prepare squash, use a large chef's knife or cleaver to split it in half. Use a sharp paring knife or heavy-duty vegetable peeler to remove the skin on smooth squash, if necessary. It's nearly impossible to peel acorn squash and other ridged varieties. Remove seeds and fibrous pulp. Cut flesh into small pieces.

Basic cooking Winter squash can be baked, steamed, boiled, stewed or cooked in a microwave oven. A quick preparation method is to bake it. Halve the squash, scoop out and discard the seeds, and place, flesh-side down, in a lightly greased baking pan. Bake at 400°F (200°C) until very tender (a fork inserted into the flesh through the skin moves easily in and out), about 45 minutes to 1 hour, depending on the size of the squash. Cut into smaller pieces to serve. To boil, place squash pieces in lightly salted water to cover. Bring to the boil, cook until tender, about 20 to 25 minutes. Add butter, salt and pepper. and mash or purée if desired.

fresh ideas

Add peeled and diced butternut squash to soups, stews, pies and casseroles.

Add peeled, grated squash to pancake batter.

Make a sauce of puréed pumpkin and grated Parmesan cheese to serve with pasta.

Cook chunks of pumpkin or squash with sugar, sultanas, red pepper and spices until tender. Serve as a chutney with meats or poultry.

A little olive oil or butter will enhance the flavor of cooked squash. You can also add any of the following seasonings.

Brown sugar

Curry powder

Honey and sage

Honey, ginger and cinnamon

Maple syrup, cinnamon and nutmeg

Jalapeño pepper and cilantro

varieties

There are many varieties of squash to choose from, each with a different shape, size and flavor. The seeds can be roasted.

acorn squash is small- to medium-sized, acorn-shaped, with dark green, orange, green and orange, or white, deeply ridged skin. Its yellow flesh is sweet and moist. Acorn squash are best baked.

banana squash is large and long, with yellow skin and orange flesh. Blue- and pink-skinned bananas are also grown in home gardens.

buttercup squash is small to medium in size, drum-shaped, with dark green skin marked with gray. Its orange flesh is dense, dry, and sweet.

butternut squash is medium-sized and shaped like a big peanut. It has smooth tan or yellow-orange skin. Its bright orange flesh is mildly sweet.

delicata squash is small to medium, elongated, and has cream-colored skin striped with orange or green. Unlike other winter squash, its skin is edible, its flesh is creamy, and its sweet corn-like flavor is very delicate.

hubbard squash is large with dusty blue-green, warty, faintly ridged skin. Its yellow-orange flesh is dry and slightly bland in flavor.

golden hubbards have dark orange skin and slightly sweeter flesh.

kabocha squash is a medium-sized Japanese hybrid, shaped like a flattened globe, with dark green, bumpy skin. Its orange flesh is dense, dry and very sweet.

pumpkins for eating are round, ridged, and have dark orange skin. Their flesh is not as sweet as that of some other winter squash.

spaghetti squash is medium-sized, oblong, with smooth yellow skin. After boiling or baking, it is halved, and the flesh is pulled out with a fork into strands that are crunchy and rather bland.

sweet dumpling squash are very small — each squash is an individual serving. Their skin is yellow with dark green strips, and their flesh is yellow-orange, sweet and moist. Sweet dumplings are best baked.

turban squash has bright orange-red skin and a decorative, turbanlike topknot. It is a relative of the buttercup squash, with dry, mildly sweet flesh.

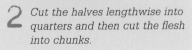
preparing squash

1 With a knife, cut off stem and halve lengthwise. Scoop out all the seeds with a spoon.

2 Cut the halves lengthwise into quarters and then cut the flesh into chunks.

glossary of good nutrition

Refer to this mini-dictionary when you come across diet and nutrition terms in this book that require explanation.

antioxidant This term refers to certain vitamins and other substances in plant foods that help prevent disease by fighting off toxic substances in the body known as free radicals, and repairing the cell damage that they cause.

beta-carotene A member of a family of substances known as carotenoids, beta-carotene is the pigment that gives the orange color to sweet potatoes, carrots, pumpkins and other fruits and vegetables. It is also found in dark green vegetables, but its color is obscured by the green color of chlorophyll that is present in those vegetables. Beta-carotene is converted to vitamin A in your body and also functions as an antioxidant to help the body fight cancer and other chronic disease.

capsaicin This phytochemical is found in all peppers and chili peppers but is most heavily concentrated in chili peppers. Capsaicin may protect against chronic diseases such as cancer and prevent blood clots.

carbohydrates The major components of foods are carbohydrates, protein and fat. Carbohydrates are either starches or sugars and are found in all plant foods – vegetables, grains, legumes and fruits. Foods that are high in carbohydrates are our main source of energy and, when carefully selected, can also be our best source of certain essential vitamins and minerals.

carcinogen A substance that causes the growth of cancer cells.

carotenoids This is a family of more than 600 phytochemicals responsible for the yellow, orange and red pigments found in vegetables and fruits. Some carotenoids, such as lutein and lycopene, function as antioxidants or have other disease-fighting properties. The antioxidant beta-carotene is the best-known of the carotenoid family.

cholesterol This waxy, fat-like substance is present in every cell in animals, including humans. Cholesterol is essential to many body functions, including the production of vitamin D, hormones and essential skin oils. Excess cholesterol in the blood can adhere to the walls of the arteries, forming a substance known as plaque that contributes to hardening of the arteries and, ultimately, to heart disease.

cruciferous vegetables This family of vegetables, including cabbage, cauliflower, broccoli, brussels sprouts and leafy greens, contains phytochemicals known as indoles that help protect against cancer.

flavonoids These phytochemicals are found in broccoli, carrots, onions, soybeans and other foods. They are the same phytochemicals that are thought to give red wine and tea their antioxidant potential to help reduce the risk of heart disease.

free radicals These unstable compounds form in the body during normal metabolism and also result from other factors such as radiation, smoking cigarettes and drinking alcohol, and environmental pollution. Free radicals set up a chain reaction of events that lead to cell destruction and potentially cause cancer. Antioxidants found in vegetables and fruits help the body repair damage done by free radicals.

homocysteine People with elevated levels of this amino acid in their blood are at an increased risk of developing heart disease. Vitamins B_6, B_{12} and folate help to convert homocysteine into a non-destructive form.

indoles Cruciferous vegetables such as cabbage varieties, cauliflower and brussels sprouts contain this phytochemical, which is thought to be protective against hormone-sensitive diseases such as breast cancer.

isoflavones These are phytochemicals present in soybeans and other leguminous plants that are called phytoestrogens – plant substances that mimic estrogen's action in the body and may protect against heart disease and hormone-sensitive cancers.

isothiocyanates These are phytochemicals found in cruciferous vegetables such as cauliflower and broccoli that stimulate the body's cancer-fighting enzymes.

legumes All beans, peas, lentils and peanuts are in the legume family. That makes them good plant sources of protein and iron, nutrients more often associated with animal foods. They are also good sources of B vitamins and fiber.

lutein This carotenoid is found in avocado, kale, spinach, parsley, red peppers and other vegetables and fruits. Lutein is thought to protect against age-related blindness resulting from macular degeneration.

lycopene This carotenoid is found in tomatoes, tomato products such as paste and sauce, watermelon, pink grapefruit and other fruits and vegetables. Studies have found that lycopene may be protective against prostate cancer and other chronic diseases.

pectin This soluble fiber, found in many fruits, vegetables and legumes, helps lower cholesterol and regulate intestinal function.

phytochemicals These plant substances help boost immunity and fight chronic disease such as cancer and heart disease.

phytoestrogens These phytochemicals, found in soybeans and other legumes, mimic the action of the estrogen produced by the human body. Because of this action, phytoestrogens may help to protect against heart disease and hormone-sensitive cancers such as breast cancer.

phytonutrients These phytochemicals have nutritional value in addition to disease-fighting capabilities.

resveratrol This phytochemical helps lower cholesterol and protect against heart disease.

sulforaphane Broccoli, cabbage and brussels sprouts contain this phytochemical, which stimulates the production of anti-cancer enzymes.

zeaxanthin This carotenoid, found in broccoli and kale, helps prevent age-related blindness due to macular degeneration.

vegetable freezing chart

Vegetables that are to be frozen must always be thoroughly cleaned and trimmed. Most need to be precooked by blanching in boiling water. Not all vegetables freeze successfully. Asparagus, for instance, breaks down and becomes limp and watery when thawed. Other vegetables that freeze poorly include beets, whole or cut-up carrots, cauliflower, cucumber, eggplant, fennel, salad greens, leeks, potatoes, radishes, zucchini and other summer squash. Here are instructions for handling those vegetables that freeze well.

beans, green	Blanch trimmed beans 3 minutes per pound (500 g). Cool completely in iced water. Drain well and place in freezer container.	Use within 12 months
broccoli	Blanch bite-sized pieces of broccoli for 3 minutes. Cool completely in iced water. Drain well and place in freezer container.	Use within 12 months
brussels sprouts	Blanch trimmed sprouts for 3 to 5 minutes, depending on the size of the head. Cool completely in iced water. Drain well and pack into freezer container.	Use within 12 months
corn	Blanch whole cobs for 4 to 8 minutes, depending on the size of the cob of corn. Cool completely in iced water. Cut off kernels or leave cobs whole and pack into freezer container.	Use within 6 months
greens, cooking	Blanch whole leaves for 2 minutes. Cool completely in iced water. Drain well and pack into freezer container.	Use within 6 months
okra	Blanch trimmed, whole okra pods for 4 minutes. Cool completely in iced water. Drain well and pack into freezer container.	Use within 6 months
onions	Pack raw, finely chopped onions, spring onions or chives loosely in freezer container.	Use within 6 months
peas	Blanch shelled peas for 2 minutes. Cool completely in iced water. Drain well and loosely pack in freezer container.	Use within 12 months
	Blanch snow peas and sugar snap peas for 2 minutes. Cool completely in iced water. Drain well. Place in single layer on a baking sheet or tray. Freeze, then pack frozen peas into freezer container.	Use within 9 months
pepper	Pack finely chopped, raw peppers in freezer container.	Use within 12 months
pumpkin, squash & zucchini	Cook pumpkin completely and purée before freezing. Cool completely before packing into freezer container. Cook squash completely and purée before freezing. Cool completely before packing into freezer container.	Use within 6 months
root vegetables	Cook carrots completely and purée before freezing. (Whole and cut-up carrots do not freeze well.) Cook parsnips completely and purée before freezing. (Whole and cut-up parsnips do not freeze well.) Cool completely before packing into freezer container. Cook turnips or rutabagas completely and mash or purée before freezing. Cool completely before packing into freezer container.	Use within 6 months
spinach	Blanch whole leaves for 2 minutes. Cool completely in iced water. Drain well and pack in freezer container.	Use within 6 months
sweet potatoes	Cook sweet potatoes completely and purée before freezing. Cool completely before packing into freezer container.	Use within 6 months
tomatoes	Blanch whole tomatoes for 2 minutes. Cool completely in iced water. Drain well and freeze for later use in cooking. Tomato sauce also freezes well.	Use within 12 months

ingredient equivalents

	amount	equivalent
apple	1 medium (165 g)	1¼ cups sliced or chopped
apricots	dried, 5 oz (150 g)	1 cup
asparagus	1 lb (500 g)	18 to 20 stalks
beans	dried, 1 lb (500 g)	2½ cups dried; 6½ to 7 cups cooked
beans	green, 1 lb (500 g)	4 cups cut-up
bread	1½ slices	1 cup soft crumbs
broccoli	10½ oz (300 g)	4 cups florets
butter	½ lb (250 g)	1 cup
cabbage	1 lb (500 g)	5 to 6 cups shredded
carrots	1½ medium	1 cup grated
cauliflower	1 lb (500 g)	4⅔ cups florets
celery	2 medium stalks	1 cup thinly sliced or chopped
corn	2 medium cobs	1 cup kernels
cucumber	1 medium	1⅔ cups chopped
eggplant	1 lb (500 g)	5⅔ cups cubed
flour, all-purpose	1 lb (500 g)	3½ cups
lemon	1 medium	2 to 2½ tablespoons juice; ½ to 1 tablespoon grated peel
mushrooms	½ lb (250 g)	3½ cups sliced
nuts	½ lb (250 g)	1⅔ to 2 cups whole; 2 cups chopped
onion	1 medium	¾ cup chopped
	amount	equivalent
parsnips	1 lb (500 g)	4 cups chopped
pasta	uncooked, ½ lb (250 g)	4 cups cooked (average)
peas, in pod	1 lb (500 g)	1¼ cups shelled
pepper, bell	1 large	1 cup chopped
potatoes	1½ lbs (750 g)	5 medium; 8 to 10 small
pumpkin	1 lb (500 g)	1¾ cups mashed
rice	1 cup uncooked	3 to 3½ cups cooked
spinach	6 oz (175 g)	5 cups uncooked
tomato	1 large	1 cup chopped
zucchini	1 large	1½ cups sliced or 1¼ cups grated

temperature

celsius	fahrenheit	
-18°C	0°F	freezer temperature
0°C	32°F	water freezes
82°C	180°F	water simmers
100°C	212°F	water boils
120°C	250°F	low oven
180°C	350°F	moderate oven
220°C	425°F	hot oven
260°C	500°F	very hot oven

index

acknowledgments

All images are Reader's Digest copyright with the following exceptions:

5 Digital Vision/Getty Images. **10** Pixtal. **12** *bottom right* Pixtal. **13** *top* Dallas Powell, Jr/ Dreamstime.com; *bottom* Pixtal. **28** *top* Royalty-Free/Corbis; *centre left* Jules Frazier/Photodisc Green/Getty Images; *bottom right* Digital Vision/Getty Images. **267** (Bok Choy) C Squared Studios/Photodisc Green/Getty Images. **273** (habanero) C Squared Studios/Photodisc Blue/Getty Images. **305** (bitter melon) Harris Shiffman/ Dreamstime.com.

The publishers would like to thank Sam and Steve Grima of Grima's farm fresh produce